THE WILES OF WAR

36 Military Strategies
from Ancient China

Compiled and Translated by Sun Haichen

FOREIGN LANGUAGES PRESS   BEIJING

First Edition   1991

ISBN 0-8351-2795-8
ISBN 7-119-01399-8

Published by Foreign Languages Press
24 Baiwanzhuang Road, Beijing 100037, China

Printed by Foreign Languages Printing House
19 Chegongzhuang Xilu, Beijing 100044, China

Distributed by China International Book Trading Corporation
35 Chegongzhuang Xilu, Beijing 100044, China
P.O. Box 399, Beijing, China

Printed in the People's Republic of China

CONTENTS

PREFACE

"Of the thirty-six strategies, running away is the best choice." This is a familiar remark, in literary works as well as in real life, from people who want to get around a situation that they are unable to cope with for the moment. The expression first appeared in the official *History of Southern Qi* about fifteen hundred years ago. Since then, it gained increasing currency until an anonymous scholar (estimated a contemporary of late Ming or early Qing) laid out the entire thirty-six strategies in a small book called *Secret Art of War: Thirty-Six Strategies*. At first it circulated only in hand-written copies and did not find its way into any bibliography of military writing. First printed in 1941 by the Xinghua Printing House in Chengdu, it did not attract general attention until after the founding of the People's Republic of China.

Apart from a preface and an afterword, the book falls conveniently into thirty-six sections, each consisting of the title, text, and comment of a strategy. The title invariably takes the form of a four-character idiom, which sometimes refers directly to a renowned battle in history. All the idioms have been in wide use among both the élite classes and the common people for at least hundreds of years; most have taken on diverse military imports. Therefore the title itself can elicit plentiful reminiscences in an average Chinese reader, who may interpret the ensuing text according to his or her own military knowledge or experience. In fact, the text of each strategy, consisting of less than a dozen characters, is so condensed that one has to read one's own thoughts into it. More often than not, the text contains a quotation from the most revered classic of China, *I Ching* (*Book of Changes*). This is followed by a relatively lengthy comment, which explicate the text and cites one or two ancient battles to illustrate the application of the strategy.

The present book offers a precise translation of the title and text of each strategy. A purport, based mainly on the original comment but also incorporating ideas from other sources, then expounds the common usage of the titular idiom and its military connotations. This is sometimes followed by quotations from various ancient military works to further exemplify the strategy. The account of a historical battle or campaign featuring the successful application of the strategy makes up the final part of each section. All the stories are adapted mainly from official history records but may also draw upon miscellaneous writings of credit.

According to a recent incomplete survey, more than twenty-three hundred titles of military writing from ancient China have survived. About fifty of them are well-known and still enjoy a broad readership among military leaders. They cover all aspects of ancient warfare: strategy and tactics, natural conditions in relation to war, manufacture and usage of weapons and gears, organization and discipline of the armed forces, tactical formations, frontier defense, training of professional troops, and military history.

All the above subjects appeal to researchers in the

history of ancient Chinese warfare, but those who look for ancient theories applicable in modern warfare generally prefer the books on strategy and tactics. In those works, one finds brilliant expositions on problems faced by military leaders of all times and cannot but marvel at the depth and scope attained by the ancient masters.

Though its technical side has undergone remarkable progress toward greater complexity and more dimensions, war as an art has certain fundamental truths that remain valid all through the ages. For instance, war is a political organ to achieve goals that cannot be brought about by peaceful means. A military leader builds up and maintains his strength and weakens that of his opponent, conceals his intentions and capabilities and endeavors to detect those of his opponent, avoids battle at his disadvantage and maneuvers to achieve superiority at the focal points where he chooses to give battle. Modern technology has greatly transformed warfare, but generals and even line officers today often face the same problems that confronted their ancient counterparts. After all, war is launched, conducted, and terminated by humans; therefore it conforms to certain intrinsic laws that are a projection of human nature. As long as human nature does not change, war as a human activity will follow some ageless rules in the course of time.

Secret Art of War: Thirty-Six Strategies was composed in conformity to the yin-yang doctrine formulated in *I Ching*. Six, the primal yin number, denotes secret ruses in military contexts, and six square means a whole bag of tricks. The summary of various strategies in terms of the yin-yang antithesis makes possible a simplistic treatment of the complex subject matter. Yin and yang represent an endless series of opposites in the universe; in warfare they are mainly embodied in the pair of *xu* (cowardice, weakness, disorder, hunger, fatigue, numerical inferiority, unpreparedness) and *shi* (bravery, strength, order, full stomach, leisure, numerical superiority, preparedness). Thus in *Li Jing's Reply to Emperor Taizong of Tang* (Tang Tai Zong Li Jing Wen Dui), the emperor observes, "In my opinion, the various military works contain nothing other than Sun Zi's *Art of War*, and the *Art of War* contains nothing other than *xu* and *shi*." Another familiar twosome is *qi* (extraordinary) and *zheng* (normal), whose relationship has been clarified in Sun Zi's well-known maxim, "Engage the enemy by your normal force and defeat it by your extraordinary forces."

Naturally, the transformation of modern warfare by technological innovations calls for a reexamination of the ancient rules. In fact, since ancient times the rules have always been flexible. They are not really rules but modes of thinking and call for the combination of common sense and extraordinary ruses, with which the military leader adjusts his decisions to the ever-changing situation in war. In this sense, the thirty-six strategies are thirty-six basic ideas distilled from military experiences in ancient Chinese warfare. Therefore they may serve to promote and activate rather than restrain military planning and decision-making today.

Strategy One
Cross the Sea Without Heaven's Knowledge

第一计 瞒天过海　备周则意怠，常见则不疑。阴在阳之内，不在阳之对。太阳，太阴。

Translation

People who take ample precautions are liable to be off guard. Familiar sights do not rouse suspicion. Yin is the inner instead of the opposite aspect of yang. The great yang contains the great yin.*

Purport

This common expression came from the story of an ingenious Tang general who devised a method to transport the emperor (regarded as the Son of Heaven in imperial China) safely across the sea, doing so without even the emperor's own knowledge. The word *heaven* may also be interpreted literally. In ancient times it was easy to conduct secret military operations on land by taking cover in natural shelters, such as mountains and forests, whereas the open water of the sea provided no hiding-place. Therefore, in order to cross the sea without heaven's knowledge, one had to move openly over the sea but

---

*Secret ruses are not incompatible to, but hide in, open acts. Utmost openness conceals utmost secrecy.

act as if one did not intend to cross it.

Each military maneuver has two aspects: the superficial move and the underlying purpose. By concealing both, one can take the enemy completely by surprise. But such ideal secrecy can seldom be attained in actual warfare. In most cases, to keep the enemy completely ignorant of one's operations is no easier than to "cross the sea without heaven's knowledge." The only alternative is to make the enemy neglect or misinterpret the underlying purpose of one's operation. In other words, if it is highly unlikely that the enemy can be kept ignorant of one's actions, one can sometimes play tricks right under its nose.

Quotations for Reference

One who is good at marshalling troops does so by putting the enemy in the unfathomable situation of fighting with shadows. He assumes no posture and reveals no shape so that there is nothing he cannot achieve. He reveals no shape and shows no move so that there is no change he cannot make. This is the supreme art of war.

Book of Master Guan (Guan Zi), Chapter Seventeen.

Yin refers to the unpredictable way. Use yang, which other people do not recognize as yang, so that the yang has also the attributes of yin. Use yin, which other people do not recognize as yin, so that the yin has also the attributes of yang. A good war strategist either practices yin under the cover of yang or uses yin to supplement yang. The essence of the method lies in seizing opportunity to make extraordinary moves, such as a surprise attack or an ambush; the enemy will surely be subdued in the end. Who can say that yin (secret) ruses cannot overcome yang (animate) spirit?

Master Jie's Canon of War (Jie Zi Bing Jing), Tome One

A good defender hides under nine layers of earth; a good attacker moves above nine layers of heaven. Thus he is able to both preserve himself and achieve a complete victory.

Wang Xi's Note: A defender perceives no chance for attack. He conceals his shape and remains quiet so that the enemy cannot detect him. An attacker perceives a chance for attack. He moves from afar in a fabulous speed and takes the enemy by surprise so that it has no time to get ready for defense.

Art of War (Sun Zi Bing Fa), Chapter Four.

Superb military maneuvers leave no trace. When leaving no trace, they cannot even be detected by deep-probing spies nor can be counteracted by persons of wisdom.

Ibid., Chapter Six.

Zhao She Rescues Yuyu

Zhao She was a low-ranking official with the Section for Cultivated Fields in the state of Zhao. On one occasion, Lord Pingyuan's family refused to pay land tax. Zhao She, dealing with the case according to the law, had nine stewards of Lord Pingyuan executed. Thereupon the lord burst into a fury. He was about to send his guards to kill Zhao She when the latter called on him in person. He pleaded with the lord, "Your Lordship enjoys the high status of a noble scion in Zhao. If you allow your house

3

servants to infringe upon public interests, the law will be undermined. If the law grows ineffective, the state will be weakened. If the state becomes weak, the neighboring powers will attack us. If Zhao is attacked and subdued, how will you be able to retain your position and wealth?"

Greatly impressed by Zhao She's argument, Lord Pingyuan discerned that he was a worthy man of honesty and wisdom and recommended him to the king. Thus Zhao She was put in charge of the state treasury. He proved his worth at his new position; before long, taxes were being collected in a well-organized and fair manner. As a result, the people of Zhao prospered and the state treasury and barns were filled to the brim. Naturally, the king included Zhao She among his most trusted courtiers.

The state of Zhao bordered on the powerful Qin to the west. In its military policy, Zhao had to give priority to checking Qin's eastward expansion. Thus a sort of alliance was established among Zhao, Hann, and Wei, the three neighboring states to the east of Qin.

In 269 B.C. the Qin army, under the command of General Hu Shang, invaded Hann and made camp at Yuyu (modern Heshun County in Shanxi Province). The King of Zhao sent for General-in-Chief Lian Po and asked, "Is it possible for us to rescue Hann?"

The old general replied, "The road is too long and dangerous." Another general, Yue Sheng, gave a similar answer. Then the king summoned Zhao She and asked his opinion. "The way is far and narrow," said Zhao. "If a battle takes place, it will be like two rats fighting in a small hole—the braver will turn out the victor." Satisfied, the king commanded Zhao She to lead troops to rescue Hann.

When the army had barely gone thirty *li* from the

capital city of Handan, Zhao She issued orders to halt and make camp. He also sternly forbade the soldiers to make any comment on the plan of battle, announcing, "Anyone who disobeys the order will be punished with death."

A band of the Qin troops, dispatched by Hu Shang to check the advance of reinforcements from Zhao, were stationed west of Wu'an, over a hundred *li* to the south of Yuyu. There they practiced military exercises to the accompaniment of drums and battle cries, creating such a clamor as to shake the roofs of the surrounding houses. A scout of the Zhao army came to Zhao She and urged him to make haste to rescue Wu'an. But Zhao She had the soldier beheaded on the spot for violating military discipline. The Zhao army was stationed there for a full twenty-eight days without advancing a single *li*. Zhao She spent all this time building ramparts to strengthen his camp site, as if he had no other intention than to stay there and protect himself.

By that time the Qin general Hu Shang had suspended the siege of Yuyu and rearrayed his troops to make ready for an engagement with the Zhao army, which to his great perplexity did not show up as expected. Thereupon he dispatched some scouts to find out the situation. They returned to report that the King of Zhao had indeed sent an army of reinforcements under the command of Zhao She, who had proceeded for no more than thirty *li* from Handan and had then made camp. Still suspicious, Hu Shang sent a trusted assistant as envoy to the Zhao army. A few days later, the envoy arrived at the camp of the Zhao army and was brought to Zhao She's presence. He said to Zhao She in a haughty tone, "The Qin army is attacking Yuyu and will capture it in no time. If you are able to fight, come quickly to meet us!"

Zhao She did not seem to be offended by this challenge. He assumed a humble air and replied, "My sovereign received an urgent call from Hann, our neighbor, and had no choice but to send me here to guard against emergencies. How can I have the impudence to fight the powerful army of Qin?" With this, he treated the envoy to a sumptuous banquet and showed him around the fortified camp.

On hearing the envoy's report, Hu Shang was greatly pleased and said to himself, "The Zhao troops are only thirty *li* from their capital, and yet they have stopped and built ramparts to protect their camp. It is all too obvious that they have no intention to fight. Now I will capture Yuyu for certain!" Thereupon he pulled back all the troops deployed to guard against Zhao and threw all his weight on the city of Yuyu, aiming to seize it as soon as possible.

After the envoy had left, Zhao She summoned the troops and led them on a forced march toward Yuyu. The vanguard, consisting of several thousand mounted archers, reached Yuyu in two days and one night and made camp about fifty *li* from the city. Hu Shang did not get the news until the Zhao army had settled down in an advantageous position. Shamed and angry at being fooled, the Qin general forthwith lifted the siege of Yuyu and led his troops in full force to challenge Zhao She.

In the meantime, a low-ranking officer named Xu Li asked permission to see Zhao She and offer his advice. Zhao She had him brought to his commander's tent. Xu Li said, "The men of Qin did not expect us to arrive so suddenly, and now in great anger they are coming to challenge us. You must arrange the troops in well-ordered formations to withstand the initial assaults of the enemy and seize the right moment to fight back and defeat them. This is the only way to cope with the superior Qin forces."

"Good!" Zhao She nodded approvingly. "However, as you have disobeyed my order, make ready to receive the punishment you deserve!"

To this Xu Li calmly replied, "I would prefer to be executed by axe."

"Well," said the general, "We'll settle the matter after our return to Handan."

"But first let me finish my suggestion. In the area around Yuyu, no place stands higher than the North Hill. By taking that position, we will have a great topographical advantage. But we have to act quickly before the Qin army gets around to it."

"Excellent idea!" Zhao She exclaimed in appreciation and forthwith sent Xu Li with ten thousand men to occupy the top of the North Hill. Soon after, Hu Shang arrived with his troops, only to find that the Zhao army had already seized the commanding ground. Losing his head in anger, Hu Shang ordered his men to besiege the hill. In response, the Zhao army rolled big stones down from the hilltop. Failing to gain any advantage, Hu Shang called off the assault to search for an easy route uphill when all of a sudden Zhao She arrived with the main force of Zhao and closed in on the flanks of the Qin troops. Hastily, Hu Shang prepared his forces to withhold the attack. At this juncture, however, Xu Li led ten thousand men in an overwhelming charge downhill. Assailed on all sides and cut into separate parts, the Qin army fell into disorder and suffered a crushing defeat. Hu Shang led the remnants of his troops in a wild homeward flight, traveling over fifty *li* before he finally threw off the pursuing Zhao army.

Thus the siege of Yuyu was relieved. The king of Hann went in person to Zhao She's camp to offer thanks, as well as handsome gifts, to the victorious Zhao army. Upon his return to Handan, Zhao She received the noble title Lord Mafu, ranking equal with Lian Po, the most distinguished general of Zhao. As for Xu Li, the soldier who achieved great merit by offering useful advice at the danger of his life, Zhao She highly recommended him to the king, who appointed him as Defender-in-Chief of Zhao.

Zhao She had a son named Kuo. Kuo had taken an interest in military science since he was only a child. He liked to discuss strategy with his father, getting to be so eloquent that Zhao She could hardly find a question to baffle him. Kuo's mother was very proud of him and once remarked to Zhao She in a contented tone, "Look at our son. How true it is that a general's family can produce another general!" On hearing this, Zhao She looked very grim, as if greatly annoyed. "Kuo should never be made a general!" he declared decisively. "It will be good luck for the state of Zhao if he is never employed to command a battle."

"But why?" asked his wife in perplexity. "Kuo has studied all your treatises and is matchless when discussing strategy. Why do you think him unfit to be a general?"

"Kuo believes that no one in the world is a match for him," explained Zhao She. "That is why he cannot be a general. War is such a perilous affair that, even when a general acts very cautiously and listens attentively to the views of others, he should still examine and reexamine his decisions to prevent possible errors in his battle plan, for the slightest mistake may lead to the downfall of the entire army. But Kuo takes war so lightly! If he is put in command of the Zhao army, he will undoubtedly be willful and strongheaded and make no use of the advice of his subordinates. This can only result in certain defeat for himself and catastrophe for our state."

Zhao She's words proved to be prophetic. A few years after Zhao She's death, the king made Zhao Kuo commander despite the objections of several courtiers as well as Kuo's mother. Zhao Kuo was thereafter lured into an ambush by the Qin army, and his defeat was complete indeed. He lost four hundred thousand soldiers and his own life. Therefore, he has been fairly well-known in China's military history as a person who could only "fight on paper."

Adapted from *Records of the Historian*
(Shi Ji), Tome Eighty-One

Strategy Two
Besiege Wei to Rescue Zhao

第二计 围魏救赵　　共敌不如分敌，敌阳不如敌阴。

Translation

Instead of attacking headlong a powerful, concentrated enemy, break it up into smaller, vulnerable groups. Instead of striking first, bide your time and strike only after the enemy has struck.

Purport

This strategy advises one to relieve the besieged by besieging the base of the besiegers. When the enemy deploys its main force to attack a neighboring state but meets with stubborn resistance, the best way to aid that neighbor is to launch an invasion into the enemy territory. The main force of the enemy will have no choice but to return at double speed; an ambush can then be effectively conducted to score a decisive victory.

In a broader sense, the strategy points to concentrating one's strength to attack at the enemy's weak point. In Chinese military literature, fighting the enemy is often compared to regulating rivers. When the enemy is as ferocious and overpowering as a big flood, one should avoid head-on confrontation and wait until it has lost its initial momentum, just like leading a flood into a dredged river to calm it down and make it controlable. As for a minor enemy, one can construct a "dike" to halt its movement and attack its vulnerable point to wipe it out.

Quotations for Reference

The motion of an army is similar to that of water. Water avoids heights and tends towards the ground. An army avoids the strong side of the enemy and tends towards its weak side. The flowing of water is determined by the terrain, the movement of the army by its enemy's situation. Therefore an army has no definite deployment, water no definite shape. A superb military commander gains victories by changing tactics according to his different enemies.

Art of War (Sun Zi Bing Fa), Chapter Six

Avoid the strong to attack the weak, avoid the solid to attack the brittle, and avoid the difficult to atttack the easy. This is the way to achieve a hundred victories in a hundred battles.

Summary of Military Canons (Wu Jing Zong Yao),
Tome Four of Part One

Sun Bin and Pang Juan

China's greatest military strategist is Sun Wu, author of *Art of War*. More than a hundred years after his death, a descendant of his, named Sun Bin, was born in the state of Qi. He studied the art of war from a Daoist hermit who styled himself Master of the Ghost Valley. Sun Bin had a fellow disciple named Pang Juan.

Pang Juan left the master and went to the state of Wei, where he soon won the king's favor by his eloquence on the subject of military strategy. Either because Sun Bin was taught more strategies after Pang had left or because he had better natural endowments, he apparently excelled Pang, who knew this all too clearly. Though he had risen to be a general and could make the king of Wei act upon whatever he suggested, Pang Juan was always worrying that Sun Bin might go to serve in another state, thereby becoming a formidable enemy.

With this fear in mind, Pang Juan advised the king to invite Sun Bin to Wei. Upon his arrival, Sun Bin was questioned by the king on matters of warfare and made replies that consistently revealed his good judgement. Convinced that Sun Bin was superior than Pang Juan as a military strategist, the king treated him as an honored guest, undecided as yet what postion to give him. Fearful that Sun Bin would take over his military command, Pang Juan decided to get rid of him.

Sun Bin came from the state of Qi, a powerful rival of Wei. Though Sun Bin actually had no close relatives in Qi, Pang Juan falsely reported to the king that Sun Bin longed to return to his native state. If Sun Bin went to serve the King of Qi, Pang warned, it would be disastrous for Wei, for he knew all the state secrets of Wei. The king was at last convinced when Pang Juan presented a forged letter, which had Sun Bin expressing his intention to leave Wei for Qi. Sun Bin was then arrested and thrown into prison.

By secret arrangement of Pang Juan, Sun Bin's knee-caps were cut off and his face tattooed on a charge of "having secret communication with a foreign state." Pang Juan hoped thus to prevent Sun Bin from appearing in public or serving in the court of any foreign state. Prison wardens were ordered to keep watch on Sun Bin night and day lest he attempt to escape.

Sun Bin had known that his fellow disciple was mean but had not imagined him capable of such monstrous deeds. He lay in the prison and swore revenge. But first he had to escape—an impossibility so long as they watched him so closely. Remembering that "there can never be too much deception in war," he formulated a plan. Feigning madness, he disheveled his hair, smeared saliva and snivel all over his face, cried and laughed alternately and assumed a blank stare; all this he punctuated with wild howls at the sky. When Pang Juan came to inspect him, Sun Bin would act even crazier. Still suspicious, Pang Juan had wine and delicious food brought to Sun Bin, who only seized them and threw them to the ground. Then feces were brought, which Sun Bin ate heartily. At this, Pang Juan was satisfied that Sun Bin was a madman and therefore no longer a threat to his position in Wei. Henceforth, the watch on Sun Bin was slackened, and he was sometimes allowed outdoor for some fresh air.

A year passed like this. Then one day an envoy from Qi came to Daliang, the capital of Wei. When Sun Bin heard the news, he crawled one stormy night to where the envoy stayed and asked to be brought back to Qi. As a disciple of the Master of Ghost Valley, Sun Bin was well-known among the states. The envoy, rejoicing at his good luck, used his own chariot to smuggle Sun Bin to Qi.

Upon his arrival at the capital of Qi, Sun Bin was introduced to Senior General Tian Ji, who consulted him on the art of war. Sun Bin talked on the subject for three days and nights, gaining the general's admiration and trust, and thereby became his guest of honor.

Tian Ji was very fond of horse races and often bet heavily with the young lords of Qi. Once, he took Sun Bin to one of these races. As usual, Tian Ji lost. Sun Bin noticed that the horses were classified into three grades, and that in each grade Tian Ji's horse was only a little inferior to those of the young lords. "In the next race," Sun Bin said, "bet as heavily as you can, for I will guarantee your victory." Tian Ji took him at his word and suggested to the young lords that they arrange another race. Confident in their horses' superiority, the young lords conceded without hesitation. At the racing ground, Sun Bin disclosed his tactics. "Arrange for your low-grade horse to race with their high-grades, your high-grade horse with their middle-grades, and your middle-grade horse with their low-grades. Thus, you shall lose the first round but win the last two and get the entire stake." The race turned out just as Sun Bin had predicted.

The news of the race spread quickly. King Wei of Qi heard of it and asked Tian Ji about Sun Bin. Thereupon Sun Bin was introduced to the king. The king could only regret that he had not met Sun Bin earlier and immediately appointed him Chief-of-Staff of the Qi army.

In the seventeenth year under King Xian of the Zhou Dynasty (352 B.C.), King Hui of Wei devised a plan to recover the state of Zhongshan. A small state to the northeast of Wei, Zhongshan had been conquered by Duke Wen of Wei (the ruling king's grandfather), who left his crown prince to rule it. When Duke Wen died, the crown prince returned to Wei to succeed to the dukedom, and the state of Zhao seized the chance to capture Zhongshan. Now that Wei enjoyed great power and stability, King Hui decided to take revenge on Zhao and bring

Zhongshan back under the control of Wei.

Pang Juan, however, held a different view. Zhongshan was small and remote, nearer to Zhao than to Wei. Capturing it would take much effort, but produce little effect among the warring states. "Your Majesty wants to attack Zhongshan only to punish Zhao," Pang Juan said, "but that small state is not really worth the effort. It would be best to strike directly at the capital of Zhao, Handan, revenging the past insult on the one hand and at the same time causing the other states to hold Wei in awe. If you want to become the overlord, this will be a good start."

"Excellent plan!" King Hui exclaimed. "I can kill two birds with one stone." He made Pang Juan a senior general to lead five hundred chariots to besiege Handan (modern Handan in Hebei Province).

The state of Zhao did not rank among the leading powers, and was no military rival to Wei. Knowing that Wei's attack was in revenge for the capture of Zhongshan by Zhao years before, the ruler of Zhao sent an envoy to ask help from Qi, offering Zhongshan as a gift in return. King Wei of Qi made arrangements for Sun Bin to lead the army to relieve the siege of Handan. "As a handi-capped person," Sun Bin said in reply, "I am not fit to command the army. I beg you to choose someone else." So Tian Ji was made commander, with Sun Bin serving as his chief-of-staff. Together they set out, Sun Bin trav-eling by a covered chariot.

When they reached the border, Tian Ji ordered the army to march toward Handan. But Sun Bin had another plan: "It is inadvisable to untie tangled cords by knocking them with fists or to mediate a fight by joining the fight oneself. If we avoid what is tangled and attack what is loose, preventing any further entanglement, matters will be easily sorted out. Right now the main force of the Wei army is out besieging Handan, so that the remaining force in Wei must be very weak. We can therefore march on Wei, take command of its vital communication lines, and create a false impression that we will attack Xianglin, thence to capture Daliang, the capital of Wei. As soon as Pang Juan hears the news, he will undoubtedly return in a hurry. Then we can prepare an ambush and defeat him completely. The siege of Handan, of course, will be relieved without our going there." Thoroughly convinced, Tian Ji ordered the army to head for Wei.

Pang Juan was startled when he heard that the Qi army was marching toward Xianglin, located a hundred and fifty *li* to the southeast of Daliang. The loss of Xianglin would expose Daliang to the enemy. He hastily issued an order: retreat immediatley to rescue Xianglin. Just as Sun Bin had planned, the siege of Handan was relieved without a single battle.

Sun Bin dispatched several subordinate officers to lure the enemy, while the Qi army waited along a vital passage in Guilin. Furious with the Qi army, Pang Juan could not wait to fight and was easily led into the trap in Guilin. Exhausted by traveling a long distance at double speed, the Wei army was all thrown into confusion when it fell into the ambush. Pang Juan tried to force his soldiers to fight, but they fled in all directions. It was a decisive victory for the state of Qi. When he retreated to Daliang with what was left of the routed Wei army, Pang Juan learned that it was Sun Bin who masterminded the scheme for Qi. He realized, a little too late, what a fool he had been to spare Sun Bin's life.

Ten years later the state of Hann, after conquering

Zheng, became very powerful. Zhao sent an envoy to congratulate the Marquis of Hann on his victory and to persuade him to take concerted action with Zhao against the state of Wei. The envoy proposed that Zhao and Hann divide the Wei territory between themselves. The Marquis of Hann, though interested, only agreed to take action the next year, for his nation had just suffered a crop failure. When Pang Juan heard this, he hurried to see the King of Wei. "I have learned that Hann and Zhao are preparing to make a joint attack against Wei," he said. "Before they are ready, we must strike first. Our state would be in great danger if we were to face the combined forces from Zhao and Hann." Taking the advice, the king ordered Prince Shen and Pang Juan to lead the Wei army to attack Xindu, the capital of Hann.

The Marquis of Hann's first impulse was to ask Zhao for help, but then he remembered that the commander of the Wei army was Pang Juan, who had once been defeated by the Qi army. It would be more helpful, he thought, to ask military aid from the state of Qi.

At that time Qi was ruled by King Xuan, the son of King Wei. He summoned all his ministers to discuss the letter from the Marquis of Hann. Opinions were divided. Zou Ji, the chief minister, thought it unwise to rescue Hann. He argued that the conflict between Hann and Wei would weaken both of them, which would be a blessing for the neighboring states. Senior General Tian Ji voted for rescuing Hann immediately. He said that if Wei vanquished and annexed Hann, it would then undoubtedly turn against Qi with the combined strength of two states, and the security of Qi would be in serious danger. Therefore, to help Hann against Wei was necessary for the very survival of Qi. Listening to all these arguments,

Sun Bin just sat there, smiling. When King Xuan noticed the smile, he knew that Sun Bin already had a well-thought-out plan.

"You smile without speaking," the king said to Sun Bin. "Does this mean that you think both opinions equally inappropriate?"

"Exactly!" Sun Bin replied, becoming serious. "The state of Wei, counting on its military strength, sent an expedition against Zhao ten years ago, and now it chooses Hann as its target. Can we say that all these actions are directed at Zhao and Hann alone? If Wei strengthens itself by gobbling Hann up, it will surely regard Qi as its next victim. Therefore it will be a great mistake not to rescue Hann. On the other hand, the siege of Xindu has barely begun, and Hann has not suffered any loss. If we go to rescue Xindu right now, the Wei army will turn against us, so that while Hann regains its peace effortlessly, we will take all the burden in its place. Therefore it will also be wrong to go to Hann's rescue immediately."

The ministers all expressed their admiration for Sun Bin's penetrating analysis, but none could come up with a new plan. The king felt anxious.

"You have denied," he said to Sun Bin, "and with good reason, both plans suggested by the others. Now what do you advise me to do?"

"First of all," Sun Bin replied, "we make a promise to help Hann. Feeling secure with the backing of Qi, Hann will muster all its forces to defend its capital, while the Wei army will launch vigorous attacks. When Hann has suffered some losses, the Wei army will also be duely weakened. If we send an army at that juncture, we can get twice the result with half the effort."

The ministers all agreed that it was a wonderful plan, and the king was very pleased. He sent for the Hann envoy and told him, "We promise to help Hann. Our army will arrive very soon."

Overjoyed at the King of Qi's reply, the Marquis of Hann gathered up all the troops of his state to resist Wei. After suffering heavy losses in a series of battles, he again dispatched an envoy to urge Qi to send out reinforcements immediately. A Qi army with five hundred war chariots at last set out, headed by Tian Ji, with Sun Bin again serving as his chief advisor.

As soon as they were across the border, Tian Ji ordered the army to head for Xindu, the capital of Hann. But Sun Bin stopped him, saying, "Ten years ago, we relieved the siege of Zhao without going there. To rescue Hann, it is again not necessary for us to go there."

Tian Ji was puzzled and asked, "Do you mean we should play the same old trick? What if Pang Juan recognizes our intention?"

Sun Bin replied, "The key in dissolving an entanglement is to attack what the enemy cannot afford to lose. Whatever Pang Juan thinks, he has to retreat from Hann if we attack Wei. That's the best plan I can think of." Tian Ji again adopted Sun Bin's advice and ordered the army to march on Daliang, the capital of Wei.

After a few victories, Pang Juan was in high spirits. "The resistance of Hann cannot last for long," he said to himself. "After the conquest of Hann, our army will ride the momentum of victory to subjugate Zhao. With the joint strength of Wei, Hann and Zhao, Qi can be vanquished at one stroke. After all this has been accomplished, the control of the all-under-heaven* will be within my reach. I will then be crowned with eternal glory." His daydream was interrupted by the report of a messenger from Wei: "The Qi army is attacking Wei and Daliang is in danger. The king orders you to withdraw the troops at once and return to rescue Daliang."

Pang Juan was furious, but he could do nothing but retreat. "I won't be a man," he swore between his teeth, "if I don't kill that puppy!" When the Wei army retreated, Xindu was left in peace. The tired army of Hann did not dare to pursue the enemy.

On hearing of Pang Juan's retreat from Hann, Sun Bin said to Tian Ji: "This is the second time that Pang Juan was compelled to give up what he regarded as an easy prey by our strategy of attacking Wei, so he must be in a frenzy of rage. I will therefore beat him just by making use of his fury." He went on, "The soldiers of Wei have been reputed to be agile and brave and tend to regard the Qi soldiers as cowards. Making use of this, we can turn our disadvantage into advantage. According to the *Art of War*, an army that rushes a hundred *li* after easy success will lose all its commanders, for only one-tenth of the soldiers can arrive in time; fifty *li*, and the vanguard commander will be frustrated, for half of the soldiers will fail to arrive. Right now we are in Wei's territory, so we can pretend to be weak and cowardly, as the enemy believes us to be, and lead them into our trap."

"What shall we do to lure the enemy?" asked Tian Ji.

"Make believe that we retreat in a panic," Sun Bin

---

*The all-under-heaven (*tianxia*) is the ancient Chinese concept of the human world, which consisted of China proper (the central plains) and the frontier regions inhabited by "barbarians."

replied. "So let us light a hundred thousand campfires today, and reduce the number in each following day. Pang Juan will be led to think that the morale of our army is sinking every day. He will pursue us with double speed right into Qi territory, where we will wait for him in ambush. I bet he won't be able to escape this time." Tian Ji acted upon Sun Bin's advice and the Qi army began to retreat from Wei.

When Pang Juan, traveling day and night with great haste, at last arrived in Daliang, he learned that the Qi army had already withdrawn. Determined to fight it out with the Qi army, he marched against Qi in hot pursuit. On the way, he carefully examined the camp fields where the Qi army had stayed the night, and had the campfires counted. At first, he was astonished to find as many as a hundred thousand campfires. "Such a large army should not be taken lightly," he told himself. On the second day, he was surprised and puzzled to find only fifty thousand campfires. On the third day, the number was reduced to only thirty thousand. Pang Juan exulted. "The decrease in the number of campfires," he said, "clearly proves that over half of the Qi soldiers have deserted. This is a great blessing for our king, and a good chance for me to revenge the insult of ten years ago!" He put his hand on his forehead and broke into a wild laughter.

"We have not seen the enemy yet," asked Prince Shen, "so what is there to be glad about?"

"I've always known the people of Qi to be cowards," Pang Juan replied, "and now the fact has been proved. The Qi army retreated in panic as soon as they heard I was returning to Daliang, and it has already lost half of its men in a mere three days. This is what the *Art of War* describes as 'falling into disorder without being attacked.'"

"But the people of Qi are very deceitful," Prince Shen warned, "and it is Sun Bin who is commanding the army. We can't be too careful in dealing with him."

But Pang Juan was too confident to listen. "Tian Ji and his army have come this time only to court death," he announced. "I won't miss this grand opportunity to get even with them. When I have caught Tian Ji and Sun Bin alive, all the state rulers will see how great I am." Leaving the main force of the army to follow behind, he picked twenty thousand men as the vanguard. He and Prince Shen, leading the vanguard army, travelled day and night with double speed in pursuit of the Qi army.

One day, one of Sun Bin's scouts reported, "The Wei army has already passed Shalu Mountain and is speedily approaching us." Sun Bin then reckoned that the Wei army would arrive at Malin at sunset. Malin (near modern Fan County in Henan Province) was an ideal place for an ambush: a narrow path went down the valley between two mountain peaks. A huge old tree stood in the bottom of the valley. Sun Bin had its bark stripped to expose the white wood, where he wrote in black charcoal, "Pang Juan will die under this tree." Then he had many trees cut down and piled in the valley to block the path and placed ten thousand archers on the two mountain peaks. He told them, "Start shooting when you see fire under the tree this evening." He ordered the assistant general, Tian Ying, to take thirty thousand men and lie in ambush three *li* from Malin to attack the Wei army from its rear after its entry into the valley.

Regardless of his soldiers' fatigue, Pang Juan impatiently drove them forward. Just as Sun Bin predicted, they arrived at Malin after twilight. It was a night in late autumn, with no moon and only a dozen stars. The soldiers at the head suddenly stopped and Pang Juan was told that the path was blocked by a pile of felled trees. Considering it to be a desperate attempt by Sun Bin to delay his pursuit, he ordered the soldiers at the head to remove the trees while the army waited in the valley. Then he was told that at the roadside there was an old tree that bore several characters. Pang Juan went to the tree, but it was too dark to read the words. "Bring fire!" he ordered, and many torches were lit at once. On reading the sentence, he exclaimed, "I've fallen into the trap of that lame and tattoo-faced traitor!" Before he could issue an order for retreat, thousands of arrows flew at them and the Wei soldiers scattered in panic. Several arrows hit Pang Juan. "I should have killed him before," he gave out a long sigh, "but now I have let the puppy make his name!" Then he cut his throat with his own sword. Prince Shen, who was in the rear, saw the confusion and immediately ordered the army to retreat. But he encountered Tian Ying and his thirty thousand men and was captured alive. Thus the entire twenty thousand crack troops of Wei were annihilated.

Adapted from *Records of the Historian*
(Shi Ji), Tome Sixty-Five

Strategy Three
Murder with a Borrowed Knife

第三计 借刀杀人　敌已明，友未定，引友杀敌，不自出力。以损推演。

Translation

When the enemy's intention is obvious and the ally's attitude hesitant, induce the ally to fight the enemy while preserving one's own strength. This can be inferred from *Sun*.*

Purport

To avoid getting incriminated for his act of murder, a person can sometimes cónduct the act with a "borrowed knife," which generally refers to someone else who holds a grudge against the victim. By inducing a third party to commit the murder, one will be able to achieve one's goal without being held responsible for it. In military contexts,

---

Sun (Decrease) is the forty-first hexagram in *I Ching* (Book of Changes). It can be deduced from *Tai* (Peace), the eleventh hexagram, in which a light line in the lower trigram is raised to the top. The judgement observes, "Décrease with honesty. Great good fortune, no blame." When the resources of the people are decreased to the benefit of the sovereign, good fortune will result so long as the sovereign remains honest to his duties, employing those resources to the ultimate interests of his subjects. In war, one can benefit from the decrease suffered by one's allies.

the idiom advises the commander to exploit the conflicts among various powers. To fight a strong enemy, he should find out the power groups that are at odds with this enemy and thereby induce them to fight it in his instead. In this way, he will get twice the result with half the effort.

According to ancient Chinese military strategists, when the two sides are evenly matched and another power suddenly enters upon the scene, the final outcome will undoubtedly depend on the posture of this third side; it should be won over by every possible means. Conversely, if a state tolerates its neighbor's continuous aggrandizement without checking or making use of it, the state is destined to deteriorate.

Quotations for Reference

Thus the superior battle plan is to attack the enemy's strategy. The next choice is to attack his associates. The next is to attack his army. The inferior plan is to attack his cities.

Art of War (Sun Zi Bing Fa), Chapter Three

To fight with an enemy near a neighboring state, use humble words and handsome bribes to ingratiate with that neighbor and obtain its cooperation. If we attack the enemy at the front and let the neighbor close in from its rear, the enemy will surely be defeated. The principle goes, "Make alliances in coverging ground."

A Hundred Marvelous Battle Plans, "Battle of Alliance" (Bai Zhan Qi Fa, "Jiao Zhan")

Entice the enemy to do what we want to do, so that its

strength is borrowed; trick the enemy into destroying the troops we want to demolish, so that its knife is borrowed; seize what the enemy possesses, so that its property is borrowed; provoke the enemy into internecine fight, so that its generals are borrowed; turn the trick of the enemy into our own trick and beat it at its own game, so that its strategy is borrowed. We need not act by our own but just sit and wait for things to happen. When something is found to be difficult to do, we simply get someone else to do it.

A Hundred War Maxims, "Borrow" (Bing Fa Bai Yan, "Jie")

To attack an enemy state, employ [the suspicion of] its sovereign is better than attack by yourself. To plot against an enemy state, employ [the infidelity of] its courtiers is better than carry out the plots by yourself. Split up the coalition of hostile powers and induce them to fight one another is better than fight them by yourself.

A Scholar's Dilettante Remarks on War
(Tou Bi Fu Tan), Chapter Five

To Protect Lu, Zi Gong Talks Four States into Fighting

In the late Spring and Autumn period (770-476 B.C.), the various feudal states were constantly fighting wars of conquest and annexation, while within the states chief ministers frequently sought to take the place of their lords.

In the state of Qi, the Tian family produced chief ministers for generations, finally becoming more powerful than the ruling house. Once, an acting chief minister, Tian Chang, was eager to get rid of Duke Jian of Qi and assume sovereignty himself. In a move to further consolidate his reputation and political power, he decided to launch an invasion against Lu, a weak neighboring state. He presented Duke Jian of Qi with a memorial, saying, "The state of Lu has many a time aided Wu to attack Qi. It would be a great shame for Qi not to take revenge." Duke Jian agreed and left Tian Chang to arrange the expedition. Tian Chang chose Guo Shu as supreme general and put him in command of an army with a thousand war chariots. "I shall not return until I have destroyed Lu," Guo Shu pledged at the banquet given him by Tian Chang.

At that time the great teacher Confucius happened to be in the state of Lu, his native place. Startled at the news that the Qi army had assembled at Wenshang (modern Wenshang County in southwest Shandong Province) to prepare for an all-out invasion, he hastily summoned his close disciples. He appealed to them, saying, "Lu is the site of our ancestral temples and tombs, the land of our parents and relatives. How could we sit here and watch it fall victim to foreign invaders, with the souls of our ancestors crying from under the earth? It would be a blessing for Lu if one of you could stand out to dissuade Qi from action."

Hardly had the Master finished speaking when Zi Lu, the most valorous of the disciples, rose to present himself, but the Master did not give his consent. Two other disciples applied for the mission, but, thought the Master, though they had more than enough loyalty and frankness, neither was a fluent speaker. The Master was glad when Zi Gong, who had a gift of repartee that never failed him, volunteered to go. On the same day Zi Gong packed up and made his way to Wenshang, where the Qi army was stationed. Only then did he learn that it was Tian Chang who had laid out the plan for invasion, so he proceeded to the Qi capital to see him.

Tian Chang, who knew what Zi Gong had come for, tried to intimidate him away from his purpose. "If I am not mistaken," he snapped when he saw Zi Gong, "you've come here only to talk in favor of Lu."

"Not really," Zi Gong replied calmly. "I have come only for the benefit of Qi."

"How could that be?" Tian Chang asked in surprise. "I beg you to speak a little more clearly."

"The state of Lu is not an easy prey," Zi Gong said. "It is small and has poorly fortified cities. Its sovereign is ignorant, its ministers incompetent, its soldiers unwarlike, and its people disloyal. Therefore it is difficult to overcome. I suggest that you attack the state of Wu instead. It has a vast territory with high-walled cities. Its weapons are sharp, its ministers wise, its generals resourceful, and its soldiers all battle-seasoned. Therefore it would be very easy to capture."

At these words, Tian Chang flew into a rage. "How dare you insult me by talking in such a way!" he roared. Zi Gong was not in the least taken aback, but quietly beckoned to Tian Chang to dismiss the attendants. Then he spoke seriously, in a lowered voice.

"Of course you have heard the saying that 'When there is external threat, attack the weak; when there is internal trouble, attack the strong.' Now you intend to be ruler of Qi and therefore have to face enemies within rather than outside the state. By attacking the powerful Wu you can turn it into a weapon against your enemies. If the Qi army wins, the victory will be yours; if it fails, resulting in the deaths of many generals and ministers, that will offer a wonderful chance for you to take control of the Qi court. If you dispatch someone to attack and overcome the weak Lu, all the other ministers will share the benefit and strengthen their positions, making it more difficult to carry out your plan."

At this, Tian Chang was silent for a moment. "Your reasoning is rather convincing," he said, sounding a little doubtful, "but I cannot see how I can act upon it right now. The Qi army has already camped at Wenshang; it would not be easy to move it toward Wu and what's more, people would talk about our indetermination and that would be damaging to our soldiers' morale."

"That's not as difficult as it seems," Zi Gong replied. "Let the troops stay in Wenshang while I go to the state of Wu and talk its king into attacking Qi. Then the Qi army will be justified in fighting Wu instead of Lu." Tian Chang gladly agreed to the plan.

Zi Gong made his way to Wu and had an interview with Fu Chai, the King of Wu. "Wu and Lu joined in an attack against Qi years ago," he said. "And Qi has been planning revenge ever since. Now at last the Qi forces have congregated in Wenshang, ready to vanquish the small Lu and thence proceed to conquer the whole land of Wu. Has Your Majesty heard any word about it?"

"I've indeed heard the news," the King of Wu replied, "and I imagine that you must have some good advice for me, since you have come all this way to see me."

"Suppose you take no action to prevent Qi from capturing Lu," Zi Gong said. "Wu will soon be attacked and overcome by the combined force of Qi and Lu. But if you take preemptive action and send a band of soldiers to aid Lu, the Qi forces can be no match for you. When you have captured the ten-thousand-chariot Qi with the thousand-chariot Lu as an ally, you will be able to challenge the powerful Jin over the control of the central plains. I beg you to consider my words."

"I've been thinking of this for quite some time," the king said. "Years ago Wu beat Qi and made it promise to pay tribute generation after generation, but now Qi is growing defiant. I decided on an expedition to punish it, but now the King of Yue, as I am informed, has been busy building the power of his state with the support of his ministers and subjects. It looks as if Yue is plotting against Wu. So I think it better to subdue Yue before proceeding north to attack Qi."

"There's a flaw in your plan," Zi Gong pointed out calmly. "When you turn to rescue Lu after the pacification of Yue, Lu would have already been swallowed up by Qi. And actually the King of Yue is no bother for you. Yue is weak and Qi strong; by attacking Yue you would gain a small profit, but by neglecting to check Qi you would come to much peril. To evade the strong and attack the weak is a sign of cowardice, something to be laughed at by rulers of the other states; to seek after a small profit and neglect a big peril is a sign of foolishness. How could Wu hope to gain hegemony over the all-under-heaven if it were cowardly and unwise? As for your worry about Yue, I will go and talk with the King of Yue and persuade him to lead a band of troops to aid you in attacking Qi. Now what do you think of my suggestion?"

"If you can really talk the King of Yue into it, then do so." the King of Wu replied. "I could not hope for anything better."

With this Zi Gong took leave and proceeded to the state of Yue. When Gou Jian, the King of Yue, heard that Zi Gong was coming, he had the road cleared and the best room in the finest inn prepared, and dispatched several officials to wait for Zi Gong at the roadside on the outskirts of the Yue capital. After Zi Gong settled down in the room of the inn, the King of Yue went down personally to see him. "You've taken the trouble of traveling a long way to our humble state," he said reverently, "so you must have some good instructions for me."

"I've come especially to express my condolences."

"I've often heard that misfortune and fortune are neighbors," the King of Yue said. "Therefore your condolences bring me good fortune. Please proceed with your instructions!"

"On my mission to the state of Wu, I persuaded Fu Chai, the king, to relieve Lu by attacking Qi. But Fu Chai suspects that Yue is plotting a revolt and plans to exterminate Yue first. If the plan were carried out, Yue would have no chance of survival."

"It is indeed fortunate for us to get your timely message," the astonished King of Yue said. "Now what shall we do to bring Yue out of danger?"

"Fu Chai is arrogant and quick tempered and Bo Pi, his chief minister, is never short of slanderous talk. If you present them with rich gifts and offer in the humblest terms to aid in attacking Qi with a band of Yue troops, they will be pleased and mollified. If the expedition against Qi proves a failure, Yue will benefit from the weakening of Wu's forces; if it turns out a success, Wu will doubtlessly venture onto the central plains to compete with the powerful Jin. Yue can thereby take advantage of Wu's internal laxity and revenge the former insult."

"You must have been sent here by Heaven!" the King of Yue exclaimed. "And your words shall be followed."

He then had handsome quantities of gold and silver brought out from his treasury and offered them, along with swords and fine horses, to Zi Gong. But Zi Gong declined and made his way back to the state of Wu.

He saw the King of Wu, saying, "The King of Yue was greatly frightened when I informed him of Your Majesty's words. He pledged deep obligation to Your Majesty and said he would rather die than play any tricks against Wu. He is now coming to wait upon Your Majesty and ask for forgiveness." The King of Wu was quite pleased, but he was still a little doubtful and asked Zi Gong to stay and wait.

A few days later, a Yue minister, Wen Zhong, presented himself to the King of Wu, saying, "Your Majesty has bestowed greatest favors on Gou Jian, a humble servant beside the East Sea, by sparing his life and allowing him to worship his ancestral shrines. To repay a ten-thousandth of such heavenly generosity, your servant is always ready to die the cruelest death. When he received words of Your Majesty's grand expedition to destroy the strong and aid the weak, he immediately sent me, his petty minister, to lay at Your Majesty's feet the spear *Qu Lu* and the sword *Bu Guang* and twenty fine suits of armor as a gift of greeting for the great Wu army. He also puts himself and three thousand Yue soldeirs at Your Majesty's disposal, ready to fight and die without regret."

The King of Wu was greatly pleased and, after the departure of the Yue envoy, sent for Zi Gong at once. "If Gou Jian comes with a band of troops and requests to join in the expedition, would it be right if we give consent?"

"By no means!" Zi Gong replied firmly. "It would be

unrighteous to employ a king in Your Majesty's service. Therefore, make use of the Yue soldiers, but not the king himself."

Though he had succeeded in inducing Wu to invade Qi, Zi Gong did not think Lu was completely out of danger. What if Wu, after defeating Qi, turned upon Lu for its next prey? He had to draw in another great power for counterbalance.

He proceeded to the state of Jin and got an audience with its ruler, Duke Ding of Jin. He said to the duke, "Your servant has often heard that 'strategies, if not carefully premeditated, will fail under emergent circumstances; soldiers, if not well-trained, will fail to defeat the enemy.' Now Wu and Qi are preparing for a war. If Wu fails to strike a victory, Yue will attack it from the rear; but if Wu defeats Qi, it will surely challenge Jin for hegemony in the central plains. Has Your Excellency thought about this?"

"What shall we do?" Duke Ding of Jin asked in consternation.

"Just prepare for battle," Zi Gong replied. "Exercise the troops, sharpen the weapons, and save up provisions."

As it turned out, Zi Gong's plan for saving the state of Lu worked perfectly, though at the heavy expenses of several other states. Fu Chai, the King of Wu, leading a hundred thousand troops in person, gained a great victory over Qi. With the central plains as his ultimate target, he preferred peaceful relations with the neighboring states and arranged for Qi and Lu to swear to be brothers. Then, with the victorious troops of Wu, he proceeded to attack the state of Jin. He engaged the well-prepared Jin army in battle at Huangchi (near modern Fengqiu County in northern Henan Province) and was severely defeated. Even then, he did not realize his role as a borrowed knife.

Adapted from *Records of the Historian* (Shi Ji), Tome Sixty-Seven

Strategy Four
Wait Leisurely for an Exhausted Enemy

第四计 以逸待劳　　困敌之势，不以战。损刚益柔。

Translation

It is possible to lead the enemy into an impasse without fighting. The active is weakened to strengthen the passive.*

Purport

The offensive and the defensive are the two fundamental elements in warfare. The offensive has the advantage of the initiative. The attacker gives battle at his own choice, to which the defender has to respond with counterstrokes. But this strategy puts stress on the advantages

---

*As stated in the comment on *Sun* (Decrease), the forty-first hexagram (cf. Strategy Three) in *I Ching*, "There are times when the active is weakened to strengthen the passive." The eleventh hexagram, *Tai* (Peace), consists of *Qian* (Heaven; the Active) below *Kun* (Earth; the Passive). It turns into *Sun* when the lower trigram has lost a light line to the upper trigram in a process of decreasing the active to increase the passive. This reveals a universal law of Nature: An overactive element will lose its momentum and grow weak, whereas a passive element will be able to preserve and build up its strength. In military terms, one should avoid engagement with an overwhelming enemy until its strength has worn out through overexertion.

of the defensive. Taking a position that the attacker cannot bypass and securing ample reserves, the defender has the opportunity to conserve his strength while waiting for the enemy to wear out until it has lost its superiorty. Then the moment will have come for the defender to counterattack.

Quotations for Reference

When engaged in battle with the enemy whose formation is in good order and whose spirit is high, we should not fight it at once but should wait till its formation endures so long that its spirit wanes. Strike the blow at this juncture to achieve certain victory. The principle goes, "Act late to wait for the enemy's decline."

A Hundred Marvelous Battle Plans, "Battle of Delay" (Bai Zhan Qi Fa, "Hou Zhan")

When the enemy has come from afar in high spirits and seeks a quick battle, we should stay on the defensive behind deep trenches and high bulwarks and ignore the enemy's challenge, waiting for it to degenerate. If the enemy challenges us by creating incidents, we must not move. The principle goes, "When secure, remain immobile."

Ibid., "Battle of Security" ("An Zhan")

When engaged in battle with the enemy, if we have suffered losses before, we must investigate the morale of the soldiers. If the morale is high, encourage the troops to fight again; if the morale is low, take time to recover and do not employ the troops until they are again employable. The principle goes, "Rest the army without over-exerting it; boost its morale to elevate its combat power."

Ibid., "Battle of Rest" ("Yang Zhan")

The enemy's esprit cannot remain always triumphant without discouragement, the enemy's precaution cannot remain always vigorous without laxity, so why don't we wait for its decline and its fault instead of trying to win by luck through a quick battle?

Strategies from the Thatched Cottage
(Cao Lu Jing Lue), Tome Six

Shake the morale of the enemy troops and weaken the determination of their general. An army is intrepid in the morning, relaxes as the day draws on, and prepares to retreat at nightfall. A master of the art of war shuns the intrepidity of the enemy and waits for its decline and retreat: This is the method for handling the troops' morale. Wait in good form for the enemy to fall into disorder, wait quietly for the enemy to howl and scream: This is the method for handling the troops' psychology. Occupy a nearby position and wait for the enemy to come from afar, take a good rest and wait for the enemy to exhaust itself, and eat plenty and wait for the enemy to starve: This is the method for handling the troops' strength. Do not intercept troops holding well-ordered banners or attack troops that are in a well-shaped formation: This is the method for adjusting strategy to different situations.

Art of War (Sun Zi Bing Fa), Chapter Seven

One who arrives first at the battleground to wait for the enemy is reposed, whereas one who arrives late at the battleground and accepts battle in haste is fatigued. Therefore, a good commander maneuvers the enemy and is not maneuvered himself.

Tempt the enemy with profit to make it come forward, forestall the enemy with danger to prevent it from coming. In this way, we can exhaust the enemy when it is reposed, starve the enemy when it is well-fed, and provoke the enemy when it is calm.

Ibid., Chapter Six

When on the defensive, make use of yin (potential); when on the offensive, make use of yang (vigor). Exhaust the enemy's yang and nourish our yin before vanquishing the enemy. This is the strategist's secret for exercising yin and yang.

Li Jing's Reply to Emperor Taizong of Tang
(Tang Tai Zong Li Jing Wen Dui), Tome Two

Wang Jian Destroys the State of Chu

Ying Zheng, the future First Emperor of China, became king of the state of Qin at the age of thirteen. He spent his first ten years getting rid of his all-powerful chief minister, Lü Buwei, who was finally exiled in 237 B.C. and later committed suicide. Starting from 230 B.C., the king launched a ten-year campaign to subdue and wipe out the six other rivaling states.

By 226 B.C., the states of Hann, Zhao, and Wei had been conquered and Yan decisively defeated. A young general named Li Xin distinguished himself in fighting the Yan army. Once, he pursued the King of Yan with a band of several thousand troops till they arrived at the Yan River. The King of Yan fled by crossing the river, but the crown prince, who led the covering force in the rear, was taken prisoner. Greatly pleased, the King of Qin decided to make Li Xin a top commander.

The king summoned his ministers and generals and declared his decision to send an expedition to conquer Chu, the most powerful state in the south. "To seize the territories of Chu," he asked Li Xin, "how many troops would you need?"

"Two hundred thousand."

A little hesitant, the king turned to Wang Jian, a much older and more experienced general.

The old man replied after a long pause. "In my opinion, an army less than six hundred thousand can achieve nothing. The Qin soldiers have won great victories, but they have also become very exhausted. The older ones are weak, and the recruits are inexperienced. The Chu army will have two great advantages of proper rest and familiar terrain. Such a battle cannot be won by mere bravery!"

"How strange!" the king exclaimed. "The numerous battles you fought only make you overcautious. General Li, though very young, is wise and brave. His words satisfy us well." With this, the king put Li Xin in command of two hundred thousand troops and ordred him to march south and attack Chu. Wang Jian, on the other hand, retired to his hometown at Pinyang (a hundred and fifty *li* northeast of Xianyang, the capital of Qin). He well knew that he would be shamed if Li succeeded and recalled if Li failed. So he kept himself well-informed of the situation by sending scouts to the battlefield.

Meanwhile Li Xin had seized two walled cities from Chu, and his assistant general, Meng Tian, had taken a third. As they had agreed to join forces at the city of Chengfu, Li led his soldiers in a forced march westward, pursued by a band of the Chu army commanded by Xiang Yan. However, Li regarded Xiang Yan as a vanquished foe incapable of any major action.

After three days of rapid marching, the Qin army stopped to make camp and take a proper rest. Scarcely had they settled down when Xiang Yan, who arrived immediately afterward, launched a violent attack. Tired, unprepared and caught in unfamiliar terrain, the men of Qin were overwhelmed. When Li Xin gathered his scattered troops again, he counted a loss of nearly half of his men and seven subordinate officers.

Shortly afterward, the King of Qin arrived at Pinyang in his royal chariot. He pleaded with Wang Jian, the old general, "Our men suffered such a disgrace, all because I refused to listen to your good advice. The Chu army is marching west toward us. I beg you to forgive my mistake and lead our men to drive back the invaders."

"I am old and sick," Wang Jian replied.

"You may have reason to turn down my request, but you cannot sit around doing nothing when Qin is endangered!"

"But I need six hundred thousand men."

"Granted."

When Wang Jian started out with his troops, the king went personally to see him off at Bashang to the east of the capital. "I will wait for news of your victory!" the king said. Wang Jian, however, seemed reluctant to set out.

"This is indeed a very arduous expedition. I long very much to be endowed with fertile fields and fine houses. That would put my heart at ease."

The king smiled. "You need not worry about this."

"But I've served you as general for so many years," the old man said, "and won no small merit. In spite of this, I failed to get the title of marquis. Now that I see you still have some use for me, I will surely take this chance to collect some fortune for my children."

The king laughed. "I will give you your fief and have the other rewards delivered to your house as soon as I return. You need only think about defeating the enemy!" At this Wang departed, but on his way to battle he sent another five memorials asking for manors and gardens.

Many people were perplexed that Wang Jian should show such extraordinary interest in wealth. That was so unlike him. To this the old general explained, "The king is very proud and suspicious. He has put me in command of nearly all the soldiers of Qin. If I do not ask for wealth and titles to show my intention of establishing myself in Qin, the king would doubt my loyalty. That would make it impossible for me to devote myself to matters of warfare!"

When Chu learned that Li Xin was replaced by Wang Jian, who was coming with six hundred thousand troops, it shifted into a defensive position and quickly mobilized its entire military force.

When Wang Jian arrived on the Chu border, he had the soldiers build and strengthen defence works, ignoring the Chu army's repeated challenges. The soldiers often took baths and ate rich food, which Wang Jian shared with them. Then one day Wang Jian asked, "What kind of games are the soldiers playing?"

"Some are throwing stones, others are practising the long jump."

"So they are ready to fight now!" Wang concluded.

For many days the Chu army had tried in vain to engage the Qin army in battle and had grown tired and low-spirited. Assuming that the Qin army had no intention to attack, Xiang Yan decided to retreat. It was at this point that Wang Jian ordered his well-rested men to attack. Xiang Yan was killed, and many of Chu's walled cities were taken. This happened in 224 B.C.

The next year, the Qin army proceeded further east, captured the King of Chu, and completely subdued this once powerful state.

Adapted from *Records of the Historian*
(Shi Ji), Tome Seventy-Three

Strategy Five
Loot a Burning House

第五计 趁火打劫　　敌之害大，就势取利。刚决柔也。

Translation

When the enemy suffers from a major crisis, seize the chance to gain advantage. Resolution prevails over pliancy.*

Purport

A burning house falls into commotion and tumult. Thus a thief can seize the chance to loot the property in the house when the doorkeeper and house guards are busily engaged in putting out the fire. The idiom therefore means to take advantage of someone's misfortune to do him harm.

In war, a burning house symbolizes a nation that is

---

*This phrase is taken from the comment on *Guai* (Determination), the forty-third hexagram in *I Ching*. The hexagram has the symbol of water (*Dui*) above heaven (*Qian*). Rising high above the sky, the water can hardly retain its position and tends to fall down. The hexagram consists of five yang lines below a yin line, which represents a ruler who has become isolated and will soon be overthrown by his subjects. In war, when a powerful enemy is suffering a major setback, one must seize the chance to attack with speed and determination.

suffering a major crisis or is on the decline. By attacking such a nation, one can get twice the result with half the effort. Thus the strategy advocates the universal principle of striking at the enemy's weak points and in this sense relates to several other strategies. For instance, when one chooses to set fire to the house before looting it unopposed instead of squaring with the house guards, one may also be said to have applied Strategy Nineteen: Remove firewood from under the caldron. If only a tactical move rather than a strategic plan is involved, Strategy Twelve is relevant: Lead away a goat in passing.

Quotations for Reference

In warfare, the situation can be exploited to our advantage. Close in on an enemy who tends toward downfall and we can rout his troops. The principle goes, "Defeat an enemy who tends toward defeat."

A Hundred Marvelous Battle Plans, "Battle of
Situation" (Bai Zhan Qi Fa, "Shi Zhan")

Confronted with an enemy whose formation is disorderly and whose soldiers are in a hubbub, we can gain advantage by launching an attack immediately. The principle goes, "Seize the enemy when it is in chaos."

Ibid., "Battle of Chaos" ("Luan Zhan")

To decide whether to launch troops and mobilize the multitudes for the purpose of protecting the people and punishing the criminal, consult heavenly conditions rather than signs of augury. Launch a punitive expedition against a rival state afflicted with an inept sovereign, muddled government, arrogant troops, impoverished civilians, exile of the wise, execution of the innocent, and calamities of drought, locusts, or hailstorms. Thus we can achieve certain victory. The principle goes, "Formulate battle plans in accordance with heavenly conditions."

Ibid., "Battle of Heaven" ("Tian Zhan")

In ancient times, one who was good at warcraft attained victories that were easily attainable. Therefore, the victory brought him neither fame for wisdom nor merit for courage. Each victory was certain, for it was gained by defeating an enemy who had already lost. Thus a victorious army gains victory before seeking engagement whereas a doomed army seeks victory during the engagement.

Art of War (Sun Zi Bing Fa), Chapter Four

The Battle of Muye

The prehistoric Shang Dynasty ruled for about five hundred years in the Yellow River valley. It was overthrown and replaced in early eleventh century B.C. by the feudal state of Zhou, which came from the west, the area of modern Shaanxi.

According to ancient tradition, the ancestor of the ruling tribe of Zhou was a semi-divine master of agriculture. Pressed by incursions of hostile tribes, his descendants moved to the Wei River basin in modern Shaanxi. There, nourished by the fertile soil of the loess plateau, a nation took shape, growing steadily in size and strength over the years. Eastward expansion brought it under the cultural as well as political influence of the Shang.

The Zhou conquest of Shang took three generations. First Jili, the chieftain of Zhou, had a military clash with

Shang. He was defeated and slain. His son, posthumously known as Wen Wang (Civil King), ruled for a total of fifty years and paved the way for the final conquest, which was to be carried out by his second son, Wu Wang (Martial King). Though Wen Wang was extolled in history as an exemplary ruler of virtue and wisdom, much credit for the establishment of the Zhou Dynasty also went to Jiang Shang, better known by his polite name Ziya. He served as councilor-in-chief for both Wen Wang and Wu Wang and played an indispensable role in formulating the policy for both the consolidation of the Zhou state and the military maneuvers against the Shang and the feudatories loyal to it.

At his ascension in 1030 B.C., Wu Wang was endowed with several legacies by his father: a wealthy and formidable state, the reputation of virtue and benevolence among the neighboring tribes, and of course Jiang Ziya, an advisor of the highest wisdom.

The rise of Zhou power coincided with the decline of the Shang kingdom under its last ruler, Zhou Wang. A man of exceptional talents and strength, he indulged himself in incessant orgies and debauchery and neglected the crying needs of his subjects. He was learned enough to refute any admonition from his courtiers and eloquent enough to justify any vile act he committed. Many of the neighboring tribes rebelled against him and much complaint rose among his own people. Zhou Wang responded with new forms of torture. He also continued to wage campaigns against unruly tribes to the north and east, thus depleting the resources of the kingdom.

In the second year of Wu Wang's reign, Jiang Ziya sent spies to Zhaoge (modern Qi County in Henan Province), the capital of Shang. They returned with the report that the Shang court was being manipulated by a group of treacherous courtiers and there was widespread discontent among the populace. In a tentative military operation to test the attitude of his neighboring feudal lords, Wu Wang led the Zhou army on a march into Shang's territory, arriving at Mengjin (to the northeast of modern Mengjin County, Henan Province). To benefit from the popularity of the late Wen Wang among the feudal lords, Wu Wang proclaimed the expedition in Wen Wang's name and set up Wen Wang's memorial tablet in a war chariot supported by the central force. He styled himself "Crown Prince Fa," Fa being his personal name.

On arrival at Mengjin, Wu Wang was joined by the troops led by eight hundred feudal lords, who gathered there of their own accord. They urged Wu Wang to advance on the Shang capital immediately. To this Wu Wang replied: "You know not the edict of Heaven. The time has not come yet."

The gathering at Mengjin caused consternation in a few sober courtiers of the Shang. However, their pressing admonitions were readily dismissed by Zhou Wang, who had full confidence in his possession of the Mandate of Heaven. Instead, he continued the costly campaign against the local tribes to the east. The few honest courtiers were either slain or thrown into prison.

In the fourth year of Wu Wang's reign, two of Shang's Three Dukes (the three most prestigious positions in court throughout imperial China) defected to join Wu Wang, bringing the musical instruments of the Shang court. Thereupon Wu Wang summoned his army and proclaimed to the allied tribes: "Shang is guilty of grave crimes. We must join forces and launch an expedition to punish the sinner and save the people!"

The expedition followed the beaten track of the trial campaign of two years before. Wu Wang mustered a force of three hundred war chariots, three thousand armed guards and forty-five thousand footmen. Feudal lords from various tribes arrived to join him, bringing a total of four thousand war chariots. With this, they started out on the eastward expedition in the first month of the year 1027 B.C. After crossing the Yellow River, they proceeded on to the north toward Zhaoge, the capital of Shang. The troops encountered no resistance, as Shang's neighboring states had no intention to fight for it and also because the main force of the formidable Shang army was engaged in yet another campaign against the "eastern barbarians."

Early in the second month, they arrived at Muye (to the south of modern Qi County in Henan Province), located only seventy *li* from the Shang capital.

King Zhou Wang was celebrating in the usual extravagant manner his victory over the "eastern barbarians" when news of the invasion reached him. He called off his celebration at once and hastened to organize the defense of the capital. By this time, he had only received news of victory and some trophies and prisoners from his latest eastern venture; the main body of the expedition had not yet returned. Forced into an impasse, Zhou Wang adopted an urgent measure that proved to be his last grave folly. He opened up the packed prisons in the capital, proclaimed a general amnesty for all the inmates and armed them with makeshift weapons. Placing these convicts and the equally reluctant prisoners of war from the east as the vanguard of the relatively small stationary army of the capital, Zhou Wang led them in person on a march westward to meet the invaders.

Before taking the field, Wu Wang assembled the allied troops in front of the memorial tablet of Wen Wang. Dressed in a suit of armor, he held a yellow axe, symbol of authority, in his left hand and a white banner in his right hand. Solemnly, he read to the warriors the famous "Oath of Muye," which expressed the following:

Brave soldiers: Raise your dagger-axes, align your shields, hold your spears straight and listen to the oath. The ancients said, "The hen should not herald the break of day. A hen that does so foretokens the ruin of the household." Now King Zhou Wang listens only to the words of a woman. He has abolished ancestral sacrifices, slain his good ministers, caused suffering to the people, and violated the dictates of Heaven.... Be as brave as the tiger and bear, as fierce as the jackal and wolf. Do not kill those who have surrendered; do not recoil from fear. Exert yourselves, or else you shall harvest the ruination of your own making!

Historians do not agree on the actual number of troops involved in the battle of Muye. An educated guess puts the allied force under Wu Wang at tens of thousands, and the Zhou troops were undoubtedly outnumbered by the opposing army of Shang by a big margin.

After the whole army had sworn to the oath, Wu Wang issued the order for attack. It was still early in the day. The four thousand war chariots pushed forward in an even, regulated pace while several hundred brave warriors headed by Jiang Ziya charged headlong at the enemy. The vanguard of the Shang army, consisting of the newly released convicts and prisoners of war, defected to join Wu Wang at the very beginning of the engagement. Thus the Shang soldiers in the rear were caught in an adverse position. Before noon the Shang army had collapsed and King Zhou Wang fled back to Zhaoge. He rushed into the palace and hastily put on his best clothes embroidered with the brightest pearls, and committed suicide by jumping into a bonfire on the Deer Terrace, his notorious pleasure ground. Thus the Shang Dynasty came to its dramatic end.

Adapted from *Records of the Historian*
(Shi Ji), Tome Four

Strategy Six
Make Noise in the East and Attack in the West

第六计 声东击西　　敌志乱萃，不虞，坤下兑上之象。利其不自主而取之。

Translation

The enemy's command becomes confused and unrestrained, with the symbol of *Kun* below and *Dui* above, signifying river water ready to overflow the bank.* Subdue the enemy when it has thus lost its discipline.

Purport

In war, surprise can be achieved by deception as well as by the troops' speed and mobility. As a Chinese saying goes, "There can never be too much deception in war."

---

*This is *Cui* (Gathering), the forty-fifth hexagram in *I Ching*. It consists of water (*Dui*) above the earth (*Kun*). As water gathers into a lake, so men get together to undertake a common cause. Therefore the hexagram signifies good luck, with its judgement declaring, "It is of benefit to set out." However, if the lake becomes too full, it will overflow the banks, resulting in disaster. Similarly, disagreement and strife may occur among a large crowd of people. Thus, a host of forces that are gathered to defend a city must have a unified leadership in order to hold back the siege of the enemy. If they become divided in opinion or hesitant in judgement, the situation will fall out of control.

However, this strategy cautions that one has to ascertain the enemy's lack of judgement before making false moves to deceive it. A commander with presence of mind knows his strong and weak points and arrays his troops accordingly; he is therefore not liable to be misled by the enemy's false gestures. He can even pretend to be deceived and turn the enemy's trick against it. Therefore, when one tries to deceive the enemy, he must bear in mind the deceitfulness of the enemy. Thus Sun Zi observes, "In the past, those who were good at marshalling warfare first made sure that they could not be defeated and then waited for an opportunity to defeat the enemy."

Quotations for Reference

In warfare, what is termed "noise" refers to false moves. Make noise in the east and attack in the west, or make noise there and attack here, so that the enemy cannot decide where to put up its guard. Thus we can attack the place where the enemy has no defense. The principle goes, "Against a good attacker, the enemy does not know where to defend."

> *A Hundred Marvelous Battle Plans*, "Battle of Noise" (Bai Zhan Qi Fa, "Sheng Zhan")

"One who is skilled at maneuvering the enemy takes a false move so that the enemy must take a corresponding move."

> *Art of War* (Sun Zi Bing Fa), Chapter Five

To make a successful attack, attack a place that the enemy does not defend; to make a successful defense, defend a place that the enemy does not attack. Therefore, against a good attacker, the enemy does not know where to defend; against a good defender, the enemy does not know where to attack.

Ibid., Chapter Six

Attack values going in. He is not a good attacker who goes in by the place where he has attacked. Defense values going out. He is not a good defender who goes out by the place where he has retaliated. Attack at one place and go in by another; retaliate at one place and go out by another. This is the artifice for attack and defense.

*A Scholar's Dilettante Remarks on
War* (Tou Bi Fu Tan), Chapter Four

The Eastern Han General Geng Yan Subdues Zhang Bu

In the late Western Han, the national resources of the empire were gravely depleted in the victorious but costly campaigns against the nomadic Xiongnu tribes to the north. Performance of the heretofore efficient government also deteriorated as a result of internecine struggles in the imperial court. Previously, intrigues by families of empresses or imperial consorts to take the throne had failed without exception, with each conspiring family being exterminated. But in A.D. 7, one such attempt saw success. Wang Mang, the usurper, was the son of the ruling empress dowager. He abolished the imperial Han house and adopted the dynastic title of Xin (meaning "new").

Wang Mang ruled as emperor for sixteen years. His drastic policies, such as the transformation of the official hierarchy, the adoption of new types of currency, and measures to curb land annexation, served only to aggravate the political and economic instability of the empire. In the last years of his reign, the nation was disrupted by widespread rebellions launched by desperate peasants as well as members of the dethroned Han imperial house. In A.D. 23 the capital Chang'an was captured by a powerful rebel band, "the Red Eyebrows," and Wang Mang was slain.

Civil warfare continued for many years, as more than one person was aspiring for the vacant throne. Liu Xiu, member of a distant branch of the Han imperial house, assumed the title of emperor of Han in A.D. 25 and proceeded to subdue other contestants for the throne. The regime founded by him, referred to as the Eastern Han, ruled for two hundred years. Liu Xiu's success had much to do with his ability to solicit capable people into his service. Among the generals who contributed to the founding of the dynasty with their military accomplishments, Geng Yan was not the least well-known.

Geng Yan was a native of Maolin in Fufeng Commandery. His father, Geng Kuang, served as a commandery governor under Wang Mang's reign. After Wang Mang's death, a member of the Han imperial house named Liu Xuan enthroned himself, taking the reign title of Gengshi; most of the rivaling bands of troops gave at least nominal allegiance to him. Geng Yan was sent by his father to pay tribute to the Gengshi emperor, but on his way he met Liu Xiu and stayed to serve him. At that time Liu Xiu was only one of the numerous military strongmen in the empire, and he also had to pay lip service to the Gengshi emperor.

As Liu Xiu gained steadily in influence and prestige, the Gengshi emperor grew anxious. He sent an envoy to summon Liu Xiu to Chang'an and appointed his trusted generals to take over the area under Liu Xiu's control. But Geng Yan persuaded Liu Xiu to defy the Gengshi emperor and to fight for control of the empire. Following this advice, Liu Xiu finally took the imperial title in A.D. 25, soon after the Gengshi emperor was killed. Geng Yan was appointed a supreme general.

In the fifth year of Liu Xiu's reign (A.D. 29), Geng Yan led troops eastward in a campaign against Zhang Bu, a recusant military leader who was stationed at Ju District in Qi Commandery in Qing Region. Zhang Bu commanded his supreme general Fei Yi to defend the district of Lixia and divide some of his troops to defend Zhu'a and Zhongcheng. On crossing a river, Geng Yan attacked the city of Zhu'a in early morning, capturing it before noon. He deliberately left a breach in his encirclement to allow some of the enemy soldiers to flee to nearby Zhongcheng. On learning of the fall of Zhu'a, the troops at Zhongcheng panicked and scattered away.

Fei Yi's younger brother Fei Gang was stationed at the city of Juli over fifty *li* to the east of Lixia. Finding Lixia well-defended, Geng Yan did not assail it but instead advanced eastward to lay siege to Juli. He ordered the troops to fell a great amount of trees with which to make war machines for attacking the city. A few days later, he learned from prisoners that Fei Yi was planning to lead a band of troops to relieve Juli. Thereupon Geng Yan announced to his officers and men that an all-out offensive on Juli would be launched in three days. In the meantime he arranged for the escape of a few captured enemy soldiers; these fled to Lixia and reported to Fei Yi about Geng Yan's plan of attack.

The plot worked out. Three days later, Fei Yi marched

towards Juli with thirty thousand crack troops. Geng Yan was highly pleased to hear the news and told his officers, "I ordered the making of assault machines with the very purpose of tempting Fei Yi to leave his nest. Now he is coming to fulfill my plan!" He left three thousand men to hold back the army in Juli and led his main force to intercept Fei Yi. He arrayed the troops on a hill, there engaging Fei Yi in battle and inflicting a crushing defeat, with Fei Yi killed on the spot. Returning to Juli, Geng Yan had Fei Yi's head displayed to the people of Juli, who became extremely fearful. Fei Gang had no choice but to desert the city; he therefore withdrew further east to join Zhang Bu. Geng Yan looted Juli's wealth and supplies to provide for his own troops and went on to destroy forty more strongholds of Zhang Bu, achieving the total pacification of Jinan Commandery. He then advanced on to the east.

At the time Zhang Bu was staying at his capital city of Ju, with his younger brother Zhang Lan defending the city of Xi'an (to the east of modern Huantai County in Shandong Province). Forty *li* to the south of Xi'an lay the larger city of Linzi, which also held a considerable body of troops. Geng Yan halted at a small town between Xi'an and Linzi and ordered the officers to rest the army for five days and prepare for an attack on Xi'an. On hearing the news, Zhang Lan put his men on a round-the-clock alert.

In the middle of the night of the fourth day, Geng Yan arranged a full meal for his troops. At dawn the next day, he led them to attack the city of Linzi. One of the generals objected, proposing that they attack Xi'an instead. To this Geng Yan explained, "Though the city of Xi'an is small, it has strong fortifications and is well prepared to defend itself. Linzi is larger but less well protected. By a surprise attack on Linzi, we shall be able to seize it within a day. When Zhang Lan loses Linzi and therefore the connection line with Zhang Bu, he will be scared into retreat. In this way we can kill two birds with one stone. On the other hand, if we attack Xi'an first, we cannot be sure of capturing it. Even if we do, it will cost us many days and heavy losses. Then Zhang Lan will fall back to Linzi and strengthen his position there against our weakened forces. Now take heed: In what a mess we would find ourselves if I adopted your suggestion!"

Thus they attacked Linzi, overcoming its defenses in half a day. When the news spread to Xi'an, Zhang Lan became frightened and pulled back to join his brother Zhang Bu at the city of Ju.

Geng Yan did not advance eastward to besiege Ju. He did not even move on to conquer its peripheral areas, which were in easy reach after the seizure of Linzi and Xi'an. Instead, he stationed the troops in Linzi, declaring that he preferred to take control of these areas after Zhang Bu arrived to strengthen them. On hearing this, Zhang Bu roared with laughter. "Big Geng has only a small and exhausted army, and he thinks I am afraid of him!" He summoned troops that reportedly numbered two hundred thousand and marched to the west with his three younger brothers, including Zhang Lan, and a general named Chong Yi.

They arrived at the east of Linzi and made ready to assail the city. Geng Yan then led a body of cavalry across the Zi River, where they encountered the enemy's vanguard led by Chong Yi. The cavalry officers asked for orders to charge forward, but Geng Yan did not allow them, saying that such a move would only result in a minor victory and make Zhang Bu cautious. So he withdrew the better part of his troops to the inner city. This convinced Zhang Bu of his superiority and he advanced straight ahead to charge at Geng Yan's camps in the outer city. Geng Yan dispatched a general named Liu Qin to check the enemy while he himself observed from an elevated terrace. After Liu Qin engaged the enemy in an entangled battle, Geng Yan commanded his crack troops to venture out of the city and attack Zhang Bu, splitting his army in the middle. Poorly coordinated and attacked on two sides, Zhang Bu's army was plunged into disorder and suffered heavy losses. In the fierce combat, Geng Yan was hit on his leg by an arrow. He cut off its protruding end with his sword and went on fighting, so that even his personal guards did not know he was injured until their return to the city after dark.

The next morning, Geng Yan was about to go out and fight the enemy again when he got word that the emperor was coming with reinforcements. The governor of Taishang Commandery, Chen Jun, who accompanied Geng Yan on the expedition, suggested that they wait for the emperor's arrival to arrange a concerted attack. But Geng Yan knew that Zhang Bu had already lost his vim and might pull away at any moment. He had no time to lose if he wanted to demolish Zhang Bu's main force once and for all. So he replied to Chen Jun in a stern tone, "A good subject should welcome the emperor with wine and beef instead of rebel troops!"

With this, he launched a major attack on the dispirited army of Zhang Bu, fighting from early morning to twilight and inflicting another grave defeat. The ditches in the outer city were filled with corpses. In the meantime Geng Yan dispatched two bands of forces to lie in ambush outside the outer city. When Zhang Bu realized he could gain no advantage and decided to withdraw the troops, he walked right into the ambush ring and was compelled to fight on both wings. He then fled eastward for over eighty *li* before he got rid of the pursuing army.

A few days later, the emperor arrived at Linzi. He highly praised Geng Yan, comparing him to Han Xin, the supreme general who helped Liu Bang found the Han Dynasty.

After that, Geng Yan proceeded further east to pursue Zhang Bu, who had retreated to the city of Pingshou in Bohai Commandery. Having lost his crack forces, Zhang Bu was utterly disheartened. He went to surrender at Geng Yan's camp, baring his chest and proffering an axe as a gesture of apology and total submission. Thereupon Geng Yan entered the city of Pingshou and gathered Zhang Bu's remaining forces, which still amounted to over a hundred thousand. He disbanded these troops and allowed the soldiers to return to their native towns. Thus the eastward campaign ended with the pacification of twelve commanderies; Gang Yan then led his victorious army back to the capital. The complete pacification of the entire empire was to take another seven years.

Adapted from *History of the Later Han Dynasty* (Hou Han Shu), Tome Nineteen

Strategy Seven
Create Something out of Nothing

第七计 无中生有　诞也，非诞也，实其所诞也。少阴、太阴、太阳。

Translation

Make a false move, not to pass it for a genuine one but to transform it into a genuine one after the enemy has been convinced of its falsity. Genuine strength grows under the cover of false appearance, just as yin growing to the extreme transforms into yang.

Purport

This idiom is generally used today to describe someone who makes a claim, usually an accusation, that is totally groundless.

In warfare, it is often necessary to feign maneuvers to distract and mislead the enemy. However, deception like this is easy to recognize and readily becomes ineffectual. Besides, the enemy can be defeated only by genuine actions, not false moves. Therefore, a wise war strategist knows not only how to deceive the enemy by false movements but also when to transform them into genuine combat operations.

Quotations for Reference

One who is good at the art of war can employ either extraordinary or normal forces on every occasion, so that the enemy is deprived of judgement. Therefore, he can achieve victory by using either normal or extraordinary forces.

Li Jing's Reply to Emperor Taizong of Tang
(Tang Tai Zong Li Jing Wen Dui), Tome One

To put up an appearance, we show the enemy our extraordinary instead of normal forces; to win a victory, we fight the enemy with our normal instead of extraordinary forces. This is the interconversion of the extraordinary and the normal.

Ibid., Tome Two

Make normal use of our extraordinary force and attack with this factual normal force, which the enemy takes to be the extraordinary; make extraordinary use of our normal force and attack with this factual extraordinary force, which the enemy takes to be the normal. This keeps the enemy in a weak position and us in a strong one.

Ibid., Tome Two

General Zhang Xun Defends Yongqiu Against Outnumbering Rebels

Zhang Xun was a native of Nanyang (modern Nanyang in southwestern Henan Province) in Deng Commandery. He took the imperial examination for civil service recruitment and gained the esteemed degree of Presented Scholar, for which he was appointed Magistrate of Qinghe

District. He distinguished himself in that position and, after his tenure was over, was recalled to the Tang imperial capital Chang'an. At that time, the emperor was indulging himself in a life of reckless orgy and dissipation with his favorite concubine, Lady Yang, to the total neglect of his regal duties. The councilor-in-chief, Yang Guozhong, Lady Yang's cousin, was an unscrupulous and corrupt man who manipulated imperial power for his own benefit. Zhang Xun was informed by his fellow officials that, in spite of his meritorious service, he could get no promotion unless he presented the councilor-in-chief with handsome bribes. Zhang Xun's refusal to do so resulted in his transfer to be the magistrate of Zhenyuan District in Qiao Commandery.

In 755, the fourteenth year of the Tianbao reign in the Tang Dynasty, a military commissioner of Tartar origin named An Lushan started a widespread rebellion that shook the entire empire to its very foundation. At that time many years of peace and prosperity had left the imperial troops in a rotten, inadequate condition, and they were fatally slow to undertake concerted action to halt the advance of the rebels. In the meantime the violent measures of An Lushan had roused general indignation, and everywhere people rose up in arms to protect themselves against the atrocious rebel troops.

Early the next year a rebel commander attacked and captured Song and Cao commanderies. The governor of Qiao Commandery surrendered to the rebels. Knowing that Zhang Xun was very talented in the art of war, the governor therefore put him in command of a body of soldiers and ordered him to proceed westward to welcome a band of rebels that was arriving. Zhang Xun seized the opportunity to turn against the governor and henceforth led his men in guerrilla warfare against the rebel troops. Soon after, near Yongqiu District, he met Jia Ben, Defender of Shanfu District (modern Shan County in southern Shandong Province), who had also collected a band of forces to harry the rebel army in the area. The two joined forces. Altogether they had about two thousand soldiers.

Linghu Chao, the magistrate of Yongqiu District (modern Qi County in mid-eastern Henan Province), believing that the Tang emperor had little chance to survive the rebellion, turned his allegiance to An Lushan and surrendered the district to the rebel army. Subsequently, he led his men in an attack against the Tang soldiers in the city of Huaiyang and captured over a hundred prisoners. He took them back to Yongqiu and had them tied up in the district courtroom. He was about to carry out their execution when an emergency call brought him out of the city to arrange his troops against the activity of some hostile forces. The captured Tang soldiers broke loose, finished off the few rebel guards, and ushered Jia Ben and Zhang Xun into the city.

Upon his return, Linghu Chao was unable to enter the city. Jia Ben had even killed Chao's wife and children and ordered their bodies to be displayed over the city gate. At this, Chao burst into a fit of uncontrolled fury and assailed the city violently. Jia Ben was killed in the tangled fight that ensued. Zhang Xun, who took over the command, was finally able to repulse the rebels. At that time Li Zhi, a member of the imperial house and Governor of Lingchang Commandery, was appointed by the emperor to supervise military actions against An Lushan in areas south of the Yellow River. At his suggestion, the emperor issued an edict making Zhang Xun a military commissioner.

In the third month, Linghu Chao gathered forty thousand men to assault Yongqiu. The city residents began to panic and even the soldiers grew fearful. Zhang Xun summoned the officers and said to them, "The rebels know pretty well that the city holds very few troops and therefore tend to underestimate us. We can strike a victory if we suddenly open the city gate and fall upon them. By such a small victory, we can reassure our people, and our city will be saved." The officers all agreed with him. Leaving a thousand soldiers to defend the city, Zhang Xun divided the rest of the troops into several bands and led them on a surprise sortie out of the city gate. This counterattack was totally unexpected by the rebels, who, as Zhang Xun had said, believed the defenders to be weak and powerless. Hence they were caught completely off guard and forced into a scrambling retreat, leaving a great quantity of provisions behind for the needy Tang soldiers.

The following day Chao returned to assail the city. The rebels used a hundred cannons to destroy the battlements on the city gate. Then they swarmed to climb up the city wall by scaling ladders. The Tang soldiers gathered stacks of straw, doused them with crude oil, lighted them, and threw them at the ascending rebels. As the rebels frantically fell back, the Tang soldiers charged out of the city gate to deal them a counterblow.

Thus, for every trick that the rebels used in their assault, Zhang Xun could always devise a quick counterstroke. Although short of food, short of manpower, and with no reinforcements whatsoever, he and his troops always got the upper hand in the hundreds of minor and major battles they fought in the next two months against the rebel army, which outnumbered them twenty to one.

Tired and discouraged, Linghu Chao withdrew his troops. Zhang Xun immediately ventured out to pursue the rebels, capturing two thousand of them. Linghu Chao was almost made a prisoner himself. Shamed into anger, Chao returned to continue his siege of Yongqiu, with the simple aim of wearing out the city.

The city began to run out of food. Zhang Xun learned that hundreds of ships of provisions that Linghu Chao had gathered for the rebel army would soon arrive along the Bianshui River north of Yongqiu. So he made conspicuous reinforcements at the southern end of the city. Fearing another counterattack, Linghu Chao hastily moved most of his men to the south. Zhang Xun then sent a band of brave soldiers to proceed secretly to the Bianshui River. There they seized over a thousand *hu** of rice and salt, burning whatever provisions that they could not carry with them.

A few days later, the city began to run out of arrows. Zhang Xun made a thousand straw figures and used ropes to send them down the city gate in the dead of night. Awakened by the sentry to find numerous dark figures slipping down the city wall, the rebel troops shot a storm of arrows before realizing they had been tricked by some scarecrows. On pulling up the scarecrows, the Tang soldiers acquired tens of thousands of arrows. The following night, the rebel troops again saw dark figures slipping down the city gate. They laughed and took no more heed. However, the dark figures turned out to be five hundred select Tang soldiers. Once safely on the ground, they flung themselves on the undefended rebel camp, setting some of the tents on fire and chasing the alarmed rebels for

---

*1 *hu* = 100 liters.

over ten *li*.

Then the city began to run out of firewood and water. Zhang Xun sent Linghu Chao a message, saying, "I cannot sustain my men and therefore want to leave this city. Please withdraw your troops so that we can get away." Chao was only too glad to get rid of Zhang Xun, so he agreed without hesitation. When the rebel troops had withdrawn, Zhang Xun dispatched his soldiers to go out and gather firewood and water. Upon his return, Linghu Chao was very indignant to find Zhang Xun still in the city. Zhang Xun explained to him, "We are only too willing to go, but we lack thirty horses." Chao took Xun at his word and gave him thirty horses. Zhang Xun distributed them among his officers and ordered, "When the rebels arrive, each of you must capture a rebel officer."

The next day, Chao arrived at the city gate and berated Zhang Xun for not keeping his promise. Zhang Xun smiled and said, "I want to leave, but my officers and men do not want to. What can I do?" Enraged, Chao challenged Xun to a fight, but he had not yet arranged his troops properly when the city gate opened and thirty cavalrymen rode out, capturing fourteen rebel officers and killing over a hundred soldiers. By this time, Linghu Chao must have realized that he was absolutely no match for Zhang Xun, for then he withdrew his troops to the city of Chenliu (modern Chenliu in Kaifeng, Henan Province) and did not venture out again to attack Zhang Xun until he was joined by another rebel general with more rebel troops.

Postscript: In 757 Zhang Xun was murdered by rebel troops when the strategic city of Suiyang, which Xun had defended for ten months, finally yielded. Historians agree that these ten months provided the Tang regime with a crucial breathing space to assemble troops and transport provisions. Therefore Zhang Xun was honored by the emperor and given the posthumous title Commander-in-Chief of Yangzhou. Today he is still remembered both as a resourceful general and a national hero.

Adapted from *New History of the Tang Dynasty* (Xin Tang Shu), Tome One Hundred and Ninety-Two

Strategy Eight
Advance Secretly by Way of Chencang

第八计 暗渡陈仓　示之以动，利其静而有主。益动
而巽。

Translation

Make a false move to tie up the main force of the enemy. It is of benefit to set forth in conformity to the situation.*

Purport

The idiom refers to the strategy used by Liu Bang, founder of the Han Dynasty, when he embarked on a campaign against his rival contender for the empire, Xiang Yu. He feigned preparation to advance along the normal path but in the meantime dispatched his army to proceed secretly by a roundabout route at Chencang, thus taking the enemy by surprise and seizing large territory at a relatively small cost.

---

*This phrase is taken from the comment on *Yi* (Increase, Benefit), the forty-second hexagram in *I Ching*. The judgement says, "It is of benefit to start out. It is of benefit to cross a great river." The hexagram consists of wind and wood (*Xun*) above and movement (*Zhen*) below. Wood that is moved by the wind symbolizes a boat, which can be used to cross a great river. In other words, conditions are ripe for undertaking a great mission.

The strategy puts stress on the application of a false move, usually a frontal attack, to conceal covert maneuvers undertaken to outflank the enemy. This basically conforms to Sun Zi's strategy of engaging the enemy by the normal force and defeating it by the extraordinary force, only in this case the enemy is contained not with the presence of the main force but with a feigned gesture, which nevertheless requires some concrete actions to establish its credibility.

Quotations for Reference

Confronted with an enemy across a river, in order to cross the river at a distant site, we should prepare many boats as if we were to cross the river nearby, so that the enemy will react by concentrating its forces. Then we can cross the river where the defense is weak. If no more boats are available, we should just use trees and bamboo, rushes and reeds, small-mouthed and amphora-like jars, urns and sacs, and spear bars to ferry across. The principle goes, "When distant, feign to be near."

A Hundred Marvelous Battle Plans,
"Battle of Distance"
(Bai Zhan Qi Fa, "Yuan Zhan")

Proceed where the enemy does not know; attack when the enemy is unprepared. Out of ignorance, the enemy cannot forestall our move; out of unpreparedness, the enemy cannot cope with our attack. Therefore we can achieve complete victory without harm.

Book of Master Guan (Guan Zi),
Chapter Seventeen

General Han Xin Captures the Area of Wei

China's first centralized monarchy, the Qin Dynasty, lasted a mere fifteen years (221-206 B.C.). Its downfall was initiated by a peasant uprising in 209 B.C., which, though finally suppressed, triggered off the rebellion of aristocratic clans of the former warring states conquered by the First Emperor of Qin. The most prominent of those rebels of nobility was Xiang Yu, a descendant of a powerful military family in the state of Chu. He emerged as the leader of all the anti-Qin troops. The Second Emperor of Qin was slain in 206 B.C., and Xiang Yu took it upon himself to confer the title of feudal prince on eighteen military commanders and divide the land of the empire among them. He set himself up as Overlord of West Chu, taking nine commanderies as his kingdom and Pengcheng (modern Xuzhou in Jiangsu Province) as the capital.

This division of the empire left quite a few officers dissatisfied, thinking that their rewards were not equal to their merits. Soon contentions broke out in the newly divided empire. Liu Bang, enfeoffed as Prince of Han, seized the chance to challenge Xiang Yu. Thus ensued a four-year war known as the Chu-Han conflict.

Xiang Yu had the best army in the empire under his command, but he was vainglorious and distrustful. Liu Bang was much more shrewd and patient, and he acquired and managed to keep the service of several remarkable advisors and generals. He mostly depended on a townsman named Xiao He for civil administration, a Daoist scholar named Zhang Liang for devising strategies within the command tent and a capable general named Han Xin for gaining victories on the battlefield.

Han Xin, who later received the title Marquis of

Huaiyin, was born into a poor family in Huaiyin (modern Huaiyin County in Jiangsu Province). Unable to support himself either by working for the government or doing business, he often had to eat at the houses of his friends, who finally got tired of him. When rebellions against Qin broke out all over the country, Han Xin went to join the troops under Xiang Yu. But he never found any opportunity to display his ability, for Xiang Yu made no use of the many suggestions he made.

After the destruction of Qin, Xiang Yu enfeoffed Liu Bang as Prince of Han. Liu Bang accepted the title and proceeded to his fief, which lay in the areas of Ba and Shu (modern Sichuan Province). Disappointed with Xiang Yu, Han Xin went to join Liu Bang. Though he impressed Xiao He favorably, he failed to attract any attention from Liu Bang. Therefore he deserted again. When Xiao He heard the news, without informing Liu Bang he hurried out to pursue Han Xin. Someone told Liu Bang that Xiao He had deserted. Liu Bang was furious, feeling as if he had lost an arm. Two days later, Xiao He returned. Liu Bang was both happy and angry to see him. "Why did you desert?" he demanded.

"I did not desert. I went after a deserter!"

"Who was this deserter?"

"Han Xin."

"Do you expect me to believe this?" Liu Bang exclaimed. "Over a dozen generals have deserted, and you never seem to care. This going after Han Xin is a lie!"

"Those generals are easy to find," Xiao He said. "But Han Xin is incomparable. If you are satisfied with your present position, you will have no use for him. But if you want to contend for the all-under-heaven, Han Xin is the only one to lay plan with."

"All right," said Liu Bang. "For your sake, I'll make Han Xin a general."

"That won't stop him from deserting."

"Then I'll make him a supreme general," Liu Bang said generously. He was about to send for Han Xin when Xiao He stopped him.

"You are always so arrogant and ill-mannered!" Xiao He said. "You want to appoint a supreme general, but you treat him as if he were a mere child. No wonder Han Xin chose to desert!"

"So what shall I do?" Liu Bang asked.

"Select an auspicious day, go on a fast, set up a platform, and conduct a proper ceremony for the appointment."

The ceremony was duly held and, each expecting to be the new supreme general, the officers were astounded when it turned out to be Han Xin.

When the ceremony was completed, Liu Bang asked Han Xin, "My chief minister has repeatedly recommended you, so what do you have to teach me?"

Han Xin replied by asking, "If you march eastward to contend for the all-under-heaven, you will have to rival with Xiang Yu, won't you?"

"That's right," said Liu Bang.

"So how do you compare yourself with Xiang Yu in bravery, kindness, and strength?"

Liu Bang was silent for a while and at last replied, "I am no match for him."

"I congratulate you for your frankness," Han Xin said, "and I also think you are no match for Xiang Yu in these respects. But I know something more about him, for I have served him before. Xiang Yu has indeed an imposing figure and when he explodes in anger he can frighten a thousand men out of their wits. But all this amounts to no more than the might of an ordinary man, for he does not know how to acquire the service of capable generals. He always treats other people with concern and respect and speaks with such kindness. When someone is ill, he will go and visit him with tearful eyes and share his own food with him. However, when it comes to conferring a title and fief to a person of merit, Xiang Yu will be very reluctant. Unwilling to part with the seal, he will keep it in his own hands, fumble with it until it becomes badly worn. This is what we call 'womanly kindness.' Though Xiang Yu has brought all the lords of the various states to submission, he has also committed several serious mistakes. First, he set his capital at the city of Pengcheng near his hometown instead of in the strategic area of Guanzhong. Second, he conferred the titles of prince according to his own preferences, in total disregard of the edict of the Righteous Emperor, whom he exiled to the south. This has caused much discontent among the lords. Also, Xiang Yu's troops loot and burn wherever they go, and the people bow to them out of fear instead of love. Guanzhong is now ruled by the three princes of Qin appointed by Xiang Yu. They used to be generals of the Qin imperial army. They were spared when they surrendered to Xiang Yu, but the over two hundred thousand Qin soldiers under their command were buried alive. Therefore these three princes were greatly hated by the Qin people. When you defeated the Qin army and marched into Guanzhong, you abolished the stringent laws of Qin and treated the people with honesty and kindness. By the edict of the Righteous Emperor, you should become the Prince of Guanzhong, and the people know this. Moreover, many of the men under your service are from the east and eager to return to their home country. If you choose to march east, it will not be difficult to recover the land of Guanzhong."

Liu Bang was greatly pleased with Han Xin's words, regretting that he had not known him earlier.

Soon afterwards, a general of Qi named Tian Rong revolted against Xiang Yu. He murdered the Prince of Qi and took the title of prince for himself. This incident touched off widespread rebellions and internecine fights among the princes. Xiang Yu, furious that his authority was thus challenged, set out north on a punitive expedition against Qi.

Liu Bang knew that his chance had come; he had to strike quickly, for the new Prince of Qi was no match for Xiang Yu. Formerly, when Liu Bang accepted from Xiang Yu the title Prince of Han and proceeded to his fief in the mountainous areas of Ba and Shu, he had all the plank roads burned down behind him, both to prevent attacks from the other princes and to show that he had no intention to march east again. At Han Xin's advice, Liu Bang dispatched a large body of troops to repair the plank roads, feigning as if he were to march out of Shu and proceed east by these roads. In the meantime his main force moved secretly by way of Chencang (near modern Baoji in Shaanxi Province). Caught off guard and without any local support, the three princes of Qin were defeated and forced to surrender to the Han army. Thus Liu Bang took control of the whole area of Guanzhong in a few months.

By that time Xiang Yu had routed and killed Tian Rong, bringing the area of Qi into submission. However, his troops again committed atrocities, burning conquered cities and looting the households of innocent civilians.

The people of Qi found it unbearable and elected a new prince, who organized a revolt against Chu. Thereupon Xiang Yu decided to stay a little longer to pacify the area, although he had already learned of Liu Bang's eastward invasion.

While Xiang Yu was thus engaged, Liu Bang was able to summon an allied army of Wei, Hann, Yan, Qi, Zhao and Han, which amounted to over five hundred thousand. With this he attacked Xiang Yu's homeland, capturing Pengcheng in the fourth month of 205 B.C. Drunk with victory and puffed with pride, Liu Bang seized the treasures and women in Xiang Yu's palace for himself and indulged in drinking parties and various other dissipations every day.

The Prince of Qi collected some thirty thousand men and maintained a resolute resistance against Xiang Yu in the walled city of Chengyang. Xiang Yu had been laying siege to the city for many days without gaining any advantage when he got word that Liu Bang had seized Pengcheng. Xiang Yu immediately left Qi and marched westward with thirty thousand crack troops. He engaged Liu Bang in battle near Pengcheng and inflicted a grave defeat. Liu Bang's troops suffered such great casualties that the Sui River was blocked by the bodies of Han soldiers. Liu Bang was compelled to pull back again and again, finally reaching Xingyang (to the west of modern Zhengzhou in Henan Province), where he was able to station his army for a rest. He set up a fortified camp, which was protected by a deep moat, and sent for provisions and reinforcements from the area of Guanzhong.

After Liu Bang's defeat at Pengcheng, the princes of Wei, Qi and Zhao turned against him, declaring allegiance to Xiang Yu. While Liu Bang was on the defensive at Xingyang, he sent Han Xin with a band of troops to advance on the area of Wei (in modern central and southern Shanxi Province). At this the Prince of Wei sent a supreme general to the ford of Puban (to the west of modern Yongji, Shanxi Province) on the Yellow River to prevent Han Xin's army from crossing it.

Han Xin arrived at the river in the eighth month. He had many banners erected along the bank and all his boats lined up, pretending to prepare for a major attack. Meanwhile he secretly dispatched his main force to proceed northward to Xiayang (to the south of modern Hancheng in Shaanxi Province). Unknown to the Wei army, they swiftly crossed the river in makeshift wooden pails. They then marched at double speed and soon started to besiege the city of Anyi (to the east of modern Yuncheng in Shanxi Province). The Prince of Wei was completely taken by surprise. In a great hurry, he led troops in person to meet Han Xin. He was gravely defeated and surrendered to Han Xin. Thus the area of Wei was restored to Han rule. After the crushing defeat at Pengcheng and the lengthy stalemate at Xingyang, the news of Han Xin's restoration of Wei sounded like heaven's blessing to Liu Bang.

Adapted from *Records of the Historian*
(Shi Ji), Tome Ninety-Two

Strategy Nine
Watch a Fire from Across the River

第九计 隔岸观火　　阳乖序乱，阴以待逆。暴戾恣
睢，其势自毙。顺以动豫，豫顺以动。

Translation

When the discord of the enemy becomes apparent,
take no action but instead wait for the oncoming upheaval. Cruel internecine struggles can only cause the enemy
to die at its own hand. Movement at an opportune moment brings happiness.*

Purport

Though great significance is attached to swiftness in
military operations, a good commander should master the
art of delay. He does not seek engagement as soon as he
can but instead chooses to bide his time and wait for the
best moment for attack—ideally, when his army is at the

---

*This phrase is taken from the comment on "Happiness" (*Yu*), the
sixteenth hexagram in *I Ching*. The judgement says, "Happiness. It is of
benefit to embark on the cause of a marquis and send forth the troops."
The hexagram has the symbol of thunder (*Chen*) above the earth (*Kun*).
It represents the period when the first spring thunder defrost the earth,
bringing new life to all creatures. Applied to warfare, the hexagram
instructs one to wait for an opportunity. As the thunder does not strike
during the winter, so a military leader refrains from taking action until
the time is ripe.

best of its strength and the enemy at its worst. Such is the underlying principle for all delay-oriented strategies.

To reap the spoils of a contest fought among others points to yet another basic law of warcraft: the use of outside forces to achieve one's goal. This puts this strategy in line with Strategy Five, "murder with a borrowed knife," which is more difficult to exercise as it often requires intricate manipulation of various powers, either friendly, hostile, or non-committal.

Quotation for Reference

When the enemy finds itself in a predicament and wants to engage us in a decisive battle, wait; when it is advantageous for the enemy but not for us to fight, wait; when it is expedient to remain still and whoever moves first will fall into danger, wait; when two enemies are engaged in a fight that will result in defeat or injury, wait; when the enemy forces, though numerous, suffer from mistrust and tend to plot against one another, wait; when the enemy commander, though wise, is handicapped by some of his cohorts, wait.

A Hundred War Maxims, "Wait"
(Bing Fa Bai Yan, "Chi")

Cao Cao Destroys the Three Yuan Brothers

Yuan Shao, the most powerful of the rivaling commanders who divided the empire among them after the fall of the Eastern Han Dynasty, had three sons, named Tan, Xi and Shang. Shang, the youngest, excelled his elder brothers in valor and military capacity and enjoyed special fondness of both his parents. Yuan Shao wanted to have Shang succeed him as the ruler of the four regions of Qing, You, Bin and Ji. However, he did not declare his intention openly but instead set about putting Shang in a position of advantage. He let Shang stay in Ji Region, the power base of the Yuan house, and sent the eldest son, Tan, to govern Qing Region to the east.

One of Yuan Shao's advisors spoke up against the plan, saying, "When a rabbit pursued by ten thousand people is caught by someone, all the others give up simply because the one who will win the rabbit has been determined. Now Tan, as the eldest son, should be your successor, but you have sent him away without confirming his position. I am afraid this may lead to disaster someday." But Yuan Shao dismissed him, announcing, "I will put each of my sons in command of a region in order to test their abilities." With this he made his second son, Yuan Xi, the Regional Inspector of You and his nephew Gao Gang the Regional Inspector of Bin.

In A.D. 200, the fifth year of the Jian'an reign, Yuan Shao suffered a crushing defeat at Guandu at the hands of Cao Cao. This marked the beginning of his end. In the fourth month the following year, he was again gravely defeated at Cangting Ford in southeastern Ji Region. Ashamed and angry of his defeat, Yuan Shao got very sick, vomiting blood. He died in the fifth month of the seventh year of the Jian'an reign (A.D. 202).

After Yuan Shao's death, his officials prepared to call back his eldest son, Tan, to succeed him. But Shen Pei, whom Tan intensely disliked, fabricated a false will of Yuan Shao with which he managed to set up the youngest son, Shang, as the successor. At the news of his father's death, Tan left the Qing Region for the District of Ye, the temporary seat of the Ji Region. While on the way, he learned that Shang had already succeeded his father as ruler of the four regions. At this Yuan Tan adopted for himself the title Horse and Chariot General and made camp at Liyang by the Baigou River to the south of the Ye District.

In the ninth month Cao Cao crossed the river to attack Yuan Tan. Tan asked help from Shang, who arrived at Liyang with reinforcing troops, leaving Shen Pei to defend the city of Ye. After losing several battles, the two Yuan brothers fell back into the fortified camp and no longer ventured out. At the same time, Shang dispatched his general Guo Yuan to join forces with Gao Gan and a chieftain of the Huns in an attack on Hedong Commandery of Si Region to the southeast of Ji. After some initial triumphs, the expedition failed miserably. Guo Yuan was killed and the Hun chieftain surrendered to Cao Cao.

In the second month of the eighth year of the Jian'-an reign (A.D. 203), Cao Cao recommenced his attack against the Yuan brothers at Liyang. He engaged them in battle in front of the city and inflicted a grave defeat. Tan and Shang had to abandon Liyang and return north to defend the city of Ye.

In the fourth month Cao Cao arrived at Ye. There he had the troops harvest all the wheat in the fields outside the city. The generals all wanted to assail the city, but an official named Guo Jia voted against it. He argued, "Yuan Shao died before he chose his successor. Now Tan and Shang are contending with each other for control of the four regions. They will put their disagreement aside and join forces if we press them too hard, but if we give them a breathing space, a fight will soon break out between them. Therefore it would be best for us to proceed southward to attack Liu Biao in the Jing Region. We can easily strike back as soon as the Yuan brothers fall on each other."

"Good!" said Cao Cao. So in the fifth month he returned to the capital of Xuchang in Yu Region, leaving General Jia Xing stationed at Liyang.

When Cao Cao's troops were pulling away, Tan went to Shang and told him, "I was defeated by Cao Cao last time because the armor of my soldiers was in bad condition. Now Cao Cao's men are retreating. They all long to go home and are no longer prepared to fight. We can easily beat them if we launch a sudden attack when they are crossing the river." But Shang was suspicious of his brother's real intention. So he neither sent him more soldiers nor gave him any new suits of armor. Tan became furious and led his men in an attack against Shang. Failing to gain the advantage, he led his troops northeast to the city of Nanpi. A couple of local officials from Qing Region arrived to join him, but most of the cities defected in favor of Yuan Shang.

In the eighth month Shang led a band of troops personally to attack Tan, severely defeating him. Tan withdrew south to the city of Pingyuan, where he strengthened the ramparts around the city to defend himself. After Shang closed up his encirclement, Tan sent an envoy named Xin Pi to seek help from Cao Cao.

Most of Cao Cao's advisors said they should put their attention on Liu Biao instead of wasting time with the Yuan brothers, who did not constitute much of a threat after all. Xun You expressed a different view, saying, "When the all-under-heaven is in upheaval, Liu Biao simply stays motionless even though he commands a most advantageous position, the prosperous land traversed by the Yangtze and Han rivers; surely he has no ambition to compete for the rule of the empire. But the Yuan brothers still possess four regions with hundreds of thousands of troops. If somehow Tan and Shang get on good terms and fully utilize what their father has bequeathed, it will be extremely difficult to destroy them. So we'd better deal with them now, when they are in discord."

Cao Cao thought Xun You's idea to be sound. But he still wanted to conquer Jing Region first and strike back when the Yuan brothers were further weakened by their infighting. When Xin Pi learned that Cao Cao did not mean to send troops to help Yuan Tan, he asked to see him.

"Why should I trust Tan? How can I be sure that Shang can be defeated?" demanded Cao Cao.

"We don't have to argue whether Tan can be trusted or not," replied Xin Pi. "The matter can be settled by a simple assessment of the situation. The dissension between the Yuan brothers has not been sowed by someone else but has resulted from their own choice, for each of them believes that he has the power to unify the world after getting rid of the other. If Tan were not forced into an impasse, he would not have sought help from you, the deadly enemy of his father. Suppose you send troops to attack Ye. Shang will be left with no base if he does not abandon Liyang to relieve Ye; whereas if he does, Tan will pursue and attack him from the rear. This is a perfect opportunity, and you cannot afford to lose it. On the other hand, the Jing Region is prosperous and stable. It would be highly inexpedient to pass over the chaotic and attack the well-disciplined. Besides, who are the most powerful strongmen in the world but the Yuan brothers? By pacifying the area north of the Yellow River, you will rock the world with your fame."

"Well said!" Cao Cao exclaimed. So he agreed to lead troops to attack Shang and rescue Tan.

In the tenth month Cao Cao arrived at Liyang. Learning that Cao Cao had crossed the river, Shang gave up his attack on Pingyuan and withdrew to Ye. At this juncture, two of Shang's generals defected and surrendered to Cao Cao. Tan secretly bestowed his seals upon them in an attempt to bring them under his service. When Cao Cao learned of this, he was further convinced of Tan's deceitfulness. In order to allay any suspicions Tan might have about him, Cao Cao arranged the marriage between his son Cao Zheng and Tan's daughter before withdrawing his army.

In the first month the following year (A.D. 204) Yuan Shang left his generals Shen Pei and Su You to defend Ye while he went northeast to assail Tan at Pingyuan. Cao Cao decided to relieve the siege of Pingyuan by attacking Tan at his base. Therefore he proceeded to the Huanshui River to the south of Ye. Su You made a plan to cooperate with Cao Cao's forces from the inside, but his plot was exposed and he had to flee the city to seek refuge in Cao Cao's camp.

On arriving at Ye, Cao Cao decided to attack the city by building earthern ramparts and digging tunnels. When he failed to gain the advantage, he left Cao Hong to continue the assault while he himself led a band of troops to seize the surrounding areas. He gained several victories, overcoming the cities of Maocheng and Handan. Then the magistrates of two nearby districts, Yingyang and She, surrendered to Cao Cao. Cao Cao granted both of them the title of Marquis in order to attract more defectors.

In the fifth month Cao Cao gave up the mounds and tunnels and began to dig a trench to encircle the city of Ye. He made it shallow at first, so that Shen Pei laughed and made no attempt to stop the construction. Then one night Cao Cao had his soldiers work with all their might. The next day the people within the city were dismayed to find themselves hemmed in by a trench nearly seven meters wide and seven meters deep that was filled with water diverted from the Zhang River. By and by, the city ran out of provisions, and over half of its residents starved to death.

In the seventh month Shang led ten thousand troops to rescue the city of Ye. Some of Cao Cao's generals proposed, "We'd better avoid them since they are a returning army that will fight to the death." Cao Cao said, "If Shang comes by the main road, we will have to avoid him; but if he arrives by way of the West Hill, we will capture him."

Yuan Shang took the mountain path to arrive at the bank of Fushui River, about twenty *li* north of the city of Ye. At night he had bonfires lighted to notify the people in the city. Seeing the fire, Shen Pei led a band out of the northern gate, endeavoring to break through the encirclement and join forces with Shang. However, both Shen Pei and Yuan Shang were defeated by Cao Cao's troops. Shen Pei pulled back into the city while Cao Cao pursued Shang, inflicting several defeats until Shang lost most of his troops and all his provisions. Shang then fled to the state of Zhongshan.

In the eighth month the city of Ye finally yielded; a subordinate officer of Shen Pei opened a city gate at night and let in Cao Cao's troops. The next month an imperial edict was issued making Cao Cao Governor of Ji Region.

Formerly, when Cao Cao was busily engaged in the siege of Ye, Yuan Tan had taken the chance to turn against him and seize control of the surrounding commanderies of Ganlin, Anping, Bohai, and Hejian—all in eastern Ji Region. Then he went to attack Shang in the state of Zhongshan. Shang lost the battle and was compelled to go further north to the city of Gu'an in You Region, where he joined his second elder brother, Yuan Xi. Tan collected the scattered soldiers left by Shang and returned to Longchou in Pingyuan Commandery. At this, Cao Cao sent Tan a letter accusing him of a breach of faith. He sent back Tan's daughter before launching a punitive expedition against him. Tan pulled back from Pingyuan and proceeded north to defend Nanpi in Bohai Commandery. Cao Cao took control of the seat of Pingyuan Commandery and went on to pacify the surrounding districts.

In the first month of the tenth year of the Jian'an reign (A.D. 205), Cao Cao led his troops in an attack on Nanpi, overcoming it. Yuan Tan fled the city but was caught and killed by Cao Cao's troops.

Meanwhile, attacked by two of his own generals who had turned against him, Yuan Xi fled with Yuan Shang to seek help from the Wuhuan, a nomadic clan in Liaoxi Commandery. By this time Cao Cao had seized control of all the four regions formally ruled by Yuan Shao. It was not until spring of the twelfth year (A.D. 207) that Cao Cao prepared an expedition against the Wuhuan. Many generals regarded the expedition as unnecessary, saying, "Shang has suffered grave defeats and lost all his territory and troops. In such dire straits, how will he be able to win the support of those barbarians, the Wuhuan, who are cold-hearted and value profit above everything else? If we go such a long distance to punish Shang, Liu Bei will probably talk Liu Biao into attacking Xuchang. That will put us in an adverse position."

At this, Libationer Guo Jia spoke up. He said to Cao Cao, "Though your fame has shaken the world, the barbarians are not on guard because they live in remote areas. So we can take them by surprise and defeat them. Besides, Yuan Shao was benevolent to the people under his rule. Now we have brought the people of the four regions into submission merely by force. If Shang gains the help of the Wuhuan and collects people who remain faithful to the Yuan family, he will be able to stir up a great furor among the populace. Then we will find the Qing and Ji regions breaking out of our control. As for Liu Biao, he is only capable of empty talk. And he knows pretty clearly that he is not capable enough to engage the service of Liu Bei. If he dispatches Bei on an important expedition with a large body of troops, he will be afraid that Bei may take the chance to break away from him. If he instead proposes that Bei be sent on a minor mission, he will be afraid that Bei may not be willing to do it. Under such conditions, why should we worry about them?"

Cao Cao adopted Guo Jia's advice, and the troops started out on the long-distance expedition. They were halted at the city of Wuzhong, where the summer rain had turned the road into pools too deep for horses and carriages and too shallow for boats. With the help of a renegade official, Cao Cao took a deserted path and pushed forward for hundreds of *li* before the Wuhuan got the news. In the eighth month Cao Cao arrived at Mount Bailang, where he engaged the Yuan brothers and the Wuhuan in battle, inflicting a crushing defeat. The chieftain of the Wuhuan clan was killed. Shang and Xi managed to escape with several thousand cavalrymen. They went east to seek refuge with Gongsun Kang, Governor of Liaodong Commandery.

Cao Cao was urged to take the chance to subdue Gongsun Kang, who had always refused to pay tribute to the imperial court at Xuchang. But Cao Cao smiled and said, "I have just ordered Gongsun Kang to deliver the heads of Shang and Xi to me. There's no need to employ troops."

In the ninth month Cao Cao withdrew his troops. Soon afterwards, the heads of Xi and Shang were brought before him, along with a submissive note from Gongsun Kang. Some generals could not help asking Cao Cao, "Why did Gongsun Kang kill Shang and Xi after our retreat?"

"Gongsun Kang has always been wary of the Yuans," Cao Cao replied. "He was afraid that Shang and Xi might usurp his position at Liaodong. If we had pressed them with violent attacks, they would have joined together in defending Liaodong. But our retreat prompted them to plot against one another."

Adapted from *History of the Three Kingdoms*
(San Guo Zhi), "Biography of Emperor Wudi"
and "Biography of Yuan Shao"

Strategy Ten
Hide a Dagger in a Smile

第十计 笑里藏刀　　信而安之，阴以图之。备而后动，勿使有变。刚中柔外也。

Translation

Reassure the enemy to make it slack, work in secret to subdue it; prepare fully before taking action to prevent the enemy from changing its mind: This is the method of hiding a strong will under a compliant appearance.

Purport

The idiom represents an archetype in world literature: a person with a smiling face and a cruel heart, dubbed a "smiling tiger" in Chinese folklore.

In everyday life, one grows wise after being tricked by a smiling tiger. In warfare, such belated wisdom has little or no use, for it may have been bought at such a high price that one can no longer afford the remedy. Therefore, before the outcome of war becomes apparent, a peace-making message is to be almost invariably regarded with suspicion. Thus, an overconfident enemy general is needed for the successful application of this strategy.

Quotations for Reference

When the enemy is strong and cannot be easily overcome, we should puff it up with humble words and ample gifts and wait until it reveals its weak point to subdue it once and for all. The principle goes, "When the enemy is humble, make it proud."

A Hundred Marvelous Battle Plans, "Battle of Pride" (Bai Zhan Qi Fa, "Jiao Zhan")

When engaged in battle with the enemy, we may send envoys to negotiate for peace. The enemy may reach an agreement with us, but among its officers different opinions will arise. We can therefore take advantage of its laxity and select crack troops to attack and defeat it. The principle goes, "An appeal to peace without concrete plans signifies a deceptive plot."

Ibid., "Battle of Peace" ("He Zhan")

Humble words and reinforcement of defense signify an oncoming attack; ... an appeal to peace without concrete plans signifies a deceptive plot.
Du Mu's Note: "If the enemy sends envoys speaking humble words and at the same time strengthens its defenses as if it is afraid of us, it must be attempting to puff our pride and make us relax before launching its attack against us."
Chen Hao's Note: "When neither army of the two states engaged in an invasive or punitive war is weakened or subdued and one side sues for peace with no apparent reason, it can only be that it has some serious trouble at home and needs a temporary peace, or that it has perceived the weakness of its opponent and sues for peace to

put it off guard so as to launch a suprise attack."

Art of War (Sun Zi Bing Fa), Chapter Nine

Lü Meng Captures the City of Jingzhou

The fall of the Han Dynasty was followed by many years of bloody strife among warlords, all of whom paid lip service to a puppet Han emperor. Only three of them survived to set up the Three Kingdoms: the Kingdom of Wei under Cao Cao, the Kingdom of Wu under Sun Quan, and the Kingdom of Shu under Liu Bei.

Liu Bei, who bore the same family name as the Han imperial house, was said to be a distant uncle of the puppet emperor. Therefore he was called "Imperial Uncle Liu." Apart from his three sworn brothers, Guan Yu, Zhang Fei, and Zhao Yun, who ranked among the best generals of the time, Liu also had in his service the military advisor Zhuge Liang, one of the best strategists and the wisest man in Chinese history.

Cao Cao is a well-known villain-hero. He was the most intelligent of the three kings; while the other two relied heavily on their advisors for plans and strategies, Cao Cao decided most of his campaigns himself. He had the puppet emperor at his mercy and could therefore issue his orders as imperial edicts.

The Kingdom of Wu under Sun Quan was never powerful enough to attempt the subjugation of its two rivals. It acted rather as a balancing power between Wei and Shu, taking advantage of their contention now and then to gain small victories. After Wei's conquest of Shu in A.D. 263, Wu managed to survive another seventeen years and then surrendered.

Lü Meng, the victor in the following battle, is but one

of the numerous capable commanders in China's long history of warfare. The loser, Guan Yu, enjoying a much more glamorous position, is known as the most glorious Chinese warrior. When he was canonized as the god of war in the Ming Dynasty, thousands of temples were constructed in his honor. His fame relied on his unswerving loyalty to his sworn brothers and his outstanding military exploits. Nonetheless, pride was perhaps his most remarkable trait, and it was pride that finally brought about his downfall.

From A.D. 219 Guan Yu led the Shu army in a series of successful campaigns against Wei, seizing several strategic cities. Cao Cao became so fearful that he wanted to remove his capital to another place. But upon the suggestion of one of his advisors, he sent another band of troops to hold back Guan Yu and at the same time dispatched a messenger to the Kingdom of Wu to persuade Sun Quan into a joint action against Shu.

For years Sun Quan had held a grudge against Liu Bei, who had "borrowed" from Wu the strategic city of Jingzhou on the Yangtze River but refused to return it under innumerable pretexts. Guan Yu was put in command of Jingzhou, and Sun Quan had enough self-knowledge to refrain from taking action. But now that Guan Yu had left Jingzhou to attack Fancheng, a city of the Kingdom of Wei, Sun Quan was all too glad to seize the opportunity for his long-awaited revenge. Therefore he disptached Lü Meng, an old, battle-seasoned general, to assail Jingzhou.

When Lü Meng arrived and made camp at Lukou, he was told by scouts that the riverbank was thickly lined with high beacon towers and that the army defending Jingzhou looked well-trained and were constantly on guard. Anxious and frustrated, Lü Meng fell seriously ill.

Sun Quan was worried to receive word of Lü's illness, but a young scholar-general named Lu Xun reassured him, "This illness of Lü Meng must be make-believe." So Sun Quan sent him to see Lü Meng.

"I have a prescription for your illness," Lu Xun told Lü Meng. Lü Meng looked up in astonishment, immediately sending away the servants, and asked Lu Xun to speak more clearly.

"Your illness, as I know, resulted from the many beacon towers across the river and the preparedness of the Jingzhou army. Now I've thought up a plan to eliminate both obstacles. Guan Yu is very conceited and there are few people whom he considers his worthy adversaries. But for you, he would devote all his efforts to fighting Cao Cao. If you pleade illness, hand over the command of Lukou to an unknown general, and pander to Guan Yu's vanity by sending him a flattering letter, he will in all probability let down his vigilance and move the better part of the Jingzhou army to reinforce the besiegers of Fancheng. Then I will use another ruse to seize the poorly guarded Jingzhou."

Immensely pleased, Lü Meng went to see Sun Quan and commended Lu Xun to replace him as commander at Lukou, saying, "If you appoint some old, prestigious general, that will put Guan Yu on guard. Lu Xun, though very wise and resourceful, is still too young and nameless to arouse Guan Yu's heedfulness. He will make out well if he takes my place."

Accordingly, Sun Quan vested Lu Xun with the commander's seal and sent him to Lukou. As soon as he took command at his new post, Lu Xun sent a messenger to Guan Yu with gifts of fine horses, brocades, and wine. At that time Guan Yu had relaxed the siege of Fancheng for a few days to nurse an arrow injury on his right arm. He had already learned that Lü Meng had fallen seriously ill and been replaced by Lu Xun. He called in the messenger, directed a finger at him, and said scornfully, "Sun Quan is brainless to use a suckling baby as general!"

The messenger knelt down, bowed his head to the ground, and brought out Lu Xun's letter, which was written in the most humble terms. When Guan Yu finished reading the letter, he gave out a vociferous laugh. The messenger returned to tell Lu Xun, "Guan Yu looked very glad and seemed to stop worrying about Wu."

Lu Xun waited until he got reliable news that Guan Yu had moved the main body of the troops stationed at Jingzhou to outside Fancheng; then he reported to Sun Quan, who dispatched Lü Meng to sail to Jingzhou in eighty swift boats with thirty thousand crack troops. Lu Xun selected hundreds of good swimmers from among the soldiers and disguised them as merchants in white robes. Then, with most of the soldiers hidden in cabins and the white-robed "merchants" on deck, the boats sailed southward across the river to the beacon towers outside Jingzhou. When interrogated by guards on the towers, the Wu soldiers replied that they were itinerant merchants driven there by an ill wind and promised to leave as soon as possible. These words were accompanied by generous gifts, so the guards let the boats stay.

At two o'clock early the next morning, the thirty thousand Wu soldiers sneaked out of the boats, captured all the guards in the major beacon towers, and marched all the way to the gates of Jingzhou completely unopposed. Some of the captive Jingzhou soldiers, threatened with death and tempted with rewards, went forward and cozened the gate guards into opening a gate. The Wu soldiers rushed in and took control of the entire city with hardly any fighting. Lü Meng made a point of keeping his troops under strict discipline with the rigid decree: "Whoever commits murder or plundering will be punished by military law."

By then Cao Cao had sent many reinforcements under the command of a capable general Xu Huang to relieve the siege of Fancheng. By a series of tricky maneuvers, Xu broke into the camp of Guan Yu's army and forced him to back off. It was at this time that Guan Yu learnd of the capture of Jingzhou by the Wu army. He roared angrily and sent a furious letter to Lü Meng, demanding an "explanation." The envoy returned with a message from Lü Meng in which he explained that though he treasured his friendship with Guan Yu, he had to obey orders. The envoy said that Guan Yu's family members and those of his officers had received ample provisions and were well treated. "This is a trick of that nasty scoundrel!" Guan Yu shouted impatiently and dismissed the envoy, who was then eagerly cross-questioned by many officers who had their families in the city of Jingzhou. Naturally, knowledge of their families' security in no wise encouraged the officers to attack Jingzhou. When Guan Yu was on his way to recover Jingzhou with his troops, many officers and soldiers actually deserted and slipped into the city to look after their families. Before he reached the city, Guan Yu was intercepted by the Wu army, which was joined by some Jingzhou troops that had defected. He fought from noon to midnight until he had only three hundred men left. Following the advice of his son Guan Ping, he retreated to Maicheng, a small town near Jingzhou, and sent a general to ask for aid from Shangyong, a nearby fortified city under Shu's control.

The commander at Shangyong happened to be Liu Bei's adopted son, Liu Feng, who held a grudge against Guan Yu. Liu Bei, after assuming the imperial title, had vacillated at the choice of the heir apparent. His own son was a muddle-headed weakling, and by comparison Liu Feng seemed much more capable. However, Guan Yu, who set great store in family ties, talked Liu Bei into making the idiot natural son his heir apparent and appointing Liu Feng the commander of a city far away from the capital. Therefore, when pleaded with to send reinforcements to Maicheng, Liu Feng replied that he did not see how he could do that, having not yet taken full control of Shangyong.

Meanwhile Guan Yu and his three hundred troops had run out of provisions in Maicheng and had to move out. He was told that the enemy troops were relatively sparse outside the north gate, which led to a small mountainous path. An advisor warned that there must be an ambush on the small path and they should take the open road instead. Guan Yu, outwitted and defeated, remained nevertheless too proud and stubborn to listen to such cautions. "What do I fear from an ambush!" he declared. As it turned out, he did fall into an ambush. No one was powerful enough to beat him in hand-to-hand combat, but the Wu soldiers stretched ropes across the grass-covered lane to trip his horse. He fell to the ground in his cumbersome armor and was captured. He was then put to death by Sun Quan.

Adapted from *History of the Three Kingdoms* (San Guo Zhi), "Biography of Guan Yu" and "Biography of Lü Meng"

Strategy Eleven
Sacrifice a Plum to Save a Peach

第十一计 李代桃僵　　势必有损，损阴以益阳。

Translation

If loss is inevitable, decrease yin to increase yang.*

Purport

War, as a contest of strength, leads to losses on the part of the winner as well as the loser. The difference lies in that the loss is inflicted upon the loser but is expected and accepted by the winner. It therefore follows that loss is always inevitable in war. By accepting this fact, a skilled commander formulates his battle plans so that he may gain a big victory at a small price. In the words of an ancient Chinese phrase, the decrease of yin (partial interest) can be made to benefit yang (overall interest). The idiom comes from a well-known Han Dynasty poem extolling brotherly love:

> *The peach grows over a well,*
> *The plum neighbors upon the peach.*
> *The peach is gnawed by bugs,*
> *And the plum dies in its place.*

---

*Make a small sacrifice to gain a major profit.

Even trees can suffer for one another,
How should brothers be mean?

A similar expression may be heard from Chinese chess players: "Give up a pawn to save a chariot." When used by a military leader, it indicates that he is ready to pay a certain price for a major victory.

Each of the two confronting parties has its own advantages and disadvantages. It is seldom that one party has advantage over the other in all respects. Though the outcome of the battle relies mostly on the relative strength of the two parties, the weaker one can strike a victory by using a small band of troops to pin down the main enemy forces while concentrating its major force to wipe out the lesser part of the enemy. Though the small band might be lost, it will be more than compensated for by the enemy's losses. After one or more such battles, the weaker party will become strong and be in a position to engage in a decisive battle and defeat the enemy once and for all.

Quotations for Reference

One who looks into the distance overlooks what is nearby; one who considers great things neglects the details. If we feel proud of a small victory and regret over a small defeat, we will encumber ourselves and lose the opportunity to achieve merits.

Li Su, a Tang Dynasty general

When observing the enemy's array, I ascertain its strong and weak points. Then I use my weak to meet its strong and use my strong to meet its weak. Taking advantage of my weakness, the enemy can at best advance for several dozen or a hundred paces. Taking advantage of its weakness, I always close in on it from its rear to deal a crushing blow. I have achieved most of my victories by employing this strategy.

Li Shimin, Emperor Taizong of the Tang Dynasty

The Fall of Shanhai Pass to Manchu Invaders

The downfall of an imperial dynasty was always the result of overall decline, never the result of any one incident. Nevertheless, traditional scholars and commentators on history have often singled out some special occurrences that they deem as chiefly responsible for the fall of the old regime, announcing that if such and such a thing had not taken place, the dynastic change would have never occurred. Thus, quite a few scholars in Qing times attributed the downfall of the Ming Dynasty to its last emperor's execution of his ablest general, Yuan Chonghuan. Another tradition, strong among popular writers, blames the Manchu occupation of China on the defection of Wu Sangui, the Ming general in charge of defending the Shanhai Pass at the eastern end of the Great Wall.

Wu Sangui was a native of Liaodong. His father, named Wu Xiang, was commander of Jing Region. Once, Xiang was convicted and put into prison in the capital Beijing. Replacing his father as regional commander, Sangui achieved great distinction and merit, especially in defending the strategic city of Ningyuan against Manchu invasion. He thereupon was granted the noble title of Marquis of Pingxi as well as the exculpation of his father, who was reappointed as a military commissioner of the imperial guards in the capital.

In the last years of its rule, the Ming regime was

compelled to wage two wars at the same time. At the northern border came the invasions of the increasingly powerful Manchu people, led by a succession of ambitious and capable rulers. In the meantime the heartland of China, including several regions north of the Yangtze, was overrun by riotous bands of hungry peasants who came to a measure of unity under two major leaders, Li Zicheng from Shaanxi and Zhang Xianzhong in Sichuan. The many costly expeditions aimed to subjugate these rebels were poorly conducted and resulted in ignominious defeats. In 1643 Li Zicheng set up his own regime in Hubei, and the next year Zhang Xianzhong followed suit in Sichuan.

In the third month of 1644 Li Zicheng advanced on Beijing with overwhelming rapidity, readily crushing any resistance on his way. Emperor Chongzhen was driven into a panic and had a message sent posthaste to Wu Sangui, ordering him to come to the rescue at full speed. On receiving the message, Wu Sangui immediately led his troops on a forced march towards the capital. On arrival at Fengdong, he learned that Li Zicheng had already seized the imperial capital. In fact, the defense of Beijing had been so ineffectual that it had succumbed without much fighting. The last Ming emperor, Chongzhen, deserted by all his guards and courtiers, had hanged himself in despair. Undecided yet in his attitude to Li Zicheng's new government, Wu Sangui pulled back to Shanhai Pass.

Soon a message from Li Zicheng arrived, demanding Wu's capitulation and threatening to slay his father if he retaliated. Still unresolved, Wu Sangui nevertheless advanced westward and arrived at the city of Luanzhou (modern Luan County in Hebei Province). There, as a story goes, he heard the news that settled his allegiance and therefore the fate of the Chinese empire. Somewhat earlier, Wu had been invited to a banquet in the house of a count while on a sojourn in the capital. There a ravishing singing girl named Chen Yuanyuan fascinated him to such an extent that he bought her on the spot for a thousand taels of silver. Just then an emergency call from the frontier prompted him to leave the capital in haste, and Yuanyuan was consigned to the house of his father, Wu Xiang. Upon the fall of the capital, Yuanyuan was captured along with other members of the Wu family, and a supreme general of Li Zicheng took her to be his own concubine.

At this, Wu Sangui immediately broke off all negotiations with Li Zicheng and returned to Shanhai Pass at full speed. Then he dispatched a messenger to implore the aid of the Manchu troops.

By this time the Manchu state had assumed the dynastic title of Qing (meaning "pure"). A child emperor ruled on the throne, while real power was in the hands of Prince Dorgon, the Regent. When Wu Sangui was commanded to abandon the stronghold of Ningyuan and bring his forces posthaste to rescue the capital, this left the Ming frontier defenses with a weak point; Dorgon perceived this as too wonderful a chance to pass up. Thus, in the fourth month he marched south with a hundred and forty thousand troops.

Then Dorgon received a letter sent by Wu Sangui from the Shanhai Pass:

> The wandering robbers have acted against Heaven, invaded the imperial palace, and usurped the imperial title. Their crimes are in the extreme and the whole world feels great indignation. Bountifully bestowed by the late monarch, Sangui desires to launch a campaign to punish the

criminals. But his force is no match for the rebels. Therefore, with tears and blood he implores Your Highness to arrange his troops and enter the Pass, joining forces with Sangui and advancing upon the capital to wipe out the evil blaze and uphold the great righteousness. This is one chance in a thousand years.

This message sounded almost too good to be true for the Manchus. The impregnable Shanhai Pass, which had defied their military ambitions for so many years, suddenly became a wide-open access leading directly to Beijing, the capital of the fallen Ming. Dorgon thus granted Wu Sangui's request at once and further promised him the title of prince. Then he led the Manchu troops on a forced march toward Shanhai Pass. As indicated in his letter of reply, Dorgon was a master statesman who knew how to exploit the political situations to his own advantage. There had been three major incursions by the Manchu army into the northern border land of the Ming. Now Dorgon announced that the present campaign had a justified aim: to punish the "robbers," avenge the Ming emperor, and save the Chinese people from misery.

In the meantime, on learning of Wu's alliance with the Manchus, Li Zicheng led two hundred thousand troops in person to besiege Shanhai Pass and dispatched an officer named Tang Tong with a lesser contingent to cross the Great Wall by a detour and assault the pass from the north. On the twenty-fourth day of the fifth month, Li Zicheng's men surrounded the Shanhai Pass. Two days later the Manchu army, led by Dorgon, arrived within ten *li* of the pass, where it engaged Tang Tong's small contingent of twenty thousand and routed it. Wu Sangui thereupon rushed out of the pass with five hundred cavalrymen to meet Dorgon in his commander's camp. There he prostrated himself before the Manchu ruler and submitted to whatever terms were dictated to him. He allowed his hair, which the Chinese regarded as a sacred part of the body, to be shaved in the Manchu fashion, with the remainder braided into a queue. Then he conducted the Manchu hosts through the pass.

During all this well-nigh effortless progress, the Manchu regent remained cautious and calculating. He was fully aware of the potency of Li Zicheng's forces, which had swept across China and beat the best of the Ming army. Besides, they outnumbered the combined forces of the Manchu army and Wu Sangui's troops. Therefore Dorgon adopted the strategy, which was to be followed throughout the Manchu conquest of China, of "employing the Chinese to fight the Chinese." He ordered Wu Sangui to stitch white cloth on the shoulders of his soldiers and take the field first.

The decisive battle took place on the twenty-sixth day of the fifth month. Li Zicheng arrayed his formidable troops in a "long snake" formation, extending from the north hill right to the mouth of the sea. The several thousand Ming soldiers under Wu Sangui's command threw themselves on the central columns of the enemy, while Dorgon stayed behind with the Manchu army and observed the contest from a vantage point. The fight went on fiercely for hours amid a violent sandstorm. Wu's well-trained soldiers fought competently enough, but they were in too great a numerical inferiority to gain the advantage. Toward midday, they had been broken up into separate parts and faced complete annihilation. At this juncture Dorgon finally gave the signal for his troops to join in. With resounding battle cries, tens of thousands of Manchu cavalrymen suddenly emerged at the right wing of Wu's beleaguered men. They were followed by a larger number of footmen.

By this time the wind had abated and the sky had become clear again. Though having gained the upper hand, Li Zicheng's men were nevertheless fairly fatigued after the morning's combat. Thus they were greatly shaken at the unexpected arrival of large hosts of Manchu warriors. As described in official history, Li Zicheng saw the oncoming Manchu army from an eminence and was the first to turn his horse and flee. But this defamatory account has been much discredited by later historians. All the same, the "pigtailed soldiers" of Manchu were regarded by the Ming Chinese with great trepidation and awe. To encounter them without warning could not but gravely demoralize Li Zicheng's weary soldiers. It was not long before the result of the battle became pretty clear. The Manchus inflicted a severe defeat on their enemy and took control of Shanhai Pass before nightfall.

After the battle was over, Dorgon fulfilled his promise by conferring on Wu Sangui the title Prince of Pingxi and put him to the task of pursuing Li Zicheng. On his way back to Beijing, Li Zicheng sent a message to Wu, appealing for peace on more favorable terms. However, there was now no turning back for Wu. He flatly rejected Li's offer and continued his headlong pursuit. Back in Beijing, Li Zicheng had himself erected as emperor in good haste; the next day he set out westward, aiming to retreat to the area of Shaanxi. Before starting on his journey, he did not forget to avenge his defeat by slaughtering Wu Xiang and all members of the Wu family. He arrived at Shaanxi but was compelled to withdraw further to Hubei, where he was killed in a close combat in 1645. The other archrebel, Zhang Xianzhong, was killed two years afterwards. The remnants of their followers were incorporated into the command of Ming generals who continued to resist the Qing army in south China.

After their occupation of Beijing, the Manchus made it their new capital. By instituting benevolent policies, Dorgon succeeded in gaining the support of the majority of the Chinese upper class in the north. However, the pacification of the south was much more arduous and sanguinary. Turncoat Chinese generals played a vital role in the process, Wu Sangui being the most outstanding among them. Subsequently, he ruled the area of Yunnan and Guizhou, the most powerful of the so-called "three feudatories." In 1673 he launched a rebellion but died of illness in the midst of contest. The rebellion was suppressed after eight years of extensive warfare. After this, the Manchu regime was finally secure in its rule of China.

Adapted from *Draft History of the Qing Dynasty* (Qing Shi Gao), Tome Two-Hundred and Eighteen; *Biography of Seven Hundred Eminent Figures in Qing Times* (Qing Dai Qi Bai Ming Ren Zhuan), "Wu Sangui"

Strategy Twelve
Lead Away a Goat in Passing

第十二计 顺手牵羊　微隙在所必乘，微利在所必得。少阴，少阳。

Translation

Take advantage of the smallest flaw; seize the smallest profit. Make use of a minor mistake of the enemy to gain a minor victory.

Purport

To lead away a goat one should choose an opportune time, a point at which there is the least chance of any intervention from a third party. If, for example, one has just got hold of the goat when a wolf appears, the result would be unpredictable. The wolf might eat both the goat and the man, or there might be a bitter struggle between the man and the wolf, while the goat gets away. In any event it is unlikely that the man will be able to lead away the goat without being hurt himself.

On the other hand, one must make certain that the goat is really a goat before he tries to lead it away. He must not take a wolf for a goat. Furthermore, the wolf and the goat are interconvertible. A goat, if not led away in time, might turn into a wolf eager to try the strength of its teeth and claws. A wolf might also turn into a helpless goat when it has outlived its strength.

In military contexts, the goat refers to any unexpected flaw of the enemy. Just as it is the chief general who decides to loot a burning house, it is usually the subordinate general who finds a goat and decides to lead it away. In a word, the strategy requires one to act according to changing circumstances. One must grasp any chance to strengthen oneself and weaken the enemy, for a small victory, like a move in a chess match, may decide the final outcome of the contest.

Quotations for Reference

An attack is planned to start from the easiest. If the enemy makes camp in several locations, it must be superior in number and strength in some and inferior in others. We should avoid the strong and attack the weak, avoid the numerous and attack the few to gain certain victory. The principle goes, "One who is good at war attains victory that is easily attainable."

> *A Hundred Marvelous Battle Plans*, "Easy Battle" (Bai Zhan Qi Fa, "Yi Zhan")

The art of war relies on variation. Wait if the enemy makes no move; when there is any variation, seize the chance to act accordingly and we will gain the advantage. The principle goes, "One who adapts to the changing situation of the enemy to gain victory is called heavenly."

> Ibid., "Battle of Change" ("Bian Zhan")

The method of being ever-victorious by changing tactics is founded on the grasping of opportunity. How can one act according to opportunity if one is not wise? To seize opportunity, nothing is more significant than the element of surprise. Therefore, when losing its natural defenses, a fierce beast may be driven away by a child with a spear; when a worm spurts its poison, even a strong man may turn pale and panic. This is because the danger emerges too suddenly for one to retain one's presence of mind.

The Art of Generalship, "Grasp
Opportunity" (Jiang Yuan, "Ying Ji")

If we fight without perceiving our advantages, we will meet defeat even if we are superior in number; if we fight when perceiving our advantages, we will gain victory even if we are inferior in number. Advantage refers to the junction when the enemy is deficient and we are sufficient. Take action when an advantage is perceived and halt when there is no advantage; perceiving advantage and seizing opportunity is the instrument of kings and emperors.

The Yin Canon of Vesper (Tai Bai
Yin Jing), Chapter Twenty-One

In battle, if the enemy makes no mistake, how can our troops gain victory? This can be compared to playing chess. When the two chess players are well matched, one mistaken move may be irredeemable. Therefore, the outcome of war both in ancient times and today is mostly determined by a single mistake, not to mention several mistakes.

Li Jing's Reply to Emperor Taizong of Tang
(Tang Tai Zong Li Jing Wen Dui), Tome Three

One who understands warfare must first guard against

surprise before he can exploit the enemy's unguardedness. Sow discords when the enemy is suspicious, attack when it is tired, besiege when it is hungry, close in when it is divided, create fear when it is weak, seize control when it is in chaos, thwart when it has not yet arrived, curb when it has not yet started out, surprise when it has just gained a victory, retreat when it has just been defeated. Therefore, in directing warfare, one should take advantage of the enemy's unguardedness rather than being taken advantage of by the enemy.

A Scholar's Dilettante Remarks on War
(Tou Bi Fu Tan), Chapter Three

Act quickly when perceiving the advantage; halt when there is no advantage. To pursue an advantage and take an opportunity does not allow the error of a moment of breath. It is too early to act an instant earlier and too late to act an instant later.

Summary of Military Canons (Wu Jing
Zong Yao), Tome Three of First Part

Tang General Li Guangbi Countervails Rebel Troops

Emperor Xuanzong of the Tang Dynasty ascended the throne as a vigorous, capable and enlightened sovereign; then he became prematurely senile and foolish, this being generally attributed to his infatuation with the lovely imperial concubine, Lady Yang. Not the least of his blunders was the appointment of An Lushan to the military governorship of three frontier prefectures.

An Lushan was a wily, ambitious man of Tartar descent. With the best army of the empire at his command, he launched a rebellion in 755 that shook the Tang at its very foundation. The next year he laid claim to the imperial title and captured the capital Chang'an, driving Emperor Xuanzong into exile. Then he fell seriously ill and was murdered by his son An Qingxu, who in his turn was assassinated by Shi Siming, a former subordinate of An Lushan. By the time Shi Siming was murdered by his son Shi Chaoyi, the rebellion had already lost its momentum. It came to an end in 763 at the defeat and death of Shi Chaoyi.

A number of military heroes emerged during the dragged-out warfare to lead the inefficient, corruption-ridden, and poorly coordinated Tang army to final victory. General Li Guangbi occupied an indisputable position of eminence among them.

Li Guangbi was a descendant of a ruling house of the Qidan. His father had received the title of duke under Emperor Xuanzong. At the outbreak of An Lushan rebellion, Li Guangbi was appointed successively to several high-ranking positions and was put in charge of the task of subjugating the rebels. He perceived the lack of discipline of the Tang army to be a major problem and took stringent measures to tackle it. The troops under his command were therefore famous for their discipline.

In autumn of the second year of the Qianyuan reign (759) Li Guangbi and several other generals laid siege to Anyang (modern Anyang in Henan Province), the seat of Xiang Region where An Qingxu was quartered. Unable to capture it, they fell back to the surrounding areas. Shi Siming, who had arrived to relieve the siege, murdered An Qingxu and proclaimed himself emperor. Then he led troops to march on to the west toward Luoyang, the eastern capital. Li Guangbi received orders to check Shi's advance.

Shi Siming first proceeded to attack Zhengzhou to the east of Luoyang. Li Guangbi arrived in Luoyang and asked Wei Zhi, the regent, "The bandits have come in a victorious spirit. It is appropriate for us to bide our time and not throw our army immediately into battle. So Luoyang cannot be defended. What then is your plan?" Wei suggested that he withdraw west to Tongguan to resist the enemy from behind natural barriers. Li opposed this plan, saying, "We should not retreat five hundred *li* gratuitously; it would only boost the morale of the enemy. We'd better move northeast to Heyang,* where we will be free to march forward or retreat according to circumstances." With this he excavated Luoyang and had provisions there transported to Heyang. He led five hundred cavalrymen to bring up the rear. By that time some vagrant soldiers of Shi Siming's vanguard had already approached the stone bridge leading to Heyang. "Shall we take a circuitous route and ferry across the river or march straight toward the bridge?" asked the officers. "Straight ahead." Li ordered. They proceeded slowly, and the rebel soldiers dared not attack. Li Guangbi arrived at Heyang at night with twenty thousand men and food for ten days.

When Shi Siming entered Luoyang, he found the city empty. Afraid that Li might retaliate at any moment, Shi did not settle down in the imperial palaces but moved the troops to White Horse Temple north of the city. There he had a crescent-shaped bulwark built to guard against Li Guangbi. Thus the two armies confronted each other across the Yellow River.

Shi Siming had over a thousand fine battle steeds, and

---

*Modern Meng County in Henan Province on the northern bank of the Yellow River.

every day he had them bathed by the southern bank of the river to show off. Li Guangbi picked out five hundred mares from his cavalry. When Shi's horses arrived at the bank, Li had the mares driven to the riverside, leaving their colts behind. The mares neighed loudly in protest. Thereupon steeds at the southern bank all broke loose and swam across the river to join the mares. Li Guangbi had them driven into the city of Heyang, gaining hundreds of horses for nothing.

Infuriated, Shi Siming sent hundreds of battle ships, pushing burning boats at the front, to attack the floating bridge defended by the Tang army. Li Guangbi prepared several hundred long poles, each with its shank made of reinforced thick wood and an iron fork attached to its head. When the burning boats approached the bridge, the Tang soldiers stuck out the poles to halt them. After a while, the fire on the boats burned them out. Then the Tang soldiers again used the poles to stop the battle ships and drew up stone catapults to attack them. Failing to gain any advantage, the rebels sailed away.

Mustering up his courage, Shi Siming finally transported his troops across the river to besiege Heyang. Li Guangbi asked Li Baoyu, the military commissioner of Zheng prefecture, "Can you defend the southern city for me for two days?" Li Baoyu promised that he could. Under the violent attack of the rebels, the city was about to collapse. Li Baoyu cheated the rebels, "I have run out of food. I'll surrender tomorrow." The rebels were overjoyed and let up on their attack. That very night Li Baoyu mobilized his men to reinforce the defense works of the city and also dispatched a band of soldiers to sneak out of the city and slip to the enemy's rear. The next morning, he emerged on the city gate to challenge the rebels. The rebels, mad with rage, charged at the city fiercely. At that moment the Tang soldiers who had hid in ambush through the night rose to assault the rebels from the rear. Caught in a two-way squeeze, the rebels suffered a severe defeat.

Dong Qin, an officer who had joined the rebels to attack Heyang, escaped one night along with five hundred followers to surrender to Li Guangbi. At that time Guangbi was taking charge of the defense of the central fortress, which was protected by stockades and a moat over six meters wide and deep. On the fifth day of the twelfth month, the rebel officer Zhou Zhi left the southern city and concentrated his men to attack the central fortress. He led his men to the fortress and ordered them to fill up the moat and tear open the stockade. Guangbi dispatched Yuan Li with a band of the strongest soldiers to defend against the rebels and went up to the northeast tower to watch. The rebels were prevailing and the situation was getting desperate, so Guangbi went down to question Yuan Li. "The rebels are filling up the moat and tearing down the stockade," he said. "But you just remain here without taking any action to stop them. Why?"

"Do you want to fight them or just defend the city?"

"Fight them, of course!"

"If we want to fight them, why should we stop them from clearing the ground for us?"

"Good idea!" Guangbi exclaimed. "I had not thought of that."

When the stockade was finally breached, Yuan Li led the dare-to-die corps to charge at the rebels, forcing them to retreat a few hundred steps. Yuan Li, realizing that the rebels' formation would not be easy to break up, withdrew again behind the stockade. Beaten by the best of the Tang army, the rebels were hesitant to launch another attack. After a time, Yuan Li's dare-to-die troops suddenly rushed out of the stockade again and threw themselves on the rebels, defeating them utterly.

Having failed two assaults, Zhou Zhi collected his men and lined them up in front of the northern gate of Heyang. Guangbi climbed up the gate with the other officers to observe. He then declared, "Though the rebels surpass us in number, they are noisy and disorderly. We have no reason to be afraid of them. I promise you that we shall overcome them by midday."

However, the fighting lasted until noon, with neither side beating the other. Guangbi summoned his officers and asked, "In which direction is the rebels' formation strongest?" They replied that it was the northwest corner. Therefore Guangbi dispatched Hao Tingyu with three hundred cavalrymen to charge it. "Where is the second strongest point?" he asked again. They replied that it was the southeast corner. So Guangbi sent another officer, Wei Zhen, with three hundred cavalrymen to charge it. Then he told the remaining officers, "I'll direct your action by my banner. When I wave it softly, you can act according to your own decision. But when I wave it vigorously and touch the ground three times with it, you must charge forward with all your might. Anyone who retreats for even a single step will be executed!"

A while later, Hao Tingyu came running back. Guangbi was startled, saying, "Tingyu has retreated! The conditions must be very bad!" With this he ordered the guards to chop off Tingyu's head. Tingyu explained, "I did not want to retreat, but my steed was shot dead." So Guangbi let him change horses and return to fight. At this time two other officers, unable to beat the enemy, fell back a few steps. Guangbi immediately sent his guards to have them executed. When the two officers saw the guards approaching, swords in hand, they hurriedly turned to fight ahead. Guangbi then waved his banner vigorously, and the Tang troops fell on the rebels with all their might. Over a thousand rebel soldiers were killed, about five hundred captured, and another one thousand drowned in their frenzied escape across the river. Zhou Zhi fled with only a handful of followers.

Shi Siming did not immediately learn of Zhou Zhi's defeat and was still attacking the southern city. Li Guangbi had the captured rebels driven to the riverside to show him. Disheartened, Shi Siming pulled off.

Adapted from *History as a Mirror* (Zi Zhi Tong Jian),
Tome Two Hundred and Twenty-One

Strategy Thirteen
Beat the Grass to Frighten the Snake

第十三计 打草惊蛇　　疑以叩实，察而后动。复者，
阴之媒也。

Translation

Ascertain the doubtful; find out about the enemy before taking action. Return and bring the enemy's secrets to light.*

Purport

This expression comes from a story in a Tang Dynasty sketchbook. The magistrate of Dangtu District, as the story goes, was a greedy man who accepted as many bribes as he was offered. Once, some locals handed in a

---

Fu (Return), the twenty-fourth hexagram in *I Ching*, has the symbol of the thunder (*Zhen*) underneath the earth (*Kun*). It represents the winter solstice in the eleventh lunar month, when everything above ground is still enveloped in cold and snow (as indicated by the five yin lines) but plant roots and seeds are beginning to grow anew deep within the earth. The hexagram therefore ushers in a new cycle of development and progress. The judgement for the yang line at the bottom observes, "Return before going too far. No remorse. Great good fortune." Just as winter grows slowly into spring, so must one act cautiously at the onset of an undertaking such as a war. He will enjoy good fortune and experience no remorse if he can turn back in time after making a mistake.

petition, accusing the assistant magistrate of taking bribes. Astounded upon reading it, the magistrate scribbled the following: "You only beat the grass, but the snake is frightened."

Sometimes one might not want to beat the grass for fear of startling the snake into preparedness or escape. Likewise, a military commander is often cautioned to refrain from minor, impulsive engagements with the enemy for fear of exposing his intentions and the deployment of his troops. This is especially true when he is preparing a surprise attack. Under other circumstances, however, it is advisable to take an open, albeit small-scale, operation to test the enemy's strength and weakness before launching an all-out offensive.

Quotations for Reference

In marshaling troops, one should first gather intelligence about the enemy, surveying its barns, calculating its food reserves, estimating its strength, assessing its heavenly and earthly conditions, and searching for its weaknesses.

Three Strategies (San Lue), Tome One

In warfare, employ both large and small forces to observe the enemy's reaction, push forward and pull back to observe the enemy's steadiness, make threats to observe the enemy's fear, stay immobile to observe the enemy's laxity, take a move to observe the enemy's doubt, launch an attack to observe the enemy's solidity. Strike the enemy when it hesitates, attack the enemy when it is unprepared, subdue the enemy when it exposes its weakness, and rout the enemy when it reconnoiters. Take advantage of the enemy's rashness, forestall its intention, confound its battle plan, and make use of its fear.

Law of Master Sima (Si Ma Fa), Chapter Five

If we and the enemy have not engaged yet and are therefore unacquainted with each other, we can sometimes dispatch a band of troops to test the enemy's strength and weakness; this is called a tasting battle. For the tasting battle, we should allow it to be neither grave nor long and should withdraw the troops after a brief engagement. Coordinating forces should be sent to cope with emergencies and prevent the loss of the tasting army, which may bring about the defeat of our main force.

An Abstract of Military Works (Wu Bei Ji Yao)

Marquis Wu of Wei asked, "Confronted with enemy forces, I know not their general and want to appraise him. What is the method?"

Wu Qi replied, "Send a brave, low-ranking officer with a lightly equipped force to make a test, aiming at defeat instead of gain so as to observe the pursuing forces. If they remain orderly in every halt and action, delay deliberately in pursuit and ignore the allurement of profit, then their general must be wise and you have to avoid him. If they make a great noise, display a disorderly array of banners and standards, make moves at their own discretion, hold their weapons both vertically and horizontally, strain their efforts in pursuit and rush forward at the sight of profit, their general must be stupid and you can capture him even if he has superior forces.

Book of Master Wu (Wu Zi), Chapter Four

The Battle of Hulao Pass

Though the Sui Dynasty (581-618) had a brief rule and comprised only two emperors, it has great historical significance as it ended nearly four hundred years of political disunity, paving the way for the glorious era of the subsequent Tang. The second Sui emperor, Yangdi, who ascended the throne in 604, certainly contributed his share in consolidating the empire. But, as accused justly by later historians, he had a weakness for pomp and glory. His grand construction projects and incessant military adventures depleted the resources of the empire and sowed the seeds of social unrest. In the end, it was the unpopular and unsuccessful campaigns against Korea that triggered the downfall of the Sui regime. Then, in the last years of Emperor Yangdi's reign, rebellions broke out all over the empire. He retired to the city of Jiangdu in the south and was murdered by a treacherous Sui general in early 618.

When Li Yuan declared himself emperor of the Tang Dynasty in Chang'an in 618, soon after Yangdi's death, he had to contend with several powerful rivals who were either commanders of the collapsed Sui regime or leaders of popular uprisings. With the aid of his lustrous sons, especially the second son, Shimin, Li Yuan adopted superior strategies in both diplomacy and warfare and was therefore able to strengthen his power base in the mountainous area of Taiyuan Commandery (in modern Shanxi), while his rivals were weakened or annihilated fighting among themselves. By 620 he was opposed by only two major contenders for control of the empire: Wang Shichong, commander of the remaining Sui army in the eastern capital of Luoyang, and Dou Jiande, the rebel .

leader who controlled the area of Hebei.

In the seventh month of 620, Li Shimin embarked on a major expedition against Wang Shichong. By seeking out weak points and striking with his concentrated force, he captured one city after another, while quite a few officers appointed by Wang Shichong capitulated with their troops. By the second month of the next year, Li Shimin had brought under his control the peripheral areas of the eastern capital of Luoyang, including the strategic Hulao Pass to its east. Then he led his army on an all-out siege against the city.

Formerly, Wang Shichong and Dou Jiande had clashed on several occasions, resulting in mutual hostility. When blockaded by the Tang army at Luoyang, Wang was compelled to dispatch an envoy, Zhangsun Anshi, to seek an alliance with Dou. The latter agreed to send reinforcements to relieve the siege of Luoyang, for he had been advised by one of his subordinates that, since the Tang was the most powerful of the three major rival regimes, the two weaker ones should join forces to halt its attempt at domination. However, Dou was at the moment busily engaged in a campaign against another rebel leader and could not proceed to rescue Luoyang immediately.

Li Shimin, after capturing the Qingcheng Palace in the Imperial Garden to the west of Luoyang, had barely time to build ramparts when Wang Shichong led twenty thousand men out of the city and arrayed them on the eastern bank of the Gu River. Shimin assured his generals by saying, "The rebels have come in the hope of winning a victory by luck. Let's beat them today and they will never dare to venture out of the city again!" He dispatched General Qutu Tong with five thousand cavalrymen to cross the river, giving the instruction, "As soon as you engage the enemy, inform me by raising smoke."

The cavalry led by Qutu Tong forded the river and charged at Wang Shichong's line. A fierce battle ensued. Then Li Shimin, upon the smoke signal, directed his main force to thrash at Wang's army from its flanks so as to disrupt its coordination. It was well over half a day before Wang Shichong's army faltered and fell back into the city of Luoyang, having suffered casualties of about eight thousand. After that, Wang stayed in the city, never sallying out again.

The city of Luoyang had been extensively rebuilt by the Second Emperor of Sui to serve as his eastern capital. It was protected by impregnable defense works and the crack troops of the former Sui imperial army, now under the command of Wang Shichong. Day and night, for over ten days, Li Shimin attacked the city vigorously but failed to gain any ground. The soldiers became tired and some officers proposed to withdraw. But Li Shimin did not waver. He observed, "Many commanderies to the east have succumbed, and Luoyang is now merely an isolated city with no external assistance. This is the best time to destroy Wang Shichong once and for all. Our withdrawal would only give him the opportunity to rest his troops and restore his control over the surrounding regions."

At this juncture, Dou Jiande finally disposed of his rival. Then he marshaled a hundred thousand troops and led them westward to relieve the siege of Luoyang. At the news of Dou's imminent arrival, Li Shimin was again urged by some of his officers to abandon the siege and withdraw the army. They argued, "Our troops are tired out and cannot readily overcome the well-protected city of Luoyang. Dou Jiande will soon arrive with his victorious army and attack us from the rear. Then we will fall into the extremely unfavorable situation of fighting two battles at the same time. Therefore, it would be best for us to pull back westward to Xin'an and wait for the enemy to grow weak."

To this Li Shimin retorted, "Wang Shichong's army is exhausted, his food is running short, and his generals are divided in opinion. We no longer need to attack the city, but can simply sit by and wait for it to yield in the ripeness of time. Dou Jiande has just waged a successful campaign; as a result, his generals are puffed with arrogance and the soldiers are extremely fatigued. We can therefore easily check their advance at Hulao Pass. If he risks launching an attack, we can surely defeat him; if he acts cautiously and refrains from battle, we will gain time to overcome Luoyang and can then, with a united force, proceed to rout Dou Jiande. If we do not act quickly to seize control of Hulao, Wang and Dou will join forces. If that happens, they will surely be strong enough to regain control of the areas surrounding Luoyang. What chance would we have to 'wait for them to grow weak' as you suggested?" With this he left his younger brother Li Yuanji to continue the siege of Luoyang and led thirty-five hundred selected troops in person to guard Hulao Pass.

Dou Jiande approached Hulao and made camp north of the Yellow River. After an initial battle in which Li Shimin lured some thousands of Dou's troops into an ambush and routed them, Dou Jiande did not venture another attack for many days. His advisor Lin Jing went to Dou and advised him to march north, cross over the Taihang Mountains, and advance on Taiyuan, the power base of the Tang. The plan, said Lin Jing, had three advantages: First, victory was certain because the Tang troops were concentrated around Luoyang, leaving a temporary military vacuum in the whole Hedong Region; second, land and people would be gained; third, the siege of Luoyang would be broken without sending troops there.

Dou Jiande, considering this to be a good plan, was about to carry it out when he was stopped by the objection of his generals, who remarked, "Lin Jing is a mere pedant. What does he know about warfare?" On hearing this, which Dou Jiande interpreted as proof of the high morale of his troops, he decided to remain in his position at Hulao. He was kept ignorant of the fact that Zhangsun Anshi, the envoy sent by Wang Shichong, had influenced the attitudes of his generals by offering them handsome bribes.

At this time, Li Shimin got a report from his agents that Dou was especially afraid of the powerful cavalry of Tang and would not advance until Li Shimin's cavalry had run out of fodder. In the fifth month Li Shimin crossed the river for reconnaissance; on his return he left some soldiers there to graze over a thousand horses.

Dou Jiande immediately responded by leading all his troops southward across the Yellow River. With the Yellow River at his back and the Sishui Stream to the front, Dou approached Hulao with his multitudinous troops arrayed in an awesome formation stretching for over ten *li*. At the sight, many Tang officers grew fearful. Li Shimin reassured them by saying, "These rebels have never fought a real grave battle. They have ventured into a position of peril and yet are making a great noise: This testifies to their lack of discipline. They have come and made camp right in front of our stronghold: This testifies to their underestimation of our strength. By waiting for them to grow tired and attacking them when they begin to falter and withdraw, we can surely defeat them. I wager we shall have them routed right after midday!" With this he sent a body of soldiers to bring back the horses from the northern bank of the Yellow River, meanwhile arraying the troops in a defensive position.

Though his troops were superior in number, Dou Jiande could find no way to deploy them against the well-guarded stronghold of Hulao. They retained their battle formation from morning to twelve noon, when the soldiers became quite tired and sat down on the ground. There was also a confused wrangle for drinking water, as the day was hot.

On perceiving this, Li Shimin decided it was time to launch the counterattack. However, to further verify his decision, he first commanded a brave officer by the name of Yuwen Shiji to lead three hundred cavalrymen on a sortie toward Dou's formation with the instruction, "Return immediately if the rebels remain still. If they become agitated, lead your troops on to the east and attack them."

The approach of the small cavalry band caused quite a commotion among Dou Jiande's troops. At this, Li Shimin at once led the main cavalry forces across the Sishui Stream and charged at Dou's formation. Several of the most valiant Tang generals penetrated all the way to the rear of the enemy, where they unfurled and waved the banners of the Tang army that they had taken with them. At this sight, the army of Dou was plunged into total commotion and started a wild flight eastward. Li Shimin led the Tang soldiers in a hot pursuit for over thirty *li* and captured Dou Jiande alive. He also took fifty thousand prisoners, though these were released by him on the same day and sent back to their native town.

Li Shimin brought Dou Jiande and the other captured generals in front of Luoyang's city gate to inform Wang Shichong. Wang summoned his generals and announced his plan to abandon Luoyang and proceed south to Xiangyang. However, his generals had all lost faith and did not want to fight. Left with no other alternative, Wang Shichong went with his officials to surrender to the Tang army. Li Shimin thereby disposed of the two most powerful rivals of the Tang regime. The complete pacification of the empire was to take another three years.

Adapted from *Old History of the Tang Dynasty* (Jiu Tang Shu), Tomes Two and Fifty-Four

Strategy Fourteen
Find Reincarnation in Another's Corpse

第十四计 借尸还魂　有用者，不可借；不能用者，求借。借不能用者而用之。匪我求童蒙，童蒙求我。

Translation

The useful declines to be used, whereas the useless asks to be used. Make use of the useless. It is not I who seek help from the callow youth but the callow youth who seeks help from me.*

Purport

According to popular Chinese myth, the spirit of a deceased, except for extreme cases when it is sent to suffer

---

*This phrase is taken from the judgement of *Meng* (Immaturity, Callowness), the fourth hexagram in *I Ching*. The hexagram has the symbol of water (*Kan*) under the mountain (*Gen*). Spring water coming out from the foot of the mountain is pure and unbridled, just as the minds of children are blank and susceptible to guidance. Therefore the hexagram also signifies education and enlightenment. The master, represented by the yang line in the second place, belongs to a lower social status than that of the pupil, the yin line in the fifth place. In familial terms, this means that when the head of the family becomes old and inept, the son can take charge of the household. In a broader sense, when a ruler has become weak and ineffectual, his authority may be taken over by a resolute subordinate, who will nevertheless act in a low profile, continuing to pay nominal homage to the ruler.

in hell or ascends to become an immortal in heaven, can find reincarnation either in a baby ready to be born or in a well-preserved corpse. Thus, when something smothered in the past is revived in a new guise, it is said to have found reincarnation in another's corpse.

The strategy advocates the use of the seemingly useless in warfare. At the downfall of a dynasty, many military strongmen will rise to contend for control over the empire. A wise leader understands that military victories are not enough to build up his strength. He must secure a measure of popular support so that he can always get people and resources to compensate for his losses on the battleground. An effective way to achieve this end is to foster a sense of his legitimacy among the common people. He might claim to be in a position to take over the empire, either as the descendant of a well-known victim of the fallen dynasty (if the latter is considered to be irredeemably corrupt) or a distant relative of the imperial house (if the fallen dynasty is considered to be a victim of vicious ministers). If unable to make such claims himself, he might set up a person who has such status as his master, whom he intends to get rid of after he has built up his strength.

Quotation for Reference

In war, it is paramount to hold on to the pivot. The pivot of war is nothing but name and righteousness. Secure a good name for yourself and give the enemy a bad name; proclaim your righteousness and reveal the unrighteousness of the enemy. Then your army can set forth in a great momentum, shaking heaven and earth and sweeping across the four corners. Wherever your command banner points, your troops will dash ahead in high spirits and break the will of the enemy.

A Scholar's Dilettante Remarks on War
(Tou Bi Fu Tan), Chapter One

The Uprising Led by Chen Sheng and Wu Guang

Chen Sheng, whose polite name was She, was a native of Yangcheng (to the southeast of modern Dengfeng County in Henan Province). Wu Guang, whose polite name was Shu, was a native of Yangxia (modern Taikang County in Henan Province).

When young, Chen Sheng worked as a farmhand for a local landowner. One day, while taking a rest in the fields, he fell into gloomy speculation. Then he said to his fellow laborers: "Let's pledge that if any of us becomes rich and noble, he shall not forget the others."

His companions responded with laughter: "You are a hired hand who plows the fields; how can you ever become rich and noble?" Thereupon Chen Sheng heaved a deep sigh and said, "Ah! What do the swallows know about the swan's aspirations!"

In the seventh month of the first year of the Second Emperor of Qin (209 B.C.), nine hundred men were conscripted for garrison service at Yuyang (near modern Miyun County in Beijing). Chen Sheng and Wu Guang were their camp leaders. Forced to halt at Daze Township (near modern Su County in Anhui Province), where the roads were blocked by torrential rain, they realized that they could not reach their destination on time. According to Qin law, notorious for its harshness, all the conscripts should therefore be punished with death.

Thereupon Chen Sheng and Wu Guang got together

to sort out the situation. They finally agreed on course of action, saying, "If we escape, we will die. If we launch a revolt, we will die. Since death is the only choice, why not die for the country?"

Chen Sheng then went on to reveal his plan, saying, "The world has long suffered under Qin. I have heard that the Second Emperor is the younger prince and should not have succeeded to the throne. The Crown Prince, Fusu, several times offered proposals that displeased his father, and so the emperor sent him to command troops far away from the capital. Now there is a rumor that the Second Emperor has murdered him, though he had done nothing wrong. The common folk have all heard of his benevolence, but very few of them know about his death. Xiang Yan, the great general of Chu, is loved by his people for his outstanding exploits and his kindness toward his men. Now some say he is dead and others declare he has fled to some remote area. If we rise up and claim Fusu and Xiang Yan to be our leaders, many people will join us."

Wu Guang agreed to Chen Sheng's plan, and together they went to consult a diviner. The diviner knew what they had in mind and announced, "The signs are auspicious, and you will succeed in your undertakings. But why not go and consult the ghosts?"

Chen Sheng and Wu Guang were pleased with the advice. "He was teaching us to create authority over the men!" They said to themselves. So they wrote "Chen Sheng will be King" in vermilion on a piece of silk and stuffed it in the belly of a fish someone had caught. When the conscripts bought the fish and prepared to cook it, they were amazed to find the silken message.

At night, Wu Guang slipped out of the camp and

made for a nearby temple, where he built a fire and cried like a fox: "The great Chu will rise again, and Chen Sheng will be King!" The next morning, the conscripts whispered among themselves and cast sidelong glances at Chen Sheng with awe.

Wu Guang was always kind and considerate to his men, and many of them would act at his beckoning. When one of the two officers in command of the conscripts was drunk, Wu Gang announced in front of the officer that he was going to escape. He said it several times, so that the officer finally became enraged and flogged him on the spot. At this juncture, the sword of the officer happened to slip a little out of its scabbard. Wu Guang sprang up, snatched the sword and killed the officer. Chen Sheng joined in by finishing off the other officer.

Then they summoned all the conscripts and said, "We have been delayed by rain and the penalty for this is decapitation. Even if we are spared, seven out of ten will die on the frontier. Now when a warrior faces death, he will die for fame and glory. Who says we cannot become kings, nobles, generals and ministers? Such men do not achieve their position by birthright!"

"We will follow you!" responded the men. They built an altar and swore their oath, offering the two officers' heads in sacrifices. Chen Sheng proclaimed himself general, while Wu Guang assumed the title of commandant. To win people's sympathy and support, they claimed to be led by Prince Fusu and General Xiang Yan and called themselves the army of "Great Chu."

This group of poorly armed, desperate men then attacked Daze Township and seized it. Thence they proceeded to capture the district of Qi and the areas to its east. As they marched on, they were joined by a multitude of people. On reaching Chen District, they had tens of thousands of footmen, more than a thousand cavalrymen and seven hundred war chariots. When they laid siege to the district seat of Chen, the magistrate was absent and only the assistant magistrate was there to defend the city gate. He was defeated and killed, and the rebels occupied the city and took control of its surrounding areas.

A few days later, Chen Sheng and Wu Guang summoned the local elders to a meeting to consult their opinion. The elders said in reply, "Wearing armor and carrying sharp weapons, the general has come to attack the despotic Qin and restore the ruling house of Chu. By his achievements, he deserves to be our king."

This proposal was opposed by Zhang Er and Chen Yu, two personages of high renown who had left their native land of Wei to join Chen Sheng at the city of Chen. They argued, "The despotic Qin has destroyed other states, demolished their ancestral altars, murdered their heirs, and exhausted the strength and resources of the people. Now, glaring in great anger, you are determined to risk your life in order to eliminate this scourge for the benefit of the all-under-heaven. But, having just reached Chen, if you declare yourself king right away, the world will suspect that you are pursuing your own selfish interest. Therefore we pray that you do not assume the title of king but proceed on to the west and dispatch envoys to restore the heirs of the ruling houses of the six states. By this action you can gain many allies for yourself in the fight against Qin. Faced with many enemies, Qin will be compelled to divide its forces. In the meantime you will grow in strength, having won many friends. Then you will encounter no resisting troops in the field and no defenders in the cities and can therefore subdue the despotic Qin with little effort. After seizing the capital Xianyang, you can issue orders to the nobles of various states who, in their gratitude to you for restoring them to power, will bow before you. In this way you can set up a new empire. But if you declare yourself king here in Chen, we are afraid that the world will fall into chaos."

Chen Sheng refused to make use of their advice and went on to set himself up as King of Zhangchu ("Upholding Chu"). The uprising of Chen Sheng and Wu Guang touched off a series of rebellions all over the empire and years of entangled warfare ensued. At the beginning, the Qin army was overpowering and victorious against the motley bands of rebels, who suffered from low strength, inferior strategy and poor coordination. Finally the Chu general Xiang Yu inflicted a decisive defeat on the crack troops of Qin and took command of the various anti-Qin forces. However, this happened after both Chen Sheng and Wu Guang had been murdered by their subordinates.

Formerly, when Chen Sheng became king and ruled in the area of Chen, one of his old acquaintances who had once worked with him in the fields heard of his success and came to call on him. The man knocked on the palace gate and said, "I want to see Chen She." The guards were about to arrest him, but he quickly explained that he was an old friend of their king. Thereupon the guards released him but still denied him entrance.

The man stayed by the roadside and called out when Chen Sheng rode out of the palace. On hearing the call, Chen Sheng ordered the man to be brought to his presence and invited him to ride in the chariot. Together they rode back to Chen Sheng's palace. The farmer exclaimed in admiration when he saw the grandeur and luxury of the great halls and spacious rooms in the palace. "What a heap of stuff you have, She, now that you are a king!" he said.

After this, the man paid frequent visits to Chen Sheng. He would ramble with ease in the palace and boast about the friendship he had had with the king in the old days. Someone went to Chen Sheng and warned him, "That silly and ignorant guest is ruining your reputation by his disrespectful blabber!"

By this time Chen Sheng had become rather arrogant. Thus he had his old friend's head cut off without the least hesitation. After this incident, all of his former acquaintances left him of their own accord and no one dared to get close with him. Chen Sheng also appointed two men to supervise the various officials and generals under his command. Any general who failed to carry out his task exactly was submitted to examination under these two men and might suffer a severe punishment for a slight offence. Thus the generals felt no security, much less attachment to their king. This partly accounted for Chen Sheng's defeat in the fight against Qin and his assassination by his chariot driver.

Though Chen Sheng died early, the various generals he dispatched on expeditions finally succeeded in destroying the Qin. Therefore he is credited with starting the anti-Qin campaign. In the time of Emperor Gaozu of Han, thirty households were assigned to take care of Chen Sheng's grave and offer him regular sacrifices.

Adapted from *Records of the Historian* (Shi Ji), Tome Forty-Eight

Strategy Fifteen
Lure the Tiger out of the Mountain

第十五计 调虎离山　待天以困之，用人以诱之。往
蹇来反。

Translation

Wait for Heaven to encumber the enemy and make
plots to allure it. When going leads to obstruction, come
back.*

Purport

In military context, a tiger in the mountain symbolizes a strong enemy who enjoys the protection of a
walled city, a fortified camp, a strategic mountain pass,

---

*This phrase is taken from the judgement of the third line of *Jian*
(Obstruction), the thirty-ninth hexagram in *I Ching*. The hexagram
consists of *Kan* (water; danger) above *Gen* (mountain; stillness). The
comment observes, "*Jian* means difficulty. Danger ahead. To stop at the
sight of difficulty is wisdom." The yang line in the third place, assisted
by the yin line at the top, aims to rise to a higher position. However, it
is confronted with the upper trigram of *Kan* representing difficulty and
danger. Furthermore, the appropriate position for a yang line in the
upper trigram, the fifth place, has already been occupied. Therefore the
third yang line should halt its advance and return to its own place. In
human terms, one is cautioned against plunging into a dangerous place
controlled by a powerful opponent. In war, one should not attack a
strong enemy who has already taken up a position of advantage.

or a wide, rushing water. One who commands a well-disciplined army is advised not to advance onto such an enemy. As a Chinese saying goes, "Stranded on the sandy beach, the dragon is teased by shrimps; descending on the plain, the tiger is bullied by dogs." Therefore, whether aiming to seize the territory of the enemy or destroy its armed forces, one should try to allure the enemy away from its impregnable position before engaging it in battle.

Quotations for Reference

When engaging the enemy in battle, if there is a position of advantage, we should capture it first and fight from there to gain a victory. If the enemy has captured it beforehand, we should not attack but should wait for a change in the situation; only then can we gain the advantage by striking at the enemy. The principle goes, "Do not attack the enemy in a contestable ground."

A Hundred Marvelous Battle Plans,
"Battle of Contest" (Bai Zhan Qi Fa,
"Zheng Zhan")

If the enemy is led on to the battlefield, its position is always weak. If we do not have to reach for the battlefield, our position is always strong. Use various methods to make the enemy come forward and lie in wait for it at a convenient locality; we can thereby achieve certain victory. The principle goes, "Maneuver the enemy instead of being maneuvered."

Ibid., "Battle of Maneuver" ("Zhi Zhan")

Supreme General Han Xin Defeats the Zhao Army

In the eighth month of 205 B.C., when Liu Bang was maintaining his line of defense against Xiang Yu at the city of Xingyang, his supreme general, Han Xin, defeated and captured the Prince of Wei and turned Wei into a prefecture under Han rule. Despite this victory, Liu Bang knew from bitter experience that Xiang Yu's personal army was all but invincible. He was therefore greatly pleased when Han Xin offered to seize the peripheral areas under Chu's effective or nominal rule before returning to join the main force of Han at Xingyang. According to this plan, Han Xin would march northward to conquer Dai, Zhao, and Yan, and then proceed east to subdue the area of Qi. After that, he would be able to go south and destroy Xiang Yu's transportation routes, then returning to Xingyang and joining forces with Liu Bang against Xiang Yu, whose army would by then be isolated and short of provisions.

Liu Bang adopted Han Xin's plan and forthwith sent him on an expedition against Dai and Zhao. Zhang Er, the former chief minister of Zhao who had surrendered to Liu Bang, was to accompany Han Xin as his guide and assistant.

Zhang Er had been good friends with Chen Yu, the Prince of Dai. In the widespread uprisings after the death of the First Emperor, they had joined the rebels together and had set up Zhao Xie, a descendant of the former royal house of Zhao, as Prince of Zhao. Later, when Xiang Yu enfeoffed eighteen princes, he transferred Zhao Xie to be the Prince of Dai. Xiang Yu had taken a liking to Zhang Er, partly because Zhang was a sociable person with many friends; therefore he made Zhang Er Prince of Changshan, a part of the Zhao area. As for Chen Yu, who did not readily follow Xiang Yu's orders, he got only three counties as his fief and the title of marquis. Chen Yu was so angry that he took the first opportunity to attack Zhang Er, driving him out of the area of Zhao and reinstating Zhao Xie as Prince of Zhao. The grateful Zhao Xie thanked Chen Yu by offering him the area of Dai. Chen accepted, but he suspected Zhao Xie's ability to govern a state not fully stabilized and decided to stay a little longer, while appointing Xia Yue, the chief minister of Dai, to govern Dai in his stead.

In the ninth month, Han Xin and Zhang Er advanced on Dai and Zhao, which were neighboring areas divided by the Taihang Mountains. They first attacked Dai, which lay to the west of the mountains, engaging the Dai army at Yuyu (modern northwest Heshun County in Shanxi Province). The Dai army was routed and Xia Yue was taken prisoner. As soon as the battle was over, the King of Han hastily sent an envoy to take command of Han Xin's best troops and bring them back to Xingyang to reinforce his own army. Left with twenty or thirty thousand men, Han Xin and Zhang Er led them eastward, planning to attack Zhao by way of Jingxing Defile.

On hearing of Han Xin's approach, the King of Zhao and Chen Yu gathered an army, which reportedly amounted to two hundred thousand, and proceeded to Jingxing Defile to halt the advance of the Han army.

Li Zuoche, a noble of Zhao, offered his advice to Chen Yu, saying, "I hear that Han Xin has crossed the Yellow River in the west, captured the King of Wei, and spilled blood anew at Yuyu, routing the Dai army and taking Xia Yue prisoner. Now, with the assistance of Zhang Er, he is planning to attack Zhao. An army like this, riding the tide of victory to fight far from its native land, cannot be met head-on. However, I have heard it said that when supplies have to be transported for a thousand *li*, the soldiers will look hungry. When firewood must be collected before each meal is cooked, the troops will sleep with empty stomachs. Now the path through Jingxing Defile is so narrow that two chariots cannot ride side by side, nor can the cavalry proceed in formation. Han Xin has marched for several hundred *li* and his provisions must be in the rear. I beg you to give me thirty thousand crack troops with which I can march by a bypass to cut off Han Xin's supply wagons. In the meantime, you just deepen the trenches, heighten the ramparts, and refuse to engage in battle. While you maintain this blockade at the front, I will cut off the enemy's supply lines in the rear. Han Xin will then be unable to advance or retreat. Running short of supplies, his troops will panic and fall into disorder, and in less than ten days the heads of Han Xin and Zhang Er will be presented before you. I pray that you take heed of my advice. Otherwise, you will surely become his prisoner!"

Chen Yu was a Confucian scholar who often declared that a righteous army had no use for deceitful tricks or unusual stratagems. He dismissed Li Zuoche's argument, saying, "Surround the enemy when you outnumber it ten to one; engage it in battle when you outnumber it two to one—that is what I have read in the *Art of War*. Now Han Xin claims an army of several tens of thousands, but in fact he has only a few thousand men. After traveling a thousand *li* to attack us, they will be worn out upon their arrival. If I were to evade such a small and tired army, how would I be able to cope with stronger foes? Taking me for a coward, the other lords would be encouraged to follow Han Xin's example and attack me."

Thus Chen Yu refused to adopt the plan. When Han Xin's spies returned to report to him that Li Zuoche's suggestion went unheeded, he was overjoyed. Only then did he dare to lead troops down the gorge. They made camp thirty *li* from the mouth of the defile. At midnight, Han Xin summoned a picked force of two thousand cavalrymen, each carrying a red banner. He ordered them to take a small path in the hills and stay at a vantage point overlooking Jingxing Defile, where the main battle was to take place. "At our army's retreat," Han Xin instructed, "the men of Zhao will leave their ramparts to pursue us. Then you must rush down at once and storm their camp, tear down the banners of Zhao and replace them with the red banners of Han."

Then he had food rations distributed among the troops and announced to his officers, "We'll have a grand feast today after we rout the Zhao army." None of the officers believed him, but they pretended to agree. Then Han Xin assessed the situation, saying, "The men of Zhao have occupied a position of advantage to build their fortified camp. They will not attack until they see my commander's flag, because they aim to destroy our main force and not just the vanguard."

With this, Han Xin sent a vanguard of ten thousand men to march through Jingxing Defile and set up battle formation with their back to the river. The Zhao soldiers roared with laughter on seeing that Han Xin had put his men in what they perceived as a suicidal position—facing the overpowering enemy hosts and with no route for retreat.

At early dawn, Han Xin set up his commander's flag and led the main body of his troops through the defile to the beating of battle drums. The men of Zhao immediately rushed out of their camp to attack, and a fierce battle ensued. Feigning defeat, the Han soldiers discarded their banners and drums and fell back to join the vanguard arrayed along the river. These ranks opened to receive Han Xin and then joined in the battle. Perceiving a chance to wipe out the Han army, the men of Zhao, including those assigned to guard the ramparts, charged forward to seize the abandoned flags and drums and pursue Han Xin and Zhang Er. However, left with no way of escape, the Han soldiers put up a desperate resistance and could not be subdued.

In the meantime Han Xin's two thousand cavalrymen, who had waited up in a mountain path till the men of Zhao left their camp in pursuit of trophies, rushed down into the empty ramparts. They tore down the flags of Zhao and set up two thousand red flags of Han. Failing to gain a victory and capture Han Xin, the men of Zhao became discouraged and were about to withdraw to their camp when they disovered that the camp was ringed with the red banners of Han. What could this mean, thought the soldiers, but that the Han troops had already seized the camp and captured the King of Zhao? The Zhao soldiers panicked and fled in all directions. The officers cut down several deserters but could not stop the stampede. Thereupon the Han forces closed in from both sides and routed the Zhao army completely. Chen Yu was slain by the riverbank and the King of Zhao was taken prisoner.

Han Xin had ordered the troops not to kill Li Zuoche, offering a reward of a thousand gold pieces to anyone who could capture him alive. When the battle was over, Li Zuoche was bound by one of the Han soldiers and brought to Han Xin. Han Xin untied his bindings, put him in an honored seat facing east and seated himself facing west. He treated Li Zuoche with great respect and asked his advice on strategies.

The officers came to Han Xin to present their captives and the heads of the slain. They congratulated him on the victory and took the opportunity to question him. "According to the *Art of War*, an army must place itself at a secure position, with the hill to its right or rear and the river in the front or to its left. But today, you ordered us on the contrary to array the army with its back to the river and announced a feast after the defeat of Zhao. We did not believe you then but it turned out that we gained the victory eventually. What strategy was that?"

"This is all written in the *Art of War*, but you simply overlooked it. Does not the book say, 'Put them at a fatal position and they will survive?' Besides, I did not have the chance to get acquainted with the troops at my disposal but had to 'drive street rabble to take to the field,' as the saying goes. Therefore I was compelled to plunge them into a desperate position where everyone had to fight for his own life. If I had provided them with a route of escape, they would have all run away before the superior forces of the enemy."

"Excellent!" the officers exclaimed in admiration. "This is really beyond us."

Adapted from Records of the Historian
(Shi Ji), Tome Ninety-Two

Strategy Sixteen
Leave at Large, the Better to Capture

第十六计 欲擒姑纵　　逼则反兵，走则减势，紧随勿迫。累其气力，消其斗志，散而后擒，兵不血刃。需，有孚，光。

Translation

Close in upon the [defeated] enemy and it will strike back; let it go and its position will weaken. Follow it closely but do not press too hard. Fritter away its strength and sap its will. After it has scattered, subdue it without staining the swords with blood. Waiting. Sincerity brings glory.*

Purport

War is an expensive cause even for the victor. Generally, it is preferable to fight a quick battle and wipe out the enemy as soon as possible. In some cases, however, one should be ready to bide one's time, waiting until the

---

*"Waiting. Sincerity brings glory and success. Peseverance brings good fortune. It is of benefit to cross a great river." This is the judgement of *Xu* (Waiting), the fifth hexagram in *I Ching*. The hexagram has the symbol of water (*Kan*) above the heaven (*Qian*). When clouds gather in the sky, it will rain. However, one cannot hasten the process but must wait for the rain to come in the fullness of time. Also, the lower trigram, *Qian*, represents strength and *Kan* represents danger. Faced with danger, a person of strength should not set forth headlong but should bide his time and wait for the right opportunity.

situation develops to one's advantage. For instance, when faced with a powerful enemy, it is sometimes inadvisable to take action immediately. Instead, use natural conditions and strategic maneuvers to consume the strength and morale of the enemy before engaging it in battle. Therefore, in an apparent contradiction to the common belief in the supreme importance of rapidity in military action, this strategy stresses the necessity of delay.

In specific, the strategy advises delaying when one has the upper hand. Under violent attack, an encircled enemy will be forced to fight to death. Encircled but not assaulted vigorously and left with an escape route, the enemy will soon lose its esprit. Therefore, in order to destroy the enemy forces that have been cornered into an adverse position, one should perpetrate this situation to wear out the enemy rather than press hard onto the enemy for fear of rousing it to desperate resistance. On the other hand, the enemy general might deliberately put his men in a position that allows no escape to encourage them to fight with all their might (cf. Strategy Twenty-Eight).

Naturally, deferment is an extraordinary method that must be used with extra caution. Before deciding to interrupt the action, one must first make sure that one's troops can afford the delay and that nothing can possibly happen during the interval to change the enemy's position for the better.

Quotations for Reference

The method for laying siege is to surround the enemy on four sides and leave one corner open as an escape route, so that the enemy will not fight desperately. In this way, the city can be captured and the enemy defeated.

The principle goes, "Always leave a way of escape for the encircled enemy."

A Hundred Marvelous Battle Plans, "Battle of Encirclement" (Bai Zhan Qi Fa, "Wei Zhan")

In warfare, if the enemy is outnumbered by our troops, it will be afraid of our strength and flee without fighting. We should not embark on hot pursuit, for anything forced to the extreme will develop into its opposite. We can achieve victory instead by leading our troops in an unhurried chase. The principle goes, "Do not press an enemy at bay."

Ibid., "Battle of Extremity" ("Qiong Zhan")

A stubborn enemy forced into an impasse will undoubtedly fight to the death. We must not engage it in battle; instead, we should press forward when it gets relaxed and pull back when it approaches to attack. By and by, the enemy will take its own life.

An Abstract of Military Works (Wu Bei Ji Yao)

Sima Yi's Expedition Against Liaodong Commandery

Sima Yi, whose polite name was Zhongda, was born of an aristocratic family in the late Eastern Han Dynasty. In A.D. 201, the sixth year of the Jian'an reign under the last Han emperor, Xiandi, Sima Yi was offered a position in the court by Cao Cao, the Minister of Works. At that time the empire was divided among several mighty warlords over whom the imperial house of Han had no control whatever. The emperor himself was a puppet of Cao Cao, the most powerful of the warlords who exerted absolute

143

authority in the court.

As he deemed the time inopportune for him to rise, Sima Yi declined the post, pleading sickness. Somewhat later, Cao Cao had himself appointed Councilor-in-Chief and again sent for Sima Yi, telling him to chose between office and prison. Thus began Sima Yi's half-hearted yet meritorious service for the Cao family.

In 220 Cao Cao's son Cao Pei deposed the last Han ruler and assumed the imperial title for himself, later known as Emperor Wendi of Wei. Sima Yi received the title of marquis and served in various key posts in the Wei court. The new emperor both liked and feared Sima Yi for his extraordinary abilities. Even so, Sima Yi played a major role in consolidating the kingdom of Wei against its two rival regimes, Shu and Wu. And he managed with success to conceal his ambition while giving full play to his talents. He was one of the three most trusted courtiers summoned before the deathbed of Cao Pei, who consigned the young crown prince to their care and assistance. The prince succeeded to the throne as Emperor Mingdi of Wei in 226.

In the first month of the second year of the Jingchu reign (238), Emperor Mingdi called Sima Yi to Chang'an and commanded him to lead a campaign against Gongsun Yuan, the governor of Liaodong Commandery who had recently renounced his allegiance to the Wei court. The emperor said, "This is no doubt beneath your ability, but I want a certain victory. So you have to take the trouble." He then put Sima Yi in command of forty thousand troops, to which several ministers objected, arguing that it would be too costly to provide for such a big army. The emperor replied, "An expedition over four thousand *li* requires not only abruptness but also sufficient strength.

We ought not to spare expense for the provisions." Then he asked Sima Yi, "What will be Gongsun Yuan's strategy to cope with your attack?"

"To abandon the city of Xiangping in a preemptive action to avoid battle and preserve his strength is the superior plan for him," replied Sima Yi. "The ordinary plan is to line up his troops behind the Liaoshui River to block our advance. If he takes no action but stays to defend Xiangping, he will soon become a prisoner."

"But which plan is he most likely to adopt?" asked the emperor.

"Only the wise can fully understand his own condition and make small sacrifices in advance. This is beyond Gongsun Yuan. Besides, he must think that our siege cannot last because of the difficulty to transport provisions across thousands of *li* for such a big army. Therefore he will first try to block us at the Liaoshui River and then pull back to defend Xiangping."

"How long will it take you to carry out this expedition?" asked the emperor.

Sima Yi replied, "I need a hundred days to arrive there, a hundred days to attack, a hundred days to come back, and sixty days to rest. Altogether, one year will be enough."

On hearing of the approach of the Wei army, Gongsun Yuan hastily dispatched an envoy to the Kingdom of Wu to offer his allegiance and ask for help. The ruler of Wu, Sun Quan, bore a grudge against Gongsun Yuan for some past insults and intended to have the envoy beheaded, but was stopped by an advisor named Yang Dao. Yang argued, "The execution of the envoy will in no wise contribute to your aspiration to rule the world. Such action only becomes an ordinary man who wants nothing more than to vent his anger. It would be better if we receive the envoy with kindness and send a band of troops to proceed to Liaodong in secret. If Sima Yi's expedition fails, we will not only gain the gratitude of Gongsun Yuan but also have our fame spread among those distant regions. If the campaign drags on with heavy losses on both sides, the surrounding areas not directly engaged in battle will become weakly defended and vulnerable. Then we can seize the chance to storm and loot these areas and revenge the past insults."

"Great idea!" exclaimed Sun Quan appreciatively. With this he mustered a band of troops for the purpose. Then he had the envoy brought to his presence and told him, "I will share the present adversity with your master and dispatch my army to aid him."

When this news reached the Kingdom of Wei, the emperor felt somewhat anxious and asked a military protector named Jiang Ji, "Will Sun Quan send troops to rescue Liaodong?"

"Sun Quan always behaves with great caution," replied Jiang Ji. "When he cannot be sure of gaining advantage, he will not move even to save his own followers. How then can he be willing to help Gongsun Yuan, who has insulted him in the past? His sending troops to Liaodong may be a mere gesture. He hopes to garner Gongsun Yuan's gratitude and loyalty if our expedition should prove a failure. He will refrain from taking action if our force keeps the upper hand and subdues Liaodong according to our plan. But if something untoward happens to make it a contracted battle with both sides suffering heavy casualties, Sun Quan will surely take advantage of the situation to ransack the peripheral areas of Liaodong."

In the sixth month Sima Yi arrived at Liaodong with

his troops. Gongsun Yuan dispatched two generals, Bei Yan and Yang Zuo, to station at Liaoshui, which was shielded by a circular entrenchment of more than twenty *li*. Together they had several hundred thousand troops, including both footmen and cavalry.

When the officers offered to attack, Sima Yi did not allow them. "The enemy has converged behind this huge defense work with the aim to wear us out. We will fall into its trap if we attack here. On the other hand, as Gongsun Yuan has sent out the majority of his forces to intercept us at Liaoshui, the defense of his own capital must be weak. Therefore we will beat him by sidestepping Liaoshui and marching on Xiangping." Thereupon he sent a small contingent of soldiers with lots of flags to move southward. Bei Yan was deceived by this and sent his men to proceed south to forestall them. In the meantime Sima Yi led his main force to the north. He crossed the Liaoshui River and advanced on the city of Xiangping.

As Bei Yan realized his mistake, he became alarmed and embarked on hot pursuit of the Wei army. A battle took place at Shoushan Mountain to the southwest of Xiangping. Just before the engagement, Sima Yi announced to the officers with full confidence, "We shall win the battle, for the enemy has come to fight out of fear." Sure enough, he inflicted a crushing defeat on Bei Yan's superior forces. Then he led troops to lay siege to Xiangping.

In the seventh month, torrential rain caused the Liaoshui River to rise sharply. Sima Yi had his troops transported by boats from the Liaokou Ford right to the city gate of Xiangping. The rain went on for over a month and water accumulated to several *chi** on level ground. The officers and men felt very uncomfortable and clamored for moving away. At this Sima Yi issued a stern order: "Anyone who talks about moving camp shall be punished with death!" When one officer disobeyed the order, Sima Yi had him decapitated on the spot. Thus the agitation among the troops died down.

The people in Xiangping took advantage of the heavy rain to venture out of the city to collect firewood in nearby hills. Sima Yi forbade his men to harass them. Gongsun Yuan's soldiers grew confident and believed that, thanks to the heavy rain, the Wei army could do them no harm.

As the stalemate dragged on, a general named Chen Gui came to see Sima Yi and questioned him, "When we attacked the city of Shangyong the other time, you divided the army into eight squads and made them charge at the city in relays day and night. Therefore we were able to capture the well-fortified city in five days and kill that traitor, Meng Da. Now we have come from a great distance but are made to act at such a sluggish pace. I am too stupid to comprehend this."

"The situations are very different," Sima Yi explained. "Meng Da had few troops and enough provisions to last a year, whereas we outnumbered him four to one but our food could hardly last a single month. Pitting a month against a year, what could we do but to fight a quick battle? And pitting four soldiers against one, we could afford to gain victory at the expense of half the army. In a word, we were compelled to race against time and we had the strength to do it. Now, however, the conditions

---

*1 *chi* = 1/3 meter.

are to the contrary. The enemy is superior in number but lacks provisions. Amid the heavy rain, we cannot launch an effective assault. And what good would it do to harass the enemy for small gains? In this campaign, I am not worried that the enemy might come forward to attack. I only fear that the enemy might come to its senses and take to its feet. Gongsun Yuan is running short of food already, but he refuses to abandon the city because he believes in his army's superiority and the protection of the rain. By looting the herds and attacking the firewood collectors, we would probably scare him into vigilance and prompt him to plan escape. Therefore it is highly inexpedient to muddle up the whole business for such small gains."

When news reached the Kingdom of Wei that the expedition was encumbered by heavy rain, a few ministers went to the emperor and advised him to call back the troops. However, the emperor had full confidence in Sima Yi's ability. He announced, "Sima Yi certainly knows how to cope with difficulties. We do not have to wait long for Gongsun Yuan to be captured alive."

When the rain finally abated, Sima Yi closed up his encirclement and began to assail the city. After a few days the city ran out of food, with some residents even resorting to cannibalism to fill their stomachs. General Yang Zuo and several other officers fled the city and surrendered to the Wei army.

In the eighth month Gongsun Yuan sent Councilor-in-Chief Wang Jian and Censor-in-Chief Liu Fu to sue for peace, pledging that he and his men would capitulate if Sima Yi would first withdraw his troops. But Sima Yi had the two envoys beheaded and sent a message to Gongsun Yuan, saying, "Chu and Zheng enjoyed equal status as feudal states, and yet the Count of Zheng, when defeated, bared his chest and carried goats to receive the Chu army. I am a grand duke appointed by the emperor, but those two envoys of yours, without the least sense of propriety, requested me to lift my siege and withdraw my troops! As they were both very senile and decrepit and must have failed to communicate your meaning clearly, I have had them executed. You may send someone younger if you want."

The next envoy, a young palace attendant named Wei Yan, duly arrived. He brought the promise that Gongsun Yuan would soon send his son to the Wei army as a hostage. Sima Yi replied, "There are only five methods in marshaling a war. If you can fight, fight. If you cannot fight, defend. If you cannot defend yourself, escape. The last two alternatives are surrender and death. Now, since Gongsun Yuan is unwilling to surrender, it can only mean that he is courting death! So what is the use of sending a hostage?"

With this Sima Yi resumed the attack relentlessly. A few days later, the city succumbed. Gongsun Yuan then led a few hundred mounted guards and broke out of the encirclement at the southeast corner of the city. But the men of Wei pursued and caught up with them. Both Gongsun Yuan and his son were put to death on the bank of the Liangshui River. Sima Yi then slaughtered over seven thousand male residents of Xiangping and had their corpses piled into a small mound to mark his glorious triumph.

Adapted from *History as a Mirror*
(Zi Zhi Tong Jian), Tome Seventy-Four

Strategy Seventeen
Cast a Brick to Attract Jade

第十七计 抛砖引玉　　类以诱之。击蒙也。

Translation

Lure the enemy with counterfeits. Punish the callow youth.*

Purport

The expression comes from a story about two poets in the Tang Dynasty. Once, a celebrated poet named Zhao Xia was about to visit Suzhou, the city of gardens in south China. When the poet Chang Jian heard about this, he knew

---

*In *Meng* (Immaturity), the fourth hexagram in *I Ching* (cf. Strategy Fourteen), the yin line at the fifth place represents an inexperienced youth who seeks instruction in a submissive manner, signifying good fortune. However, sometimes the youth may become arrogant and disrespectful, as represented by the yang line at the top, violating the propriety of behavior. Then he should be duly punished. Even then, the punishment must be meted out as a preventive against further offense; it is inappropriate to counter evil by evil means. Thus the judgement of the sixth line observes, "Punish the callow youth. It does no good to commit a violation but is of benefit to resist one." In military context, against the invasion of a hostile power, one should refrain from launching an attack into the enemy territory. Instead, it is best to allow the invading army to move in and then defeat it on one's own ground.

that Zhao was sure to stop by the Lingyan Temple (Temple of Intelligent Rock). So he went there at once and wrote two lines of poetry on the wall. When Zhao Xia arrived and saw the two lines left by Chang, he wrote two more lines, completing the poem. It is generally agreed that the last two lines are far superior to the original lines of Chang Jian. Therefore Chang Jian is said to have "cast a brick to attract jade." Today, the expression is still used by people who want to sound modest. For example, a person who is asked to speak first at a meeting might say, by way of modesty, that he is going to "cast a brick to attract jade."

In a military context, the brick and the jade refer respectively to false and actual maneuvers. To use another popular idiom, it is a trick of "passing off fish eyes as pearls." First, the commander offers the enemy some bait, which can be a body of weak troops, poorly guarded provision carts, or a herd of oxen or horses that seem to be unprotected. At the prospect of gain, the enemy will advance to swallow the bait. Thus the commander has gained the initiative by maneuvering the enemy at his will, and the battle has actually been half won before it is fought.

Quotations for Reference

When engaged in battle with an enemy whose general is too stupid to act according to circumstances, we may tempt it with profit. When it eagerly pursues profit to the neglect of danger, we may then prepare an ambush to strike and defeat it. The principle goes, "Give profit to the enemy to lure it."

A Hundred Marvelous Battle Plans, "Battle of Profit" (Bai Zhan Qi Fa, "Li Zhan")

In warfare, the so-called baiting does not refer to poisoning the enemy's food. Instead, any force used to tempt the enemy with the prospect of gain is called a bait army. If, during an engagement, the enemy troops scatter oxen and horses, desert property, or jettison supplies, we must not seize them, for that would lead inevitably to our defeat. The principle goes, "Do not swallow the bait army."

Ibid., "Battle of Bait" ("Er Zhan")

When engaged in battle with an enemy whose camps are faraway and whose strength is equal to ours, we may dispatch a small body of light cavalry to challenge it and arrange an ambush to wait for it; thus the enemy can be overcome. If the enemy employs this tactic, we should not retaliate with our main force. The principle goes, "When the enemy comes from afar to challenge, it aims to entice you to advance."

Ibid., "Battle of Challenge" ("Tiao Zhan")

Abandon goods to throw the enemy into disorder, abandon troops to entice it, and abandon fortresses and land to encourage its arrogance. When it is expedient to apply abandonment, success can hardly be won with too much attachment, and nothing can be accomplished without forbearance.

A Hundred War Maxims, "Abandon"
(Bing Fa Bai Yan, "Wei")

One who is good at maneuvering the enemy makes a move so that the enemy must make a corresponding move, offers bait so that the enemy must swallow it, or lures the enemy with the prospect of gain and waits for it with one's main force.

Cao Cao's note: Entice the enemy with profit, lead it away from its fortress, assume a vantage point, and attack when the enemy is weak and lacking in support.

Art of War (Sun Zi Bing Fa), Chapter Five

General Li Mu Wards off the Xiongnu Invaders

Li Mu was a renowned general of Zhao in the Warring States period. He remained for years at Yanmen in the area of Dai to guard the northern border against the warlike Xiongnu people. He exerted full authority over the border region under his command and appointed officials by his own decision. Moreover, he had the local tax revenue brought to his headquarters to meet the expenses of his officers and men. He also had several oxen slaughtered each day to feast the soldiers. Thus, he treated the troops generously and they followed his orders with gladness.

Li Mu made a point of training his men in mounted archery, the expertise of the Xiongnu invaders. He also reinforced the beacon system and employed many secret agents, thereby always learning beforehand if the Xiongnu were about to launch an attack. As the troops were not strong enough to make any counterattack, he forbade them to give battle. He issued a stern order: "When the Xiongnu come for a raid, retreat quickly behind the ramparts. Whoever dares venture out to fight the enemy will be punished with death."

Thus, whenever the Xiongnu came on a raid, the Zhao soldiers lit the beacon fires to pass the warning and withdrew behind the ramparts, where they could easily repulse the enemy's assaults. Li Mu employed this strategy for many years, keeping the Xiongnu safely away from the border land. The local people therefore suffered little loss from the Xiongnu's repeated raids. However, because Li Mu refused to give battle, the Xiongnu regarded him as a coward. Even his own soldiers thought that Li Mu, though undoubtedly a generous and kindhearted man, did not have the courage and valor befitting a good general.

Several courtiers who were jealous of Li Mu took the opportunity to talk ill of him in front of the King of Zhao. Thereupon the king sent a messenger to reprimand Li Mu and urge him to counterattack the Xiongnu invaders. But Li Mu ignored this order and continued to act his own way. Then the king angrily recalled him to the capital and appointed another general to guard Yanmen in his place.

For over a year, whenever the Xiongnu horsemen arrived to raid the northern border land of Zhao, the new general always ventured out of the ramparts to meet them in battle. He suffered many defeats, resulting in great losses. The local people could no longer raise cattle and work the fields in the frontier area. Their grievances finally reached the court of Zhao.

The king realized his mistake and decided to reinstate Li Mu. When the king's messenger called on Li Mu, the latter pleaded illness and refused to see him. When the king insisted, Li Mu said, "If my lord really wants to let me take command, I ask permission to carry on just as before." To this the king readily gave his consent, and Li Mu returned to take charge of the defense at Yanmen.

For the next few years the northern border land of Zhao enjoyed peace and security. The Xiongnu, however, still regarded Li Mu as a coward, since he did not give battle. By this time the well-fed and well-trained Zhao soldiers were eager to take to the field.

Thereupon Li Mu selected thirteen hundred war chariots, thirteen thousand horsemen, fifty thousand brave soldiers and a hundred thousand archers. Having trained them for a major battle, he allowed cattle and farmers to scatter all over the plain to lure the Xiongnu. The Xiongnu immediately arrived to make a small incursion. Li Mu feigned defeat and discarded several thousand men and numerous cattle to the enemy. On hearing the report, the Xiongnu chieftain mustered more than a hundred thousand cavalrymen to launch an all-out invasion. Employing unusual stratagems, Li Mu enticed the Xiongnu into an ambush and outflanked them on both sides. Thereby he wiped out the entire Xiongnu cavalry and, riding the crest of victory, proceeded to subdue three large Xiongnu tribes to the north. Though the Xiongnu chieftain escaped, for more than ten years afterwards his men dared not approach the frontier of Zhao.

Li Mu was to achieve even greater military exploits, mainly in conducting successful battles against Qin, which by then had become powerful enough to embark upon the task of subjugating the rivaling states and unifying the all-under-heaven. For this he was honored with a noble title. In 229 B.C., a Qin general named Wang Jian led troops on a major offensive against Zhao. When Li Mu was put in command of the Zhao army, Qin bribed a favorite courtier of Zhao and used him as agent. The courtier then went to the King of Zhao to slander Li Mu, accusing him of plotting treason. So the king sent two generals to take over Li Mu's command. However, Li Mu refused to obey. Thereupon the king sent men to strike him by surprise and kill him. Three months later, Wang Jian launched his attack, routing the Zhao army and capturing the King of Zhao. The state of Zhao was thus destroyed.

Adapted from *Records of the Historian*
(Shi Ji), Tome Eighty-One

Strategy Eighteen
To Catch Bandits, First Catch the Ringleader

第十八计 擒贼擒王　　摧其坚，夺其魁，以解其体。龙战于野，其道穷也。

Translation

Crush the enemy's main force and capture its chief to disintegrate its body. A dragon compelled to fight on land is faced with an impasse.*

Purport

This expression is taken from a poem by the Tang poet

---

*This is the symbol of the top line of *Kun* (Earth, the Receptive), the second hexagram in *I Ching*. The hexagram consists of six yin lines, with the upper and lower trigrams being both *Kun*. Thus it represents the primal yin nature. In human terms, it denotes a person who is yielding, submissive, and always ready to serve the others. However, the line at the sixth place has developed into the very extreme of the yin principle. It takes hold of a position of leadership, which is unsuitable for its yin nature, and attempts to contend with the yang principle for supremacy. This can only lead it to a dead end. Thus a person who tries to secure a position to which he is not entitled will soon find himself challenged by the authorities, resulting in a contest that he has no hope to win. In military context, a leader who undertakes a cause that is far beyond his means will evoke the attention and anger of the strong and, in the ensuing contest, will be destroyed or swallowed up.

Du Fu:

> *To draw a bow, draw one that is powerful;*
> *To pick arrows, take those that are long;*
> *To shoot horsemen, first shoot their steeds;*
> *To catch bandits, first catch the ringleader.*

The word *bandit* here is a derogatory name for enemy forces that will scatter and flee after their leader is captured. When fighting such an enemy, one may simply catch the ringleader, and his followers will succumb.

In general, the enemy's headquarters is situated at its strongest point. In order to beat such an enemy, one has to destroy its armed forces first. Such direct contention is undesirable but often necessary in warfare. It can be avoided when the hub of the enemy happens to be in a weak point. Finding a breach in the enemy's defense line, one may bypass its strongholds and attack its base by a circuitous path. After the enemy commander is captured, his subordinates will not be able to fight on their own.

Quotations for Reference

When our troops have penetrated deep into the enemy's territory and the enemy strengthens its defense works and refuses to engage in battle for the purpose of wearing us down, we may attack its sovereign, storm its headquarters, block its return route, and cut off its provisions. Thus it will be compelled to fight, and we can employ crack forces to defeat it. The principle goes, "When I want to fight, the enemy cannot avoid me in spite of his deep gullies and high ramparts, for I attack

159

the place that he must salvage."

A Hundred Marvelous Battle Plans, "Battle of
Necessity" (Bai Zhan Qi Fa, "Bi Zhan")

Break up one camp and all the other camps submit;
overcome one place and all the other places topple down.
This is because you have destroyed the enemy's mainstay.

A Hundred War Maxims, "Situation"
(Bing Fa Bai Yan, "Shi")

There are ten thousand artifices of war, and one
should not stick to any one of them. First seize the
enemy's mainstay, and its strength will be weakened by
half.

Canon of the General (Hu Qian Jing)

When asked, "If the enemy troops are superior in
number and about to advance in an orderly formation,
how shall I cope with them?" I reply, "Seize something
they treasure and they will become maneuverable."

Art of War (Sun Zi Bing Fa), Chapter Eleven

Li Su Captures Caizhou by a Surprise Night Attack

The An Lushan rebellion gravely damaged the prestige of the Tang empire. To fight the rebels, the government had to mobilize the military governors, who grew
inordinately powerful in the process. Many of them took
complete control over the area under their command and
thereafter defied the authority of the imperial government.

Among those small, semi-independent realms, Huaixi

Defense Command, comprising three prefectures, stood out as a major problem for the Tang emperor. For more than thirty years it had been ruled by successive warlords in all but open confrontation with the Tang court.

Wu Shaoyang, the military commissioner of Huaixi, had inherited his position from his brother Wu Shaocheng and shared in the ambition to rule independently from the central government. Without the emperor's consent, he organized a band of his personal army to strengthen the military defense of Huaixi. He even encouraged his men to raid adjacent regions and rob traveling merchants. The emperor was fully aware of Wu Shaoyang's disloyalty but refrained from denouncing him openly.

Wu Shaoyang died in 814. His son, Wu Yuanji, knew that the emperor would not allow him to succeed to his father's place. Therefore, he did not report his father's death to the court immediately but instead made haste to seize control of the command of Huaixi in secret.

The emperor was enraged on hearing of Wu Yuanji's behavior. He ordered the troops surrounding Huaixi to be mobilized against the further expansion of Wu Yuanji. In the next three years, the Tang army launched many campaigns against Huaixi. News of victory kept pouring into the court, but the emperor felt doubtful, as there seemed to be little genuine progress. Then there was a defeat too severe to conceal, and it became known that the past victories were mostly exaggerated.

In 816 a military governor named Yuan Zi was appointed to the task of subjugating Wu Yuanji. Cautious to the point of cowardice, Yuan Zi was mainly concerned with his own safety and forbade his men to venture into the territory controlled by the rebels. When Wu Yuanji arrived to launch an offensive, Yuan Zi submitted an obsequious letter begging Wu to withdraw. Consequently, Yuan Zi was soon demoted and replaced by Li Su.

Li Su, whose polite name was Yuanzhi, was the son of the famous Tang general Li Mao. When the Tang army suffered a grave defeat at the hands of Wu Yuanji, Li Su presented a memorial to the emperor to recommend himself for the task of pacifying Huaixi. Pei Du, the Councilor-in-Chief, also spoke in his favor. Thereupon the emperor appointed him as military commissioner of the three prefectures of Sui, Tang, and Deng. At that time the governors of two other localities, Li Shidao and Wang Chengzong, also ruled semi-independently from the imperial government. Like Wu Yuanji, they had their personal armies and frequently looted in the neighboring areas. The emperor realized that he could not afford to fight three governors at the same time and therefore ordered Li Su to concentrate his forces to destroy Wu Yuanji first. Wu was then staying in the city of Caizhou, which was protected by many surrounding fortresses.

When Li Su arrived in Tangzhou in the first month of the twelfth year of the Yuanhe reign (817) to take up his post, the Tang troops had not yet recovered from the previous year's defeat. The soldiers were all afraid to take the field. They feared that Li Su, newly arrived and eager to prove his merit, might lead them to attack the rebels immediately. At this Li Su announced, "Knowing me to be soft and timid and capable of bearing humiliation, the emperor has sent me to look after you. As for wars and attacks, these are not my business." On hearing this, the soldiers were relieved.

Li Su showed great consideration to his men and often went personally to comfort the sick and wounded. And he made no attempt to enforce stringent military rules among the troops. When someone criticized him for this, Li Su explained, "Indeed, I know the significance of military discipline! But my predecessor tried to appease the rebels with favor, and the rebels looked down upon him. Upon my arrival the rebels become wary and undertake to strengthen their defenses, for they expect me to reorganize and outfit the troops against them. Now that I feign timidity and tolerance, they will soon despise me and lose their vigilance. Then I will have the chance to gain victory."

After a few days, the Tang troops began gradually to recover from their fear and frustration and, handsomely treated, were ready to follow Li Su's command. He then had them daily trained to prepare for combat. In the meantime he had various war machines brought to his camp and collected horses and provisions.

In the second month, Li Su presented a petition asking for reinforcements. The emperor had two thousand soldiers from other prefectures transferred to Li's command. Thus Li Su began to carry out his plan to capture Caizhou. First he set out to seize control of the strongholds that served to shield the city. He conducted a series of successful campaigns and made a point of treating the prisoners with kindness and trust. In this way he was able to learn much about the typographical features and military deployment around Caizhou.

One day, a rebel officer named Ding Shiliang was captured. Li Su consented when his officers asked to have Ding killed by gouging out his heart. But when the man was brought to his presence, Li Su took a liking to him, finding him bold and honest, and freed him on the spot. Ding Shiliang was greatly moved and said, "I am not a native of Huaixi but come from Anzhou. When I was captured in a battle against Wu's army, I thought I was going to die. But they set me free and offered me a post. That's how I came to serve the Wu family. Yesterday I used up my strength and was captured, and again I prepared myself to face death. Now that you have released me, I will not spare my life to repay your favor."

Then he told Li Su that Wengcheng, a hundred and twenty *li* to the southwest of Caizhou, was a major stronghold upon which Wu Yuanji relied. Its commander, Wu Xiulin, with the help of a resourceful advisor named Chen Guangqia, had been successful in warding off the Tang army. But Chen liked to lead small groups of men to fight and therefore could easily be lured into an ambush and captured alive. So Li Su put Ding Shiliang to the task. A few days later, Chen Guangqia was brought to Li Su's presence.

Having lost his advisor, Wu Xiulin grew discouraged. In the third month he surrendered the stronghold of Wencheng with three thousand soldiers. Greatly encouraged by this victory, the Tang soldiers were eager to give battle. A few days later, the army under the Tang general Li Guangyan routed thirty thousand rebel troops near Yancheng to the north of Caizhou. Early in the following month, the city of Yancheng yielded.

At the loss of Yancheng, Wu Yuanji felt very much afraid. He sent his ablest officers and large numbers of troops stationed at Caizhou to the city of Huiqu to strengthen his defense line in the north. In the meantime Li Su sent his men to seize several strongholds to the west of Caizhou. He treated Wu Xiulin handsomely and consulted him on the plan to attack Caizhou. Wu replied, "If you want to capture Caizhou, you must get Li You. I myself can be of little help."

Li You was a cavalry officer stationed at a fortress near Zhangcai Village on the outskirts of Caizhou. Brave and ingenious, he was proud of his ability and scornful of the Tang army. One day in the fifth month he led a few men to harvest wheat at Zhangcai Village. Li Su sent three hundred cavalrymen to lie in ambush in the woods by the field. Then several Tang soldiers rushed out, waving flags, and made to the piles of collected wheat as if they were going to set fire to them. Li You, leading several men to pursue the Tang soldiers, fell into the ambush and was caught alive. Being a good fighter, Li You had killed many people of the Tang army, so Li Su's officers and men hated him intensely and asked to have him beheaded. But Li Su set him free and treated him as an honored guest.

With great secrecy Li Su began to work out the plan of a surprise attack on Caizhou. He discussed the matter only with Li You and another rebel officer who used to serve under Chen Xiulin at Wencheng. The Tang officers all thought Li You unreliable and expressed their doubts to Li Su, who responded by placing more trust in Li You. This caused anxiety and indignation among the troops and a rumor was started that Li You was a secret agent dispatched by Wu Yuanji.

Li Su knew that, if the rumor reached the court before he presented his report, the emperor might accept the rumor and dismiss his argument. Therefore he immediately had Li You bound up and escorted to the capital. In the meantime he sent a secret memorial to the emperor to explain the case, adding, "If Li You were to be killed, we would be unable to win the battle." The emperor issued an edict ordering the release of Li You, who then returned to Wencheng. Overjoyed, Li Su said to him, "It is good luck for our nation that you are out of danger!"

Late in the fifth month Li Su sent an army to attack the stronghold of Langshan. The campaign failed because the rebels received timely reinforcements. The officers and men felt frustrated and angry, but Li Su laughed and said, "This is part of my plan!" He then picked out three thousand brave soldiers to set up a dare-to-die squad, training them in person. However, heavy rainfall blocked the roads and the plan to attack Caizhou had to be put off.

In the ninth month Li Su marched east to attack the stronghold of Wufang. He captured the outer city and killed over a thousand rebels. The rest withdrew to the inner city, where they put up a stubborn resistance, refusing to come out and fight. Thereupon Li Su feigned retreat. When the rebels sent out a band of cavalry to pursue him, he fought back and routed them. Some officers urged Li Su to take the chance to capture the inner city, but he smiled and said, "That would go against my plan."

Li You then urged Li Su to attack Caizhou, saying, "Wu Yuanji has stationed his best forces at Huiqu and entrusted the defense of Caizhou to some weak and decrepit soldiers. If we advance directly on Caizhou in a surprise attack, we have a good chance to capture Wu Yuanji before his men from the surrounding areas come to his rescue." To this Li Su agreed.

On the fifteenth day of the tenth month, Li Su led nine thousand picked troops out of Wencheng. Li You, in command of three thousand dare-to-die soldiers, was in the vanguard. When asked where to go, Li Su ordered, "To the east!"

They marched for sixty *li*, arriving at Zhangcai Village in the evening. Taking the enemy off guard, they easily finished off all the rebel troops stationed there, including the men in charge of beacon fires. Thus the people in Caizhou could not be informed of the fall of Zhangcai Village. Li Su ordered the troops to eat some food and take a short rest. He also left five hundred men to destroy the bridges connecting Huiqu and other strongholds to Caizhou. Then, in the dead of night, he issued the order to set out again.

The officers, who had been kept ignorant of the battle plan, asked where they were heading. Li Su replied curtly, "Enter Caizhou to catch Wu Yuanji!" The officers all turned pale with fright and the army supervisor wailed tearfully, "We've fallen into Li You's trap!" They all believed that they were going to die, but none dared disobey Li Su's orders.

A heavy snowstorm arose. Many flags were torn apart, and now and then the men saw the frozen corpses of people and horses along the road. At midnight the snow became even more relentless. They marched for seventy *li* until they reached the city of Caizhou. Outside the city there was a pond of ducks and geese, which had the habit of raising a clamor of squawks now and then at night. Li Su sent some soldiers to stir up the ducks and geese, making them squawk loudly, to conceal the sound of the marching troops.

Ever since Wu Shaocheng had turned a deaf ear to the Tang emperor more than thirty years before, Caizhou had not seen a single government soldier. As a result, the residents had long lost their vigilance. In early morning on the sixteenth day, Li Su arrived at the city gate of Caizhou to the total ignorance of the rebels. Li You led some brave soldiers to break holes on the city wall and climb into the city. The gatekeepers were caught in their sleep and finished off without a sound. The gate was opened and the troops proceeded into the outer city. They entered the inner city in exactly the same way.

At cockcrow the snow stopped. Wu Yuanji was lying in bed when the Tang troops attacked his fortified residence. "The emperor's army is come!" reported a guard.

"It must be some criminals who are making trouble!" laughed Wu. "I'll have all of them decapitated in the morning."

"The enemy has occupied the city!" reported someone else.

"It must be my men at Huiqu who have come to ask for winter clothes!" Wu Yuanji said. But when he got up and went to the window, he was stunned to hear a resounding battle-cry raised by nearly ten thousand men. He sent for his subordinate officers and went out to organize the troops for resistance. Soon after, the Tang soldiers destroyed the outer gate and seized a storehouse of weapons. The attack continued the next day. Li Su ordered his men to set fire to the south gate, and many local people assisted by carrying firewood. Arrows fell like rain on the gate, making it as prickly as a hedgehog. Eventually the gate was destroyed, and Wu Yuanji surrendered. Li Su had him put into a prison van and escorted to the capital Chang'an.

When the battle was over, the officers asked Li Su, "When we met defeat at Langshan, you did not worry. When we won at Wufang, you did not want to capture it. When the snowstorm arose, you ordered the troops to march on. And you were not afraid to lead an isolated force deep into the enemy territory. Even now, though we have gained a great victory, we still cannot understand how it worked."

Li Su replied, "Our failure at Langshan made the rebels underestimate our strength and lose their vigilance. If we had captured Wufang, the rebels there would have retreated to Caizhou and reinforced its defense. The violent snowstorm made it impossible to light beacon fires, so that we could march all the way to Caizhou unannounced. As you know, we were launching a surprise attack and had to conclude it before the rebels from the surrounding areas came to rescue Caizhou. Our soldiers fought bravely and took the city in a mere day. That was because we were an isolated army in constant danger of being besieged ourselves. Under such conditions, each man had to fight for his own life. When we have a great cause in mind, we should not be troubled with petty things. If we are proud of a petty gain and worried over a petty loss, how can we ever concentrate our minds to achieve a great victory!"

In the eleventh month Wu Yuanji was taken to the imperial ancestral altar in Chang'an and beheaded there.

Adapted from *History as a Mirror*
(Zi Zhi Tong Jian), Tomes Two Hundred
and Thirty-Nine and Two Hundred and Forty

Strategy Nineteen

Remove Firewood from Under the Caldron

第十九计 釜底抽薪　　不敌其力，而消其势，兑下乾上之象。

Translation

Avoid a contest of strength with the enemy but seek to weaken its position in accordance with the image of *Dui* underneath *Qian*.*

* *Lü* (Conduct), the tenth hexagram in *I Ching*, consists of *Dui* (lake, the yielding) under *Qian* (heaven, the strong). The yang line in the fifth place, a strong element in a position of power, is here compared to a tiger. As the lower trigram, *Dui*, is yielding and joyous in nature, it meets with success rather than danger by treading upon the tiger. Therefore the hexagram signifies good fortune, with its judgement observing, "One steps on the tail of a tiger. It does not bite one. Success." The yin line in the third place represents a person who overexerts himself. Its symbol states, "An one-eyed man can see, but not clearly. A lame man can travel, but is no good company. He faces the danger of being biten because he occupies an improper position." On the other hand, the yang line in the fourth place brings good fortune, for it takes up a humble position even though it has inner strength. Its judgement observes, "One steps on the tail of a tiger. He is cautious and fearful. Good fortune in the end." Therefore, standing up against the strong, the weak will meet danger if it overreaches itself but will attain good fortune if it acts with fear and circumspection.

Purport

The man must be completely foolish who attempts to cool water in a caldron on the stove by scooping it up and pouring it back repeatedly. A military leader who confronts a superior enemy head-on commits the same kind of blunder at a much greater cost. Thus the strategy instructs him not to seek engagement with the enemy until he has successfully reduced its combat strength, mainly by undermining the morale of its forces.

Quotations for Reference

When we confront the enemy in siege warfare the result of which is still uncertain, the side that has food will win. We must carefully protect our line of food transport to prevent the enemy's intrusion. We should send crack troops to block the enemy's path for provision transport. Running out of food, the enemy troops will retreat, so we can strike and defeat them. The principle goes, "The army that lacks food will perish."

A Hundred Marvelous Battle Plans, "Battle of Food" (Bai Zhan Qi Fa, "Liang Zhan")

One who is good at fighting battles concludes them before the army is dispatched; one who is good at eliminating perils deal with them before they burgeon; one who is good at defeating the enemy gains victory unnoticeably. The best war strategy is to win without war. Therefore, one who vies for victory by naked swords is not a good general, and one who makes preparations after defeat is not a person of wisdom.

Six Strategies (Liu Tao), Chapter Twenty-Six

Attack not only can be directed at the enemy's city or battle formation but also includes ways to subdue its heart. Defense means more than protecting one's city wall or maintaining one's battle formation but also includes ways to keep up one's spirits to wait for opportunity.

Li Jing's Reply to Emperor Taizong of Tang, (Tang Tai Zong Li Jing Wen Dui), Tome Three

In directing warfare and assessing the enemy, one should try to undermine the enemy's morale and destroy its discipline, so that it looks intact but loses its utility. This is the method to win by political strategy.

Book of Master Wei Liao (Wei Liao Zi), Chapter Four

The Small State of Lu Defeats the Powerful Qi

In spring of the tenth year of Duke Zhuang of Lu (684 B.C.), the Qi army invaded Lu.

Duke Zhuang wanted to lead an army in person to meet the enemy and consulted Shi Bo, one of his ministers. "I recommend a man who can help you win the battle," Shi Bo said.

"Who is this?" asked the duke.

"He is named Cao Gui and lives in a village. Though he has never held any office, he has the talents that become a minister or general."

Thereupon the duke sent Shi Bo to call on Cao Gui. A fellow villager said to Cao Gui, "Warfare is the business of the meat eaters. Why should you meddle with it?"

"The meat eaters are constipated and incapable of making farsighted plans," replied Cao Gui. "That is why I have to help them." And so he received Shi Bo in his house. Shi Bo told him that the duke need his help in the coming battle with Qi. Cao Gui smiled and said teasingly, "So the meat eaters have run out of their plans and a vegetable eater has to come to the rescue?"

"Well," Shi Bo replied, "If the vegetable eater comes up with a good plan, he will soon have meat to eat."

When Cao Gui was ushered into the palace, the duke treated him with great respect and could not wait to ask how to fight the battle against Qi. But Cao Gui gave an unexpected reply. "Before I talk about how to fight the battle," he observed, "I beg Your Lordship to answer a question. What makes you believe you can fight the battle at all?"

The duke was surprised. He hesitated for a minute before replying, "I dare not enjoy good food and fine clothes alone but always share them with my subjects."

Cao Gui did not look impressed. "These are but petty favors," he remarked. "Besides, only the few people around you enjoy them. The common people are in no wise indebted to you and may not answer your call to arms."

"Well ...," the duke again paused. "When I offer sacrifices to the gods, I always see to it that the oxen, goats, jade ware, and silk are in appropriate order. When making prayers, I use words that are true to the facts. Therefore the gods will bless my nation."

"That may not be," announced Cao Gui. "I have heard that the gods judge a man by his deeds rather than his words. They are not to be coddled by handsome sacrifices. Therefore you should not count on the gods' blessing when estimating your strength."

"I am careful in dealing with legal cases, big or small," said the duke. "Though I cannot investigate every one of them thoroughly, I try my best to handle them in accordance with reason."

At this Cao Gui nodded approvingly and said, "This is a very worthy deed. Since you have worked for their benefit, the people must be grateful to you. This will enable you to gain victory over Qi."

Duke Zhuang's face brightened on hearing this. He said eagerly, "Now you may tell me how to handle the battle."

"In warfare, one has to know the actual situation before he can make decisions with certainty. Therefore I beg to accompany you in the expedition. I will then offer my suggestions on the field."

The duke agreed. He let Cao Gui ride in the same chariot with him, leading the Lu army to Changshao to meet the Qi troops.

The two sides confronted each other in battle formations. Because of past victories, the Qi general held the men of Lu in contempt. As soon as the two armies had arrayed themselves, he ordered drums to be beaten, and the Qi soldiers marched forward to attack. Cao Gui calmly watched the approaching enemy troops but said nothing. Duke Zhuang of Lu, fretting impatiently, roared out his order, "Let the drums be beaten! We will advance to meet the enemy!"

But Cao Gui stopped him and said, "Tell the troops not to move. Tell everyone to stick to his position and make no noise. Cut down anyone who dare disobey." There was such authority in his voice that the duke followed his advice without hesitation. Then the duke looked at Cao Gui inquisitively. To this Cao Gui explained, "The Qi forces outnumber us and are in high morale at this moment. I can see no advantage in engaging them in a tangled fight. It would be better for us to stay still."

The men of Qi charged forth vigorously. The Lu soldiers did not advance to meet them but retained their defensive formation. They fought only to defend their position, without moving a single step or uttering a single battle cry. Failing to penetrate into the formation, the Qi soldiers fell back. The Qi general rearranged his troops and ordered them to charge forth at the second beating of drums. Again, the Lu army retained its formation and did not venture out to give battle.

The Qi general did not take caution after two assaults had failed. Instead, he announced with great confidence, "The men of Lu are afraid to fight. Another beating of drums will send them into flight."

When the Qi soldiers came forth to attack for the third time, Cao Gui told Duke Zhuang, "Let's beat the drums! It's time to rout the enemy!" At the beating of drums, the men of Lu rushed on the enemy with great intrepidity. The Qi soldiers were caught off guard at this sudden retaliation and turned to flee. At this, Duke Zhuang wanted to lead the troops in pursuit, but Cao Gui told him to wait. Cao Gui climbed up on the front bar of the chariot and watched the retreating Qi forces carefully. Then he got down and said, "We can chase them." Thereupon the Lu army pursued the enemy for over two dozen *li*, capturing numerous weapons, chariots, and provisions.

Duke Zhuang returned to the capital with his victorious army. He did not quite understand how the victo-

175

ry had been achieved and asked Cao Gui, "The enemy beat drums for three times, but they lost. We beat the drums only once, but we won. Can you explain why it was so?"

To this Cao Gui replied, "The outcome of a battle is determined not only by strength but mainly by the courage of the contestants. A commander whose men are courageous will gain victory, and the one whose men have lost courage will lose the battle. When two armies confront each other in the field, the beating of drums is not merely a signal for attack; it can serve to boost the morale of the soldiers. The soldiers have come to the field fully prepared to give battle. When the drums are beaten for the first time, they go out to fight with all their strength. If they fail in the first assault and have to listen to the drums beaten for the second time, they will feel frustrated, and their morale will be impaired. When the drums are beaten for the third time, they cannot but lose their esprit. We won the battle of Changshao just because we engaged the men of Qi when their morale was at the lowest while that of our soldiers was at its best."

"When the men of Qi retreated, you climbed up the chariot and watched for a while before sending the troops in pursuit. What did you see that caused you to make the decision?"

"The men of Qi are deceitful," replied Cao Gui. "I thought that they might be feigning defeat in order to lure us into an ambush. But when I ascended the frontal bar, I saw crisscross chariot tracks and drooping banners. That convinced me that the Qi army was in headlong flight."

After hearing Cao Gui's replies, Duke Zhuang exclaimed in admiration, "You are a real master of the art of war!" He appointed Cao Gui as a minister and bestowed handsome rewards on Shi Bo for recommending Cao Gui.

Adapted from *Zuo's Spring and Autumn Annals* (Zuo Zhuan), Tome Three

Strategy Twenty
Muddle the Water to Seize Fish

第二十计 混水摸鱼　　乘其阴乱，利其弱而无主。随，以向晦入宴息。

Translation

Take advantage of the enemy's internecine fight and make use of its weakness and lack of judgement. *Sui*: At nightfall, return home to rest.*

Purport

A regular element in offensive operations, surprise can be effected by the deception of the enemy as well as the mobility of one's own troops. A cautious commander understands that, in general, deception can be employed but not relied on. Namely, he can hope to gain advantage

---

*Sui (Following), the seventeenth hexagram in *I Ching*, has the symbol of *Zhen* (thunder, movement, eldest son) under *Dui* (lake, joy, youngest daughter). Its comment observes, "Thunder under the lake symbolizes *Sui*. At nightfall, the superior man returns home to rest." A movement that is joyous will attract many followers. *Dui*, the upper trigram, represents the moment of sunset during the day or the autumn season of the year. As thunder grows weaker in autumn, so a person should retire to rest in the evening. One who wants to be followed must first be a follower himself; only then will he able to gain from others the necessary trust for them to follow him. Here in this strategy, one is advised to conceal the identity of his troops until the moment of attack.

if the deception works but must be prepared for its failure. However, he may be willing to take a greater risk if the enemy forces become disorderly due to internal strife; at this, he can plan a surprise attack that depends entirely on deception. In a typical employment of this strategy, one dresses his forces in the enemy's uniforms, penetrates into its territory and attacks its vulnerable point.

Quotation for Reference

One who is good at combatting the enemy fools it with inscrutable moves, confuses it with false intelligence, makes it relax by concealing one's strength, causes it to hesitate by exposing one's weakness, deafens its ears by jumbling one's orders and signals, blinds its eyes by converting one's banners and insignias, eases off its vigilance by hiding what it fears, saps its will by offering what it likes, confounds its battle plan by providing distorted facts, and breaks its courage by showing off one's power.

A Scholar's Dilettante Remarks on War
(Tou Bi Fu Tan), Chapter Eight

Cao Cao Beats Yuan Shao at Guandu

In the late Eastern Han Dynasty the empire was divided among several warlords, who fought intermittent wars to contend for supremacy. The ruin of the imperial house was prompted by peasant uprisings and internecine struggles within the court. Unlike the First Emperor of Qin, whose death sparked off revolts all over the country, the ruling emperor of Han was not universally denounced as a despot and had not lost his legitimacy. Therefore he

179

remained the nominal ruler of the empire, and the warlord who had the emperor under his protection could hope to greatly enhance his prestige among the people.

Cao Cao was the warlord fortunate to have the emperor under his control. Though in name he was only the councilor-in-chief, he drafted most of the imperial edicts himself and then gave them to the emperor to sign. Naturally, the other warlords became jealous and indignant. Among Cao Cao's rivals, Yuan Shao was the most powerful. Coming from a very influential family, he controlled the four regions of Ji, Qing, Bin, and You (covering modern Hebei, Henan, Shanxi, northern Shaanxi, and Shandong provinces) through a number of outstanding advisors and generals and several hundred thousand well-trained troops. He wrote a memorial asking the emperor to move to his place, but Cao Cao flatly refused on behalf of the emperor. This incident brought to the surface the conflict between the two rivals.

In the fifth year of the Jian'an reign (A.D. 200), Yuan Shao embarked on an expedition against Cao Cao, advancing on the city of Xuchang, Cao Cao's power base and seat of the Han imperial court. Tian Feng, Mounted Escort of Ji Region, tried to dissuade Yuan Shao, observing, "Though Cao Cao has few troops, he is skilled in military strategy and can always come up with a lot of tricks by which to conduct his inferior army to his advantage. You are endowed with the people and resources of four regions, so you should first build up your strength by enlisting talented people into your service and promoting agriculture to provide ample provisions for the troops. Then you can dispatch a force to attack Cao Cao by using extraordinary methods, feigning maneuvers on the left and advancing toward the right. In this way you will be able to destroy Cao Cao within three years without venturing out in person. But now you launch this campaign in the hope of gaining victory by a fluke. The result would be unthinkable if you fail!"

This advice did not sound pleasant to Yuan Shao's ear, and he refused to make use of it. When Tian Feng, undaunted, came to repeat his warning again and again, Yuan Shao became enraged and had Tian thrown into prison. Then he issued a proclamation enumerating Cao Cao's crimes. In the second month he led troops and arrived at Liyang (modern Jun County in Henan Province).

His first encounters with Cao Cao resulted in a series of ignominious defeats in which he lost two of his most prestigious generals. This was mainly due to his refusal to adopt the sound advice of his advisors and officers. However, Yuan Shao failed to learn his lesson and, relying on the numerical superiority of his troops, was still determined to crush Cao Cao by sheer force. After a short period of rest and rehabilitation, he marched with a hundred thousand troops to the town of Yangwu (modern Yuanyang in Henan Province) north of the Yellow River and prepared to attack Cao Cao, who had made camp at Guandu (modern Zhongmou County in Henan Province) on the southern bank.

Yuan Shao was eager to advance and give battle, but his advisor Ju Shou tried to dissuade him, saying, "Our troops are superior in number but cannot compare with the enemy in valor. On the other hand, Cao Cao has doughty soldiers but inadequate provisions. Therefore it is expedient for Cao Cao to fight a quick battle and for us to wait and bide our time. If we can maintain our position for months until Cao Cao runs out of food and provisions, we will be able to beat him without much fighting."

"So you've joined the others in demoralizing my troops!" Yuan Shao exclaimed, his face flushed with anger. With this he had the poor advisor thrown into prison. "To teach you a lesson, I will not punish you until I have routed Cao Cao!" Thereupon he crossed the river and made camp right in front of Cao Cao's army.

Having only about thirty thousand soldiers, Cao Cao was bent on a quick battle. He ventured out to fight but, failing to gain any advantage, was compelled to retire behind his ramparts. Yuan Shao tried several tactics to seize Guandu, but Cao Cao could always devise an effective counteraction. Cao Cao held out successfully for over two months, but then his food and provisions began to give out. He considered abandoning Guandu and pulling back to his capital, Xuchang. Unable to reach a decision, he wrote a letter to a trusted advisor Xun Yu in Xuchang, asking for advice. Xun Yu wrote in reply:

"Formerly, Emperor Gaozu and Xiang Yu were stalemated in the area around Xingyang and Chenggao for years, yet neither of them would weaken his position by withdrawing first. Now for half a year you have confronted Yuan Shao, whose troops outnumber yours ten to one, not allowing him to advance a single step. This kind of situation will not last long, so you should employ extraordinary plans to bring about a favourable turn."

Cao Cao was greatly pleased with this reply and immediately sent a few scouts to spy out Yuan Shao's army. They returned with the report that a contingent of supply wagons was coming to Yuan Shao's camp and that General Han Meng, who was put in charge of the contingent, happened to be a man of reckless courage. Hence Cao Cao ordered one of his best generals, Xu Huang, to intercept and burn up all the supply wagons.

On hearing the report from Han Meng, who had managed to flee and return alone, Yuan Shao flew into a rage and wanted to have Han beheaded. Upon the supplication of many of his generals, he finally agreed to spare Han's life. He then dispatched a general named Chunyu Qiong with twenty thousand troops to reinforce the defense at Wucao, his provisions base. General Chunyu was tough and severe and therefore dreaded by his men. Even worse, he had a weakness for liquor.

A few days later, Cao Cao's provisions gave out. An envoy sent to Xuchang to ask for help was caught by Yuan Shao's men and brought to Xu You, one of Yuan Shao's military advisors who had been a childhood friend of Cao Cao. Xu You immediately went to see Yuan Shao and persuaded him to assail Xuchang, saying, "Cao Cao has concentrated his main force here at Guandu, therefore the defense at Xuchang must be relatively weak. It would be better to send troops in a surprise night attack on Xuchang than to stay here at Guandu without taking any action."

Yuan Shao replied he had to give the matter some more thought, for he suspected that the captured envoy might be a spy sent deliberately by Cao Cao. At this juncture a messenger arrived with the news that some of Xu You's relatives had been thrown into prison because of misconduct. At this, Yuan Shao burst into fury, accusing Xu You of conspiracy with Cao Cao and warning him to take care of his head. Filled with shame and indignation, Xu You decided to leave Yuan Shao and seek refuge with Cao Cao, his childhood friend.

Cao Cao was resting in bed when the guards reported

that Xu You had come secretly to see him. Cao Cao jumped out of bed and, with no time to put on shoes, rushed out barefoot to meet Xu. When he accompanied Xu You into his room, he bowed deeply, treating Xu You as his superior. This courtesy on the part of the Councilor-in-Chief toward a cloth-gown friend did not fail to move Xu You. Xu was then very willing to help Cao Cao at the expense of his former master, Yuan Shao.

"Please teach me how to beat Yuan Shao," Cao Cao asked.

"But I've already advised Yuan Shao to attack Xu-chang."

"Indeed!" Cao Cao gasped. "If he adopts your plan, I would get into serious trouble."

"How much provisions do you have?"

"They will last a year."

"That sounds improbable."

"Well, actually, they will last only half a year."

Xu You got up and made for the door. "I come to you with sincerity and you treat me with deceit!"

"Don't get angry," Cao Cao said. "To tell you the truth, they will only last for three months."

Xu You laughed. "I've heard people call you a 'wily hero,' and I see the name befits you well."

Cao Cao also laughed. "War is a game of deception, isn't it?" Then he lowered his voice. "They will hold out for only this month!"

"Don't you try to fool me!" Xu You exclaimed. "You have already run out of food!"

"How do you know?" Cao Cao asked in astonishment.

Xu You told him about the captured envoy.

"What is the strategy that you are going to teach me?" asked Cao Cao, taking Xu You by both hands to show his sincerity.

"You lead a small army to fight an overpowering enemy but do not seek for a quick solution. This is a suicidal way to conduct war! I will offer you a plan that can throw Yuan Shao's men into disorder within three days."

"Tell me about it!"

"Yuan Shao has most of his provisions stored at Wucao, and General Chunyu is the commander there. But Chunyu Qiong drinks too much to maintain proper vigilance. You can dispatch a band of troops disguised as Yuan Shao's men. They will claim to be led by an officer named Jiang Qi to reinforce the army at Wucao. Chunyu Qiong will be taken off guard, and your men will have a good chance of burning Wucao to the ground. How can Yuan Shao's troops help panicking when they hear of the destruction of their base of provisions?"

Greatly delighted, Cao Cao immediately set about putting the plan into practice. He left his brother Cao Hong and a trusted advisor, Xun You, to guard the camp at Guandu. Then he took charge of five thousand men that were dressed as Yuan Shao's soldiers, leading them to Wucao in the dead of night. On the way, because of their disguises, they passed several major enemy posts with little difficulty. Arriving at Wucao, they quickly scattered and set fire all over the place. General Chunyu Qiong was lying in bed after an evening of carousing with his officers when he heard the commotion outside. He jumped out of bed and tried to summon his men to cope with the surprise attack.

On hearing that Wucao was on fire, Yuan Shao declared, "Cao Cao's men are engaged at Wucao, so we can take the opportunity to storm his camp at Guandu, leav-

185

ing him with no place to return to." With this he commanded two generals, Gao Lan and Zhang He, to attack Cao Cao's camp.

"But we must rescue Wucao first!" Zhang He said. "Cao Cao has devoted his best troops to the attack on Wucao and General Chunyu cannot hold out for long. If Wucao is lost, we will be definitely done for." However, another advisor named Guo Tu voted for attacking Cao Cao's camp. So Yuan Shao dispatched his main force to assail Guandu and only a few light-equipped cavalrymen to rescue Wucao.

As it turned out, Cao Cao's fortified camp at Guandu was well-prepared, and the Yuan army failed to gain any advantage. Afraid that he might be blamed for his wrong advice, Guo Tu intimated to Yuan Shao that Zhang He had not fought hard enough because he was secretly in sympathy with Cao Cao. Frustrated by Yuan Shao's refusal to adopt his advice and enraged by Guo Tu's false charge, Zhang He burned up his weapons and went with Gao Lan to surrender to Cao Cao's army.

In the meantime Cao Cao was engaged in a close battle at Wucao when he was informed that Yuan Shao's cavalry was coming. A general asked Cao Cao to send part of the troops to guard against the upcoming cavalry, but Cao Cao dismissed him impatiently. "Do not trouble me until the enemy has arrived right at my back!" he shouted. Realizing the urgency of the situation, his soldiers fought with all their might, and therefore it did not take them long to rout Yuan Shao's army and kill its general, Chunyu Qiong. Then Cao Cao turned back and routed the cavalry sent by Yuan Shao to rescue Wucao.

Yuan Shao had by then lost his provisions base as

well as some of his best generals. The troops were despondent and scared. Then they were alarmed by a rumor, spread by Cao Cao's secret agents, that Cao Cao had sent troops to seize two cities at Yuan Shao's rear and block his path of retreat. At this moment Cao Cao launched his major offensive on the panicking enemy and inflicted a grave defeat, annihilating about eighty thousand enemy soldiers. Yuan Shao himself escaped across the river with only a few hundred mounted guards.

Among the numerous trophies, a well-adorned chest caught Cao Cao's eye. On opening it, he found stacks of letters from his subordinates, both those who remained in the capital Xuchang and those on the expedition, pledging allegiance to Yuan Shao. He immediately ordered the letters to be burned, observing, "Yuan Shao was so strong and I so weak that I could hardly protect myself. How can I blame the others?"

Yuan Shao retreated north into Ji Region, arriving at Liyang. There he was able to collect some of his scattered troops. Tian Feng, who had insistently opposed the expedition, was informed of Yuan Shao's defeat by the prison guard. "Now you will receive handsome rewards and a high position!" said the guard in congratulation.

"Now I have no hope to live!" Tian Feng replied calmly. "Our master is generous in appearance but jealous in disposition. He does not understand my loyalty but only remembers how I have offended him with my warnings. If he were returning victoriously, he might have spared me out of sheer good humor. Now that he has suffered a decisive defeat, shame and jealousy will get the better of him. That means the end of my life." No sooner had Tian Feng finished his words than a messenger from Yuan Shao arrived to carry out his execution.

Adapted from *History as a Mirror*,
(Zi Zhi Tong Jian), Tome Sixty-Three

Strategy Twenty-One
The Cicada Sloughs Its Skin

第二十一计 金蝉脱壳　　存其形，完其势，友不疑，敌不动。巽而止，蛊。

Translation

Maintain the original shape and play out the original pose, so that the ally does not doubt and the enemy does not move. Submission and stillness lead to decay.*

Purport

From a distance, the newly sloughed skin of a cicada looks like the cicada itself. One who wants to catch the cicada may be distracted by the skin while the cicada flees. Thus the idiom points to a method of escape: Maintain the appearance of inaction while taking action in secret.

In warfare, to withdraw is no easier than to advance.

---

*This line is taken from the comment on *Gu* (Decay, Removing Decay), the eighteenth hexagram in *I Ching*. The hexagram consists of *Xun* (wind, submission) under *Gen* (mountain, stillness). The judgement observes, "Removing Decay. Great success. it is of benefit to cross a great river. Before the beginning, three days. After the beginning, three days." It is submission within and inaction without that have brought about decay. To remove decay and start anew, one must act with great caution. Do not plunge ahead rashly but allow some time for inner readjustment.

A retreating army is exposed to attack from its rear; the retreat may turn into a stampede if the superior enemy forces follow up to attack. Therefore one has to arrange a "surprise retreat" by pulling away all of a sudden and in the meantime maintaining the appearance of inaction. In a broader sense, the strategy instructs one to conjure up false appearances for the concealment of secret military maneuvers.

Quotation for Reference

When confronted with an enemy superior in number and strength, we should set up a great quantity of banners and standards and double our cooking stoves to flaunt our strenghth. Thus, the enemy will be unable to ascertain our actual number and strength and will think twice before seeking an engagement with us. Then we can withdraw quickly to get away from peril and preserve our forces. The principle goes, "Strength or weakness depends on dispositions."

A Hundred Marvelous Battle Plans, "Battle of Weakness" (Bai Zhan Qi Fa, "Ruo Zhan")

Wu Han Regains the Initiative by a Covert Maneuver

Wu Han, whose polite name was Ziyan, was born of a poor family in Wuan District of Nanyang Commandery (modern Nanyang in Henan Province) during the late Western Han Dynasty. He once served as a neighborhood head. In the reign of Wang Mang, the "usurper," he had to flee his hometown because of some legal offenses. After that, he made a living by working as a horse dealer. He traveled a lot and made quite a few friends. These were mostly persons of ability, ambition and resolve, bound to distiguish themselves in a tumultous age.

In A.D. 23 Liu Xuan, scion of a collateral branch of the old imperial family, declared himself emperor with Gengshi (New Beginning) as the title of his reign. Many pro-Han military leaders declared allegiance to him. At the time Liu Xiu, who was to become the first emperor of Eastern Han Dynasty, was also exploiting the popular sentiment for the restoration of Han to expand his personal power. However, he was wise enough not to assume the imperial title before the ripeness of time.

Wu Han offered his service to Liu Xiu instead of the Gengshi emperor. Though a person of wisdom and valor, he was artless and reticent in nature and did not know how to promote himself. After repeated commendations from his fellow officers, he finally got an interview with Liu Xiu, who highly appreciated him. After that, Wu Han soon distinguished himself in his military exploits and was promoted to be a supreme general. When Liu Xiu set out on a campaign to pacify the area of Hebei, Wu Han led the vanguard of five thousand cavalrymen, gaining many victories. In the sixth month of A.D. 25, Liu Xiu declared himself emperor and appointed Wu Han to be commander-in-chief.

In the twelfth month of the eleventh year of the Jianwu reign (A.D. 35), Wu Han led thirty thousand men and marched up the Yangtze River to attack Gongsun Shu, a recalcitrant warlord in Sichuan.

In the first month the following spring, Wu Han engaged Gongsun Shu's generals Wei Dang and Gongsun Yong in battle at Yupei Ford and routed them. He then proceeded to besiege the city of Wuyang. Gongsun Shu sent Shi Xing, his son-in-law, to relieve Wuyang. Wu Han routed Shi Xing and then pushed further north. Thereupon all the strongholds under Gongsun Yuan took defensive positions behind closed gates. At the emperor's order, Wu Han attacked and seized the strategic city of Guangdu to the south of Chengdu. He then dispatched light cavalry to burn the bridges in Chengdu. The officers under Gongsun Shu became very much afraid and many deserted him. The emperor wanted to entice Gongsun Shu to surrender and sent him a letter, saying, "If you turn yourself over in time, you shall be able to preserve your family. This handwritten imperial edict will not be issued twice." However, Gongsun Shu refused to yield.

The emperor then gave Wu Han an instruction concerning strategy, saying, "Chengdu has a force of over a hundred thousand and should not be taken lightly. Establish yourself firmly at Guangdu and wait for Gongsun Shu to come forward and attack you. If he dare not come out, you can push forward to threaten him. Do not give battle until he has become fully exhausted."

Wu Han led twenty thousand men on a march to Chengdu. He stopped about ten *li* from the city and made camp on the northern bank of the river. He had a pontoon bridge built over the river and sent a subordinate officer named Liu Shang with ten thousand men to make camp on the southern bank. When the emperor learned about this, he was startled and forthwith sent a message to berate Wu Han, saying, "I have cautioned you a hundred times, and you still muddle things up like this! You underestimate the enemy and penetrate too deeply into its territory. Moreover, you and Liu Shang camp separately, so that if anything inopportune happens, you will not be able to aid one another. If the enemy sends troops to tie you up while focusing its main force on Liu Shang, he will lose the battle, and this will bring about your defeat. If, out of good fortune, nothing has happened yet, you should return to Guangdu with all dispatch."

The emperor's letter had not reached Wu Han when Gongsun Shu sallied out on the offensive. His tactics, however, fell short of those predicted by the emperor. He dispatched Xie Feng and Yuan Ji with over a hundred thousand troops to surround Wu Han. At the same time he sent another ten thousand men to tie up Liu Shang and prevent him from coming to rescue Wu Han.

Wu Han fought strenuously for a whole day and, failing to gain the advantage, pulled back into his fortified camp. There he summoned his officers and gave them a speech. "We have fought our way through a thousand *li* and cut deep into the enemy's territory. Now we are separated from Liu Shang's men. This puts us in an adverse situation. We have to move secretly to the southern bank of the river and converge with Liu Shang's forces to fight the enemy together. If we can fight as one, we will be able to achieve a great victory. Otherwise we will meet a crushing defeat. The result of this maneuver will therefore decide our destiny."

The officers replied in unison, "We understand!"

For the next three days Wu Han kept the soldiers and horses well fed and ordered the troops to remain behind the ramparts. No one was permitted to go out to fight the enemy. He also had numerous flags set up all over their encampment and kept the stoves burning so that there was always cooking smoke drifting up from the camp.

On the third night Wu Han led troops to leave the camp by a narrow path and, crossing the river in the quiet darkness, joined forces with the men of Liu Shang.

The next morning Xie Feng saw that Wu Han's camp was still strewn with flags and shrouded in cooking smoke. He left his main force to surround Wu Han while he crossed the river to guide the smaller part of his army to attack Liu Shang. However, he met with the joint force of Wu Han and Liu Shang. The battle lasted from morning to twilight. Realizing the danger of their position, Wu Han's men fought to the best of their strength. Thus they brought about a hard-won victory, killing Xie Feng and Yuan Ji. Leaving Liu Shang to check Gongsun Shu, Wu Han pulled back to Guangdu. There he wrote a report to the emperor in which he criticized himself for his grave mistake.

The emperor, who appreciated Wu Han's timely maneuvers to get out of his predicament, responded with praise and encouragement. "It is very expedient for you to return to Guangdu," he wrote in the edict. "Surely Gongsun Shu dares not bypass Liu Shang to attack you. If he attacks Liu Shang first, you can then march the fifty *li* swiftly and rout him when he is busily engaged."

After that, Wu Han fought with Gongsun Shu between Chengdu and Guangdu, gaining eight victories in eight battles, and finally captured the city of Chengdu.

Adapted from *History as a Mirror* (Zi Zhi Tong Jian), Tomes Forty-Two and Forty-Three

Strategy Twenty-Two
Bolt the Door to Seize the Thief

第二十二计 关门捉贼　　小敌困之。剥，不利有攸往。

Translation

Force the small enemy into a quagmire. *Bo*: It is not favorable to set forth.* [It is disadvantageous to pursue a weak, tottering enemy for long distance.]

Purport

When you return home to discover that a thief has broken into your house, you may either step aside to let him go before calling for help, or bolt the door to block his way of escape and go on to seize him. With the former strategy you have little hope to catch the thief even if you can later enlist the help of many people. Therefore, if you think yourself capable of dealing with him single-

---

*This is the judgement of *Bo* (Disintegration), the twenty-third hexagram in *I Ching*. The hexagram has the symbol of a mountain (*Gen*) that stands alone on the earth (*Kun*), exposed to the errosive impacts of the elements. The shape of the hexagram, featuring five yin lines underneath the only yang line, also resembles a house whose foundation is being undermined. Therefore the overall condition of the hexagram is decay, disintegration, or splitting apart. It is unfavorable to undertake anything in such adverse conditions.

handedly, or if prompt help is at hand, you may adopt the latter plan to catch the thief on the spot.

To apply the strategy to warfare, it is paramount to ascertain beforehand whether the enemy is small or big. Of course, this refers to combat strength rather than the number of soldiers. The word *thief* or *bandit* designates a small body of troops that carries out sporadic, guerrilla-style operations. Because of its small size, it has unusual mobility and speed and can seize every chance to harass its opponent. The strategy points out that encirclement and annihilation is the best method to deal with such a guerrilla force. A typical application involves leaving the door open, luring the thief into the house and barring the door to catch him. For instance, on learning of the enemy's plan for a night attack on your camp, you can pull away the troops and leave the camp empty. When the enemy enters the camp, you can then lead the troops to close in from all sides and form a tight encirclement. Or you can use a bait army to lure the enemy into an ambush ring that allows no way of escape.

The Battle of Haoshui River

Compared with its predecessor, the powerful Tang, the Song Dynasty (960-1279) was generally known as a feeble regime because it never effectively fended off the military incursions from semi-nomadic peoples in the north. It suffered ignominious defeats first at the hands of the Qidan people of the Liao Dynasty and the Tangut of the Xia Dynasty, then the Nuzhen of the Jin Dynasty, and finally the Mongols, who conquered all of China. Such military incapacity resulted mainly from the Song emperors' distrust of military commanders. The emperor himself controlled the military forces of the empire and his generals had little power to act on their own. Furthermore, the positions of the officers were constantly shifted, so that they never knew their men very well. The practice was meant to prevent the commanders from nurturing their own power bases in the army, but it greatly reduced the army's combat strength. The infirmity of the Song was clearly manifested in the humiliation it suffered from the small kingdom of Xia to the northwest.

The Xia Dynasty was proclaimed in 1038 by Yuanhao, chieftain of the ruling Tuoba tribe of the Tangut people. The earliest official record of the Tuoba tribe comes from the late sixth century. At that time the tribal leader paid tribute to Tang and was honored with the family name of the Tang imperial house, Li. But the Tangut allegiance was only nominal and came to an end along with the decline and fall of the Tang empire.

Yuanhao's grandfather, Li Jiqian, was a warlike ruler who conducted vigorous, though smallish, campaigns against the Northern Song Dynasty with the sole purpose of plunder. He suffered a severe injury in his last battle and died soon afterwards. While on his deathbed, however, he told his son Li Deming to adopt a policy of reconciliation with the Song, for he had come to realize that the Tangut people were not in a position to rival the Song. Besides, the Liao Dynasty of the Qidan people to the north was rapidly gaining in strength and would not hesitate to attack Xia when there was a chance of gaining advantage.

Li Deming ruled for almost thirty years, a time of peaceful development for the Tangut people. In mutual antagonism, both the Song and the Liao sought the friendship of the Tangut, who benefited a great deal from their trade with the Song.

Yuanhao did not like his father's submission to the Song. He tried to talk Deming into strengthening the army and adopting a more active military policy. To this his father replied: "Our people have dressed in brocade and silk for thirty years. We have got all this from Song, and we must not be ungrateful!"

"To wear animal skin is the very nature of our tribal people," said Yuanhao in retort. "A hero should aspire to rule the world. What's the use of brocade and silk!"

Li Deming died in 1032. Before that, he had already accepted the title of King of Xia from both the Song and the Liao. In that same year Yuanhao succeeded to the throne. He at once undertook to pillage and plunder the border land to the west and southwest, which was inhabited by various nomadic tribes. A series of tentative incursions into Song territory were also conducted to seek out the weak points along the border.

In 1038 Yuanhao proclaimed himself emperor of the Xia Dynasty. The next ten years under his reign was marked by incessant clashes with the Song to the south and the Liao to the north. Mostly, Yuanhao was on the offensive. He launched the first major southward campaign in 1039. After a few initial victories, he lost the last battle and failed in his attempt to seize the land of Yan Region.

In the early spring of 1041, Yuanhao led a hundred thousand troops in person to march south again. It seemed an unlikely time for such a major operation, for a piercing north wind still carried the chill of winter, and the rivers had not yet melted. Therefore they were able to penetrate nearly two hundred *li* into Song territory, encountering little resistance, and arrived at the stronghold of Huaiyuan.

When news reached Han Qi, Assistant Pacification Commissioner of the Jingyuan Circuit, he hastened to the stronghold of Zhenrongjun to collect the few forces there. In the meantime he recruited some young, able-bodied peasants from local villages. Thus he managed to assemble a motley band of eighteen thousand men. He appointed Ren Fu, an officer from another circuit who had come to Jingyuan to attend a military conference, to be the commander. Several local officers were appointed to assist him. These included Geng Fu, as the adjutant; Shang Yi, as the vanguard leader; and Zhu Guan, Wu Ying, and Wang Gui.

Experienced in dealing with the men of Xia, Han Qi knew that they were fierce on the offensive but lacked the endurance to fight under adverse conditions. He therefore decided to delay engagement with the enemy until its strength and morale were worn out. He ordered Ren Fu to proceed toward Huaiyuan, turn west to the stronghold of Deshengjun and on to the south to station at Yangmulong. Around that area there were several well-equipped strongholds, about thirty to forty *li* from one another and interlinked with secure routes for the transport of supplies. Ren Fu was to camp there, at the enemy's rear, and refrain from giving battle until the situation changed for the better. In the meantime Han Qi would mobilize the frontier troops to withstand Yuanhao's attack. When Yuanhao retreated after failing to capture land, an ambush could be arranged to destroy his tired and hungry troops.

Right before Ren Fu started out, Han Qi admonished him: "Whoever disobeys orders will be beheaded no matter what distinction he may achieve."

Yuanhao feigned a move toward Wei Region, as if determined to capture it. However, his real aim was not to seize territory but to destroy the Song troops under Han Qi, who had been preparing a major offensive against the Xia. A few days after he reached Huaiyuan, Yuanhao learned from his scouts and spies about the maneuvers of Ren Fu's army. Thereupon he led his main force on a swift march southwest to the city of Yangmulong, where he arrayed the troops to wait for the Song army. In the meantime he dispatched his assistant general with a couple of thousand horsemen to cross the Liupan Mountain and march on Wei Region to distract Han Qi's attention.

When Ren Fu arrived at the Liupan Mountain with his vanguard cavalry, he encountered two other Song generals, Chang Ding and Liu Su, who were engaged in battle with the Xia forces to the south of Zhangjiabao. Ren Fu's cavalrymen charged at the enemy and routed it. The Xia soldiers abandoned many sheep, horses, and camels and fled westward along the northern bank of the Haoshui River.

That night Ren Fu stationed the troops by the Haoshui River, while Zhu Guan and Wu Ying made camp on a tributary of the river. They were about five *li* apart. Scouts reported that the Xia forces were inferior in number and seemed rather fearful. At this Ren Fu lost his vigilance and grew contemptuous of the men of Xia. He did not stop his officers and men from pursuing the Xia army and capturing its abandoned provisions. Geng Fu reminded Ren Fu that the men of Xia had always been deceptive and advised him to bring the troops under discipline and advance slowly in a regular formation. Scouts should also be dispatched to probe further into the surrounding areas in order to find out what tricks the enemy was up to. However, Ren Fu ignored this advice. He made arrangements with Zhu Guan to proceed by separate routes to pursue the enemy and join forces at the mouth of Haoshui River the next day.

The Xia horsemen feigned defeat, emerging now and then four or five *li* in front of the Song army. Ren Fu and Zhu Guan marched swiftly in a hot pursuit, eventually arriving to the north of the city of Longgan. There the Xia soldiers suddenly vanished from sight. Ren Fu realized at last that he had been deceived and decided to pull the troops out of the mountainous region.

The next day Ren Fu led his men to move westward along the Haoshui River. They finally got out of the Liupan Mountains and proceeded towards the city of Yangmulong. At this juncture Ren Fu got reports of enemy activity in the vicinity. He had to call the troops to a halt about five *li* from the city and array them in a defensive formation. Just then, several large wooden boxes were discovered lying by the road. The boxes were tightly sealed and rustling sound came from within. Curiously, Ren Fu ordered the boxes to be opened. All of a sudden, dozens of pigeons fluttered out of the boxes and flew high into the sky, with loud tinkling sounds coming from the small bells attached to their claws. All the Song soldiers looked up in astonishment, when large hosts of Xia soldiers appeared in every direction to form a complete encirclement.

On hearing the pigeon bells, Yuanhao knew that the Song army had entered his ambush ring. Thereupon he sent an assistant general with fifty thousand men to surround and assault the band of troops led by Zhu Guan and led the other half of his troops in person to attack

Ren Fu, whom he considered a tougher opponent than Zhu Guan.

By this time Ren Fu's soldiers were pretty much worn out from the days of trudging through the mountains. Besides, many of them had barely any combat experience, as they had just been recruited and had received no training at all. Thus Ren Fu found it difficult to coordinate the troops for even the simplest tactical moves. Though some officers and men fought competently, the Song army as a whole was not capable of coping with such an adverse situation. The battle started in early morning; before long the men of Song were cut into several sections.

At noon Ren Fu perceived that the battle had already been lost. To avoid total annihilation, he made a desperate attempt to lead the army to break out of the encirclement. However, Yuanhao had his command banner set up on top of a nearby hill. Wherever the Song army charged, the observing Xia officer would point the banner in that direction, and the Xia troops would move to reinforce the corresponding area. The Song soldiers failed to penetrate the encirclement and were compelled to continue the tangled fight. Many were killed and some even threw themselves down the precipice in despair. Ren Fu himself was hit by over a dozen arrows. One of his guards urged him to surrender, which seemed the only way to save his life and the remnants of his men. But Ren Fu sighed and said, "I am a general of the Song and shall pay for this defeat with my life." With this he brandished his mace and fought fiercely until he was mortally injured on the face by a spear. Then he took his own life by strangling himself. All of Ren Fu's subordinate officers died in combat, and his army was completely wiped out.

In the meantime Zhu Guan's men had also fallen into ambush. Deploying some experienced soldiers to defend the wings, Zhu Guan managed to maintain his ground and sent several bands of cavalry to charge at the Xia army in an attempt to break up its formation. But the men of Xia, superior in number and enjoying a topographical advantage, gave full play to their ferocity, and their formation remained impregnable. At this critical juncture Yuanhao led his victorious troops to attack the Song army from its rear. The Song army collapsed and a scene of rout and slaughter ensued. Thousands of Song soldiers, along with their officers, were killed. Zhu Guan fell back with a thousand men behind a stretch of earthen walls, where they checked the advance of the Xia army by letting loose a rain of arrows. It was getting dark by this time. Having learned of the battle, a contingent of Song army stationed in a nearby stronghold arrived to provide reinforcements, whereupon Yuanhao pulled away his troops.

The grave defeat in the battle of Haoshui River caused consternation among the Song emperor and his ministers. Han Qi was demoted, along with several other commanders in charge of frontier defense. On his way to receive the remnants of the troops from Haoshui River, he was stopped by thousands of local people who had lost their sons or husbands. Carrying clothes of their beloved dead and ghost money,* they gathered by the road to express their bereavement. On seeing Han Qi's contingent, some cried out aloud: "You have gone to battle with General Han. Now General Han is back, why don't you come back

---

*Paper money that is burned to provide funds for a deceased in the afterworld.

with him?" Overwhelmed with shame and sorrow, Han Qi could not utter a single word in reply.

The poor performance of the frontier army of Song, such as displayed in the battle of Haoshui River, was to repeat itself again and again during Yuanhao's rule over the Xia kingdom. To the Song people who suffered greatly from this "barbarian" archbandit, it might seem a sign of justice that at the end of his ten-year reign Yuanhao was murdered by his own son.

Adapted from *Biography of Yuanhao*
(Yuan Hao Zhuan)

Strategy Twenty-Three
Befriend Distant States While Attacking Nearby States

第二十三计 远交近攻　　形禁势格，利从近取，害以远隔。上火下泽。

Translation

When circumscribed in situation and restricted in disposition, seek profit from nearby and keep peril at a distance. Fire above the lake.*

Purport

In the late Warring States period, Qin emerged as the most powerful state and proceeded to destroy its rivals to gain control of all China. Though superior to any other

---

*Kui (Opposition), the thirty-eighth hexagram in I Ching, consists of the upper trigram of Li (fire) and the lower trigram of Dui (lake). Thus its symbol reads, "Fire above the lake symbolizes opposition." The comment indicates that things opposite in nature can serve the same end. Heaven and earth are opposite, yet they share the same function of nourishing life; man and woman are opposite, yet they share the same will to live and prosper; the multitudinous things in the cosmos are all different, but they share a similar course of development. In a utilitarian point of view, such as adopted in this strategy, totally different approaches can be used to achieve one and the same purpose.

single state, Qin was no match for the combined power of all the other states. Therefore it adopted the plan of eliminating the rival states one by one. A key strategy it employed in the process was to befriend distant states while attacking those nearby. It was proposed by the famous statesman of the time, Fan Sui. The successful application of this strategy led to the unification of China under the Qin Dynasty.

Even a strong army cannot afford to fight several battles at the same time. Therefore the strategy instructs the military leader to deal with his enemies one by one. Also, one is cautioned against seeking superficial victories that do not bring about any concrete profit. By launching an expedition against a distant state, one may gain great fame. But the campaign will be both costly and risky. Even when it turns out a success, one cannot gain a single foot of land. It would be better to attack a neighboring state and in the meantime secure friendly relations with distant states so that they may not come to rescue the beleaguered.

Quotation for Reference

Procure the enemy's trusted followers to keep you informed, procure the enemy's warriors to make concerted action, procure friendly states to support your cause, procure neighboring powers to assist in your attack. One who wants to gain the mastery of the world must make use of the world and not rely merely on one's own strength. Nevertheless, procurement is a risky strategy and precautions must be taken to guard against possible change in situation. Make sure that you have endowed enough benefits to befriend or have enough power to control those you want to procure.

A Hundred War Maxims, "Procurement"
(Bing Fa Bai Yan, "Gou")

Qin Subverts the Qi-Chu Alliance Before Attacking Chu

Zhang Yi, a native of Wei, was a disciple of the Master of Ghost Valley. After finishing his studies, he set out traveling to the various states and selling his ideas to their rulers.

On one occasion, Zhang Yi was drinking wine with the chief minister of Chu when the latter found his jade missing. His attendants said, "Zhang Yi is poor and unscrupulous. He must have stolen the jade." So they bound him up and flogged him several hundred strokes. As Zhang Yi would not admit to the theft, they finally let him go. When he returned home, his wife exclaimed, "Ah! Stop reading books and canvassing, will you? Then you can at least avoid such insult and humiliation!"

"Is my tongue still in its place?" asked Zhang Yi.

"Why, it is still there." replied his wife.

"I am all right then," announced Zhang Yi. Later he went to Qin to serve as chief minister there.

In 313 B.C. the King of Qin planned to attack Chu, but was worried over the military alliance between Chu and Qi. In order to destroy the alliance, he announced the dismissal of his chief minister, Zhang Yi, and sent him as an envoy to Chu.

The King of Chu had Zhang Yi accomodated in the best inn and, summoning him for an audience, inquired about his intentions. Zhang Yi answered, "Your Majesty numbers the first among the people that my king likes and respects, and I have no greater ambition than to become your house servant. The King of Qi numbers the first among the people that my king dislikes and I also dislike him intensely. Unfortunately, your alliance with him makes it impossible for my king to attend to you and for me to be your house servant. If you break with Qi, you can send an envoy to go west with me and receive six hundred *li* of the land of Shang and Yu, which Qin took from Chu in the past. In this way you will benefit from the decline of Qi in the north and the gratitude of Qin in the west, in addition to recovering the land of Shang and Yu."

Immensely pleased, the King of Chu appointed Zhang Yi as his chief minister and gave banquets day after day, boasting proudly, "I have regained the land of Shang and Yu!" The courtiers all came to offer congratulations, but Chen Zhen approached the king with a solemn face and offered condolences.

"Why is this?" the king asked in surprise.

Chen Zhen replied, "Qin regards you with respect just because you have Qi as your ally. However, you have abandoned Qi and isolated yourself before obtaining the land of Shang and Yu. Now that Chu is all alone, how can it retain the respect of Qin? As I see it, if you demand to get the land before breaking with Qi, Qin will surely refuse. If you break with Qi before getting the land, you are bound to be cheated by Zhang Yi. Then you will become enraged and regard Qin as an enemy. When we confront with Qin in the west and lose the alliance of Qi in the north, Wei and Hann will seize the chance to attack us. For this reason I have come to offer my condolences."

The King of Chu refused to believe this and sent a general to go with Zhang Yi to accept the land of Shang and Yu.

Upon his return to Qin, Zhang Yi feigned a fall from his carriage out of drunkness. He then stayed in his house and refused to meet anyone, pleading illness. Therefore the Chu general could not get the land that had been promised. At this the King of Chu said to himself, "Maybe Zhang Yi thinks my breakup with Qi is not thorough enough." So he sent a brave man to the court of Qi to abuse its king. The King of Qi flew into fury and sent an envoy to seek alliance with Qin.

After the establishment of the Qin-Qi alliance, Zhang Yi promptly showed up at the court of Qin. He sent for the Chu general and said to him, "Why don't you go and get the land? It's as big as six *li* in such-and-such an area." The astonished Chu general replied, "I received orders to get land of six hundred *li*, not six *li*." With this he left the Qin court and returned to Chu empty-handed.

The King of Chu, bursting into rage, mustered his troops to attack Qin. Chen Zhen advised against it, saying, "It is inexpedient to attack Qin. It would be better if we bribe Qin with a large city so that it will join us in an expedition against Qi. In this way we can gain from Qi what we lose to Qin and thus preserve the strength of our nation. If you cut off relations with Qi and launch a campaign against Qin, you will bring Qi and Qin into a coalition against us. Chu will suffer greatly."

"It is Qin who has cheated me," the king said. "What wrong has Qi done? I would be ridiculed by all the world if I adopt your suggestion and attack Qi instead of Qin." With this the King of Chu ordered his army to march westward. Qin also dispatched a band of troops to meet the challenge of Chu.

A mighty battle took place at Danyang in the spring

of 312 B.C. The Chu army was routed, losing eighty thousand footmen and more than seventy generals. Hanzhong Prefecture was seized by the victorious Qin forces. Thereupon the King of Chu summoned all the troops of his state in a second attack against Qin. The Qin army engaged the Chu forces at Lantian and gained another major victory. When Hann and Wei learned about Chu's predicament, they launched raids against Chu from the south. The King of Chu was compelled to call back his expedition.

The following year Qin proposed to make peace with Chu, offering half of the land of Hanzhong as a gift. The King of Chu replied, "I would rather have Zhang Yi than the land." At this, many courtiers of Qin who were jealous of Zhang Yi persuaded the king to send him to Chu, saying, "It is most profitable to exchange a single person for several hundred *li* of land!" The king was still hesitating when Zhang Yi himself volunteered to go. "But what if Chu wants to get even with you?" the king asked.

"I am familiar with Le Shang, a court eunuch of Chu, who is assigned to wait upon the king's favorite concubine, Zheng Xiu. This Lady Zheng is well-known for her jealousy and artfulness. Once, the King of Chu was enamored of a new beauty to the neglect of Lady Zheng. Lady Zheng went to see the beauty and told her, 'You are very lucky to have gained the king's favor, but you must be careful about one thing. The king does not quite like the look of your nose. You should conceal your nose in his presence to please him better.' The beauty was very grateful. A few days later the perplexed king came to ask Lady Zheng, 'Why does the new beauty always cover up her nose in front of me?' And Lady Zheng replied, 'She does not like your smell.' The king was so furious that he had the beauty's nose cut off. I can make use of Lady Zheng's jealousy to protect my safety. You should also send troops to the border and pretend to prepare for another attack on Chu. In this way I will be able to get back safe and sound."

Upon his arrival at Chu, Zhang Yi was immediately thrown into prison. The King of Chu then selected an appropriate date on which to hold a ceremony at the ancestral temple for the execution of Zhang Yi.

Zhang Yi sent a follower to seek help from Le Shang, the trusted eunuch. Le Shang paid a visit to Lady Zheng and said to her, "You will soon lose the king's favor!"

"How come?" Lady Zheng asked anxiously.

"Qin did not know that our king is very angry with Zhang Yi and wants to have him beheaded. Now the King of Qin regrets having sent Zhang Yi here and has offered, in exchange for Zhang Yi, six districts in the area of Shangyong, a princess to marry our king and several singing girls as his concubines. When the maidens of Qin arrive, our king will undoubtedly treat them with respect and devotion in order to maintain good relations with Qin. How will you be able to retain the king's undivided favor?"

Lady Zheng was startled. "I must stop this! Tell me what I should do."

"Just behave as if you knew nothing of the matter," Le Shang said. "Go to the king and persuade him to release Zhang Yi for the benefit of Chu."

Thereupon Lady Zheng went to see the king. On reaching his presence, she got down on her knees and broke into tears. She said weepingly, "I beg my lord to allow me and my son to flee to the south. Qin has shown its respect for Chu by sending Zhang Yi as you required.

Now if you kill him, Qin will be infuriated and come to attack us."

The king did not want to displease his favorite, though he felt reluctant to accept her advice. Then Le Shang came to see him, saying, "The King of Qin is very fond of Zhang Yi and must be angry to learn of his imprisonment in Chu. If we offend Qin for the mere purpose of revenge and lose the chance to make peace with it, the other lords will despise us." So the king had Zhang Yi released and treated him kindly.

With his glib tongue Zhang Yi talked the King of Chu into signing an agreement with Qin. Then he left Chu for Qin. He had been gone two days when Qu Yuan, Left Minister of Chu, returned from a mission to Qi. "Why didn't you have Zhang Yi decapitated?" he demanded. Overcome with regret, the king hastily sent a band of soldiers to chase Zhang Yi. But it was already too late.

Adapted from *Records of the Historian* (Shi Ji), Tome Seventy

Strategy Twenty-Four
Attack Hu by a Borrowed Path

第二十四计 假途伐虢 两大之间，敌胁以从，我假以势。困，有言不信。

Translation

A small state is sandwiched between two great powers. If one of them attempts to bring it to submission, the other will be able to take control under the pretext of aiding it. *Kun*: When one utters words, one is not believed.*

Purport

The battle from which this idiom originated took place in the Spring and Autumn period, when warfare was evolving from a seasonal sport of the nobles into a practical means to gain power and resources. Aiming to swallow up Yu and Hu, two small neighbors, the big state of Jin first borrowed a path through Yu to attack Hu. After the conquest of Hu, the Jin troops attacked and destroyed

---

*This phrase is taken from the judgement of *Kun* (Oppression), the forty-seventh hexagram in *I Ching*. The hexagram has the symbol of *Kan* (water) under *Dui* (lake), indicating a lake that has dried up. Therefore it represents a time of adversity. Caught in an unfavorable situation, a person should improve his lot by taking action; mere words will produce no effect.

Yu on their way back.

The strategy instructs one to adopt a piecemeal solution when faced with more than one enemy. Even a powerful state cannot afford to fight two wars at the same time. In laying out its plan for aggrandizement, it has to select one foe at a time. It may befriend a distant state while attacking one nearby, as in the last strategy, or it may borrow a path from a nearby state to attack a distant one.

Jin Borrows a Path Through Yu to Attack Hu

The first half of the Eastern Zhou Dynasty, known as the Spring and Autumn period, saw the decline of the prestige of the ruling house of Zhou and escalating wars of conquest and annexation among the various feudal states.

The state of Jin, located in modern Shanxi, grew steadily in strength by swallowing small neighbors. There were two small states, Hu and Yu, to its south. In the spring of the nineteenth year under King Hui of Zhou (658 B.C.), Duke Xian of Jin sent for a trusted minister, Xun Xi, and declared his intention to attack Hu.

"We have little chance to gain advantage," observed Xun Xi after a pause. "Hu and Yu have always been very close. When we attack one of them, the other will surely come to its rescue. Pitched one to one, neither of them is our match, but the result is far from certain if we fight both of them at the same time."

"Surely you are not saying we have no way to cope with these two small states?" asked the duke.

Xun Xi thought for a while before replying, "There is a plan, but it will take time to carry it out. First we can send a few beautiful maidens to the Duke of Hu. He will become infatuated with them, which will cause complaints among his subjects. Then we can bribe the Quan-rong tribe to the northwest into attacking Hu. Hu will become a much easier prey if it is weakened by both internal and external troubles."

The Duke of Jin adopted this plan, which proved successful. He then summoned Xun Xi and asked, "Now we may attack Hu, I suppose?"

"Not yet," replied Xun Xi, "for Hu still has Yu as its ally. I have thought up a plan by which we will be able to subdue both Hu and Yu. For the first step we should present the Duke of Yu with handsome gifts and ask him to lend us a path by which we can attack Hu."

The duke asked, "But we have just offered gifts to Hu and signed a friendly agreement with it. We can hardly make Yu believe that we want to attack Hu instead of Yu itself."

"That is not so difficult to work out," replied Xun Xi. "We may secretly order our men on the border to make raids on Hu. When the men of Hu come to protest, we may use that as a pretext to attack them. In this way Yu will be convinced of our professed intention."

The duke considered it a good plan. Before long, armed conflicts broke out along the Jin-Hu border to the south. Thereupon the duke asked, "Now we have good reason to convince Yu of our intention to attack Hu. But it will not lend the path to us unless it receives a good profit in return. So what shall we use to bribe the Duke of Yu?"

Xun Xi replied, "Though the Duke of Yu is known to be very greedy, he will not be moved unless our gifts are extremely precious. So why not offer him fine horses from Qu and jade from Chuiji?"

The duke looked reluctant. "But these are the best treasures I have. I can hardly bring myself to part with them."

"I am not surprised by your doubts," said Xun Xi. "Nevertheless, we are bound to subdue Hu now that it has lost the shield of Yu. After Hu is conquered, Yu will not be able to survive on its own. Therefore, when you send these gifts to the Duke of Yu, you are simply consigning the jade to your external mansion and the horses to your external stable."

The duke was satisfied by this reply but had one more doubt. "What about Gong Zhiqi? I have heard he is a very shrewd minister and the Duke of Yu places great trust in him. He will surely advise his duke against lending the path to us."

"I know a lot about this Gong Zhiqi," said Xun Xi. "He has grown up in the Duke of Yu's company. The duke treats him with familiarity but not respect and does not take his words seriously. Besides, Gong is a timid man who dares not insist upon his advice. He will keep his mouth shut once the Duke of Yu refuses to listen to him."

Fully assured, the Duke of Jin dispatched Xun Xi as an envoy to borrow a path from Yu. When Xun Xi was ushered into the court of Yu and presented the gifts, the Duke of Yu's eyes bulged. He happened to be a great lover of horses. Finally, he turned to ask Xun Xi, "Why has your lord sent me such incomparable gifts?"

"My master entertains the uttermost respect for Your Highness' virtue and with great eagerness seeks to establish good relations with your great state." Xun Xi thus replied in a humble tone.

"Even so," the duke said, "he must need me to do

something for him in return. What is it?"

To this Xun Xi replied, "The men of Hu have repeatedly worked up disturbances along our border. To protect our people from the calamity of war, we have exerted the highest restraint and concluded a peace treaty with Hu. Nevertheless, the impudent Hu takes our restraint for weakness and is now creating new troubles by making invidious charges against us. Therefore my lord was compelled to order a punitive expedition against Hu, and he dispatched me to ask your permission to let our troops pass through your land. This way, we can get around our border with Hu, where its defense is strong, and launch a surprise attack at its weak point. When we have defeated the men of Hu, we shall present you with splendid trophies to testify to our mutual alliance and friendship."

Immensely pleased, the Duke of Yu was about to give his consent when Gong Zhiqi spoke up against the offer. "Your Highness must never gratify their wish!" he exclaimed. "You must have heard the saying that 'If the lips are gone, the teeth will be cold.' Hu and Yu are close neighbors that share a common lot and depend on each other for security. If Hu is destroyed, how will Yu be able to survive on its own?"

The duke retorted, "The Duke of Jin has shown his good will by offering such munificent gifts, so how can I deny him the simple favor of lending a path? Besides, Jin is ten times more powerful than Hu. Is it not a good deal to secure an alliance with Jin at the expense of our relationship with Hu? Now step aside and do not meddle in my business anymore!"

Gong Zhiqi was about to speak again when he was stopped by Bai Lixi, a fellow courtier and good friend. After they took leave of the duke, Gong Zhiqi asked his friend anxiously, "Why did you stop me from speaking up? I think you should have spoken up yourself to support my argument."

"Can you not see the duke was blinded by those gifts from Jin? " replied Bai Lixi. "To offer good counsel to a stupid man is like throwing pearls and jade on the road. By insisting upon your objection, you cannot save Yu but can only endanger your own position."

"So Yu is doomed!" deplored Gong Zhiqi. He was at a loss what to do.

That summer the Jin troops attacked Hu by way of Yu. The Duke of Yu led a band of force in person to join in the expedition. They defeated the Hu army and captured Xiayang, one of Hu's two major cities. The Duke of Yu received his share of the booty and believed he had nothing to regret for.

Soon afterwards the men of Hu engaged the Quanrong tribe in battle and gained a victory. At this the augurer of Jin observed, "The state of Hu is destined to fall into destruction. At the loss of Xiayang, it was not shaken into fear and vigilance and inspired to guard its security, but instead launched an invasion. This shows its lack of fear for the powerful Jin and consideration for its people. Hu cannot last more than five years."

In autumn of the twenty-second year under King Hui of Zhou (655 B.C.), the Duke of Jin again sent an envoy to borrow a path from Yu, and again the Duke of Yu gave his consent. At this Gong Zhiqi offered his objection, saying, "Lending a path to a state with ulterior motives can only lead to our downfall. Once is already too many times; how can you do it twice?"

"Jin borrowed a path from us three years ago," said the duke. "We gained much profit and never came to any harm. So why not lend them the path again?"

Back home, Gong Zhiqi said to himself, "This must be the end for Yu! The men of Jin will not need another expedition but can destroy Hu and Yu once and for all." He summoned all his clansmen and together they moved out of Yu.

In the eighth month, the Duke of Jin led six hundred war chariots and proceeded by way of Yu to attack Hu. They laid siege to Shangyang, the capital of Hu. With inferior troops and no reinforcements from outside, the city, after holding out for nearly four months, finally yielded. The Duke of Hu fled to take refuge in Luoyang, the dynastic capital of Zhou, and Hu as a feudal state was destroyed.

On their way back, the Jin troops halted at Yu. The Duke of Yu came to welcome them, receiving the Duke of Jin into the capital. The Jin troops seized the chance to storm into the city. Taken totally off guard, the Yu army submitted with little resistance, and the Duke of Yu was taken prisoner.

Duke Xian of Jin was extremely pleased when Xun Xi returned to present him with the horses and jade as well as the captured Duke of Yu. At first he wanted to have the Duke of Yu executed. But Xun Xi advised against it, observing that a great power should use its force stringently. Thus the duke allowed the ruling house of Yu to continue its ancestral worship. He also offered the tariff collected from the land of Yu to the King of Zhou.

Adapted from *Zuo's Spring and Autumn Annals* (Zuo Zhuan), Tome Five

Strategy Twenty-Five
Steal the Beams and Change the Pillars

第二十五计 偷梁换柱　频更其阵，抽其劲旅，待其自败，而后乘之。曳其轮也。

Translation

Change the enemy's formation frequently, dislocate its main force and deal the blow when it tends toward defeat. Stop the wheel.*

Purport

Battle formations are a common feature in early military history of China. A typical formation has a central

---

Wei Ji (Before Completion), the sixty-fourth and the last hexagram in *I Ching*, is composed of *Li* (fire) above *Kan* (water). This hexagram, with all its yang lines in yielding positions and its yin lines in strong positions, represents a time of transition when everything is tending toward change. For the yang line in the second place, the judgement reads, "Stop the wheel. Good fortune." Located in a yielding position and sandwiched between two yin lines, it resembles a cart wheel that becomes obstructed and cannot run smoothly. Here, a person of strength in an unfavorable situation is advised to proceed slowly and cautiously. He may attain good fortune by preserving his strength and waiting in patience until the time to act has come. In the strategy, the enemy's troops are compared to a chariot and the main axles of its battle formation to the wheels. By stopping the wheels, one can put the chariot to a halt. By dislocating the main axles of the enemy's formation, one can throw the enemy into disorder and defeat it.

axle (heavenly beam) extending from the front to the rear and a horizontal axle (earthly pillar) connecting the left and right flanks. The two axles, formed by the best combatants, serve to maintain the structure of the formation. When assaulted, a formation will not yield until its axles become dislocated. Therefore the attacker should employ a shock force to break into the enemy's formation and displace its axles. He can also use tricks to throw the enemy's formation into disorder before launching a frontal attack. The strategy also points to a general principle: Throw the enemy into confusion before engaging it in battle. For this purpose, one can find out and strike at the vital part of the enemy's formation.

Quotation for Reference

Man depends on his throat for fluent breathing and the maintenance of life. When his throat is strangled, his five sense organs will lose their sensibility and no longer function normally. He will not be able to stretch his limbs, which become numb and paralyzed. The man can therefore rarely survive. Thus, when the banners of the enemy come into sight and the beating of its battle drums can be heard, we must first ascertain the positions of its back and throat. Then we can attack it from the back and strangle its throat. This is an excellent strategy to crush the enemy.

Essentials of War (Bing Lei), Chapter Thirty-Two

The Battle of Feishui River

After the Western Jin was overthrown by northern tribal people, the prominent clans immigrated to the south and joined forces with local landowners to establish the Eastern Jin Dynasty, with its capital at Jiankang (modern Nanjing in Jiangsu Province). While the Eastern Jin maintained a relative stable rule in spite of internal power struggles, north China became the fighting ground among various non-Han tribes. Sometimes a distinguished ruler would conquer all his rivals and achieve a measure of unified rule over the north, but most of the time several rival regimes coexisted.

Fu Jian, the second emperor of the Former Qin, a regime of Di people founded in A.D. 351, employed a great Han scholar named Wang Meng as prime minister. Wang Meng served his sovereign wholeheartedly. He reformed and upgraded the semi-primitive socioeconomic and military structures of the Di people. Over the years the Former Qin grew into a great military power and succeeded in unifying the greater part of the north. On his deathbed, Wang Meng cautioned Fu Jian, "Do not seek for any object beyond your reach. Do not ride south across the Yangtze River."

Though he held his prime minister in great respect, Fu Jian was too willful and ambitious to listen to such counsel. In the tenth month of 382, he summoned all his ministers to the court and announced his intention to attack the Eastern Jin. He said, "I have ruled for nearly thirty years and pacified the four corners of the world; only the southeast remains to be conquered. I have calculated my soldiers and found them to be nine hundred and seventy thousand. I want to lead them in person on an expedition. What is your opinion?"

One or two courtiers voiced their support, but the majority objected to the plan, arguing that, though the Jin was weak and corrupt, it had not committed any grave atrocity so as to lose its people's support. Besides, it had a very capable minister, Xie An, as well as the natural barrier of the Yangtze River. Therefore it would not be easy to subdue it.

On hearing this, Fu Jian sneered contemptuously. "With my men, I can block the river by throwing our whips into it!" Then he dismissed the audience and beckoned for his younger brother, Fu Rong, to stay.

After the courtiers left, Fu Jian said to Fu Rong, "Since ancient times, every great cause has been planned by only one or two courtiers. Today, the confusion at the court only serves to ruin the whole matter for me. Let the matter be settled between the two of us."

Fu Rong replied, "To attack Jin, we are faced with three problems. First, the heavenly conditions are inappropriate. Second, the Jin is not suffering from internal strife. Third, our troops are exhausted from several battles and the common people have an aversion to warfare. The officials who objected to the expedition are dutiful and loyal to you, and I beg you to listen to their counsel."

At this reply, Fu Jian was disappointed and angry. "Even you are talking like this!" he exclaimed. "Is there no one whom I can lay plan with? Look, I have a million mighty troops and heaps of wealth and provisions. Though I dare not compare myself to the ancient sage rulers, I am certainly neither stupid nor immoral. Riding the crest of victories to attack a kingdom at the brink of ruin, I see no reason why I cannot destroy it for good. Why should I continue to put up with these remnants of rebels, who are a constant threat to my country?"

Fu Rong pleaded, "The Jin cannot be subdued; this is for sure. A large expedition will not achieve its aim. But I also worry over something else. You have placed trust in the Xianbei, the Qiang and the Jie people, who bear intense hatred against us. If the crown prince is left to guard the capital with a few tens of thousands of weak soldiers, I fear that rebellion will break up at our home. Then it will be too late for us to regret. Of course I am stubborn and foolish, but what about Wang Meng? You are wont to compare him to Zhuge Liang. Then do you still remember his last words?"

Fu Jian was·unmoved. When more ministers came to advise him against the expedition, he became indignant. "Considering the relative strength of Qin and Jin, our expedition will be like the autumn wind sweeping away fallen leaves! I cannot understand why so many in and outside the court speak against it!"

There was a general of Xianbei origin named Murong Cui, who voted for the expedition with unusual enthusiam. He said to Fu Jian, "The weak will be swallowed up by the strong, and the small by the big. This is the way of heaven. Your Majesty has brought the whole world into submission and achieved matchless exploits. How can you leave the petty kingdom of Jin for your descendants to conquer? The ancient sages have said that too many advisors result in no strategy. So why ask for the opinions of the courtiers? Your Majesty can simply decide the matter with his supreme judgement."

Fu Jian was overjoyed to find such a warm supporter. "You are the only one I have to help me pacify the all-under-heaven!" he said. He then endowed Murong Cui with a gift of five hundred bolts of silk. Little did he suspect that Murong Cui harbored an evil motive against him.

In the summer of 383, Fu Jian issued the edict for an all-out southward campaign against the Eastern Jin. He started out from Chang'an with six hundred thousand footmen and two hundred seventy thousand cavalrymen. The gigantic columns of the expedition stretched for hundreds of *li*. In the ninth month Fu Jian arrived at the city of Xiangcheng. Fu Rong led three hundred thousand men as the vanguard and reached Yingkou at the mouth of Huaihe River.

The Jin emperor appointed Xie Shi as the general-in-chief and Xie Xuan as the vanguard general, the two leading a total of eighty thousand troops to counter the invasion of Qin. Another general, Hu Bin, was put in command of five thousand troops to reinforce Shouyang.

As the Qin army outnumbered the Jin by over ten to one, the whole capital of Jin was overcast with fear and apprehension. When General Xie Xuan went to ask advice from Xie An, the prime minister, the latter appeared very calm and tranquil as if nothing were happening and nonchalantly ignored Xie Xuan's eager inquiry. When Xie Xuan got back, he sent a subordinate to see Xie An again. Thereupon Xie An arranged an excursion to his cottage in the hills. Many friends and relatives were present. Xie An played go with Xie Xuan. A much more skilled player than Xie An, Xie Xuan could nevertheless gain no advantage. After that, Xie An set out to explore the natural charms of the surrounding area and did not return until late at night. As the most powerful and renowned figure in the Eastern Jin, Xie An calmed his people by assuming a cool pose. This had some favorable effect, though at the same time a few people felt even more worried, thinking that Xie An was taking the destiny of Jin too lightly.

In the tenth month Fu Rong attacked and seized Shouyang, the seat of Huainan Commandery, capturing

Jin general Xu Yuanxi and some of his subordinate officers. Fu Rong then appointed his advisor Guo Bao as governor of Huainan. Murong Cui, leading another band of the Former Qin army, seized the city of Yuncheng in Jiangxia Commandery. The Jin general Hu Bin, who was marching westward to meet the Qin army, pulled back to defend Jiashi on hearing the fall of Shouyang. The Qin general Lian Cheng led fifty thousand men to Luojian Ford. Arriving there, he had stockades constructed to block the traffic on the Huaihe River. Xie Shi and Xie Xuan stationed their troops about twenty-five *li* from Luojian and dared not advance further.

Running short of provisions, Hu Bin sent a letter to Xie Shi, saying, "The enemy forces are very strong, and I have run out of food. I fear that I will not be able to meet with you." The messenger was captured by the Qin army. On reading the letter, Fu Rong felt exalted and went at once to see Fu Jian. "The enemy troops are few and can be easily defeated," he said. "The problem is to prevent them from escaping. We have to attack them as soon as possible." Thereupon Fu Jian left his main force at Xiangcheng and led eight thousand lightly equipped cavalrymen to Shouyang. Then he dispatched Zhu Xu as an envoy to the Jin army to persuade General-in-Chief Xie Shi to give up resistance and surrender.

Zhu Xu had been an Eastern Jin general in charge of the defense of Xiangyang. When the city was captured by the Qin army, he was taken prisoner and compelled to surrender. But he remained loyal to Jin and did not want to serve his captor. On arriving at the Jin army, he did not advise Xie Shi to submit to the Qin. Instead, he described the conditions of the Qin forces, saying, "When all of the one million Qin troops arrive, you will have no chance to survive their attack. Therefore you should set out immediately to give battle before the various sections of the Qin troops get together. By routing its vanguard, you can break the morale of the entire Qin army. Then it will be much easier to subdue."

When told that Fu Jian had arrived at Shouyang, Xie Shi became fearful and intended to stay immobile and put up a passive resistance. But Xie Yan urged him to follow Zhu Xu's advice.

In the eleventh month Xie Xuan sent a brave officer named Liu Laozhi with five thousand crack troops to advance on Luojian. The Qin general Liang Cheng lined up his men along the river to stop the Jin army from crossing it. Undaunted, Liu Laozhi charged headlong at the Qin troops and routed them. He also dispatched some of his men to block the enemy's path of escape. Thus he gained a major victory, killing fifteen thousand Qin soldiers.

Much heartened, Xie Shi mustered his courage and pushed forward with his troops. Standing on the city of Shouyang, Fu Jian and Fu Rong observed the approaching Jin army. They were somewhat dismayed to find such orderly formations advancing in a well-regulated pace. Fu Jian came to realize the strength of his enemy. Staring anxiously into the Bagong Mountains across the river, he even began to suspect that enemy forces were hidden behind the trees and grasses. He turned to his brother and observed, "This is surely a formidable enemy. And some fools told me the Jin is small and weak!" For the first time, he felt a little afraid.

After the defeat at Luojian, the Qin troops grew cautious. They assumed a battle array on the western bank of the Feishui River so that the Jin army could not cross it. Thereupon Xie Xuan dispatched an envoy to see Fu Rong and say to him, "You have come a long way to arrive at our land, but now you line up your troops along the river to block our path. This is the method for fighting a protracted war and will not bring about a quick solution. Would it not be better for you to pull back a little and let our men cross the river, so that we can fight it out once and for all?"

When Fu Jian consulted his officers, they all objected, saying, "Now that we outnumber the enemy, we had best stay here to check them. This would be a surefire plan."

But Fu Jian believed he could turn the enemy's trick against it. "We may just fall back a little bit to allow the enemy troops to cross the river and attack them with cavalry when they are halfway in the water. In this way we will gain a certain victory." Fu Rong also voted for the plan, and the order was issued for the Qin army to pull back.

It turned out that Fu Jian had too high an opinion of the morale and discipline of his troops. Once the order was given to withdraw a little, the men thronged back in such haste that the formations fell into disorder. At this moment Zhu Xu, who had stayed in the rear, had his followers shout aloud, "The Qin army is defeated!" At this the Qin soldiers began to flee helter-skelter. In his attempt to stop the stampede, Fu Rong was knocked down by his own frenzied cavalry and then killed by the pursuing Jin soldiers.

In the meantime Xie Shi and Xie Xuan led their men to rush across the river and charge at the chaotic Qin troops. Some Qin soldiers were killed by the pursuing Jin army; more were stamped to death as others tried desperately to escape. Fu Jian was wounded by some stray arrows but managed to flee back to Luoyang. There he collected the remnants of his troops, which amounted to a hundred thousand. His ignonimous defeat drastically undermined his position as ruler of the Former Qin. The next year, he was assassinated by his own cohorts.

Adapted from *History as a Mirror* (Zi Zhi Tong Jian), Tome One Hundred and Five

Strategy Twenty-Six
Point at the Mulberry and Abuse the Locust

第二十六计 指桑骂槐　　大凌小者，警以诱之。刚中而应，行险而顺。

Translation

The strong may use punishment to lead the weak into submission. Proper severity obtains response; risky action meets no obstruction.*

Purport

In the old Chinese family, a concubine dissatisfied with the domineering principal wife usually dared not confront her face to face. She might instead find fault

---

*This phrase is taken from the comment of *Shi* (The Army), the seventh hexagram in *I Ching*. The hexagram has the symbol of *Dui* (water, danger) under *Kun* (earth, the yielding). As water collects in the earth, so amid obedient peasants are hidden soldiers, who will be assembled into an army during a war. The yin line in the fifth place represents the sovereign, who has delegated his power to the general, the yang line in the second place. Being the only yang line in the hexagram, the general has received the supreme authority necessary to carry out his duty. Holding the second place, which is neither too weak nor too strong, the general will therefore conduct himself with proper severity. Thus he will achieve success even in a risky undertaking.

with the wife's maid. This is the household application of Strategy Twenty-Six. In military contexts, the phrase conveys an idea similar to another common expression, "Kill the chicken to scare the monkey." Compared with the chicken, the monkey is much more difficult to kill, but it can be scared into submission by the killing of the chicken. More frequently, the killing of a chicken is used to scare a whole group of chickens, monkeys and others.

A military commander can scare two kinds of people into submission: his own troops or power groups without formal allegiance. In the latter case, he must have an advantage over the people he wants to frighten. For instance, when a leader of an alliance of bandit groups wants to bring the various group leaders into total submission, he can pick out the most powerful of those groups and destroy it completely. He will not choose to destroy all of them, partly because they are useful to him, but mainly because it is beyond his capacity to fight with all of them at once. With the possible exception of the First Emperor of Qin, most empire founders in China adopted this strategy in eliminating their many rival contenders.

The strategy may also be used to strengthen military discipline, when the commander severely punishes someone whose high connections make him irreverent of military rules and defiant of the commander.

Quotations for Reference

When fighting with the enemy, our soldiers will advance and dare not back up if they are more afraid of us than of the enemy. If they dare back up but not advance, that is because they are afraid of the enemy but not of us. Authority and rigor compel the soldiers to go through fire and water without disobedience. The principle goes, "When severity surpasses solicitude, victory is certain."

A Hundred Marvelous Battle Plans, "Battle of Severity" (Bai Zhan Qi Fa, "Wei Zhan")

In warfare, make our soldiers dare advance but not retreat when encountering the enemy. Those who retreat for a single *cun* must be severely punished. In this way, victory can be achieved. The principle goes, "Punishment must be promptly carried out."

Ibid., "Battle of Punishment" ("Fa Zhan")

In warfare against the enemy, if there are cowardly soldiers in our ranks who do not advance on hearing the drum and retreat before the gongs are beaten, we must select a few of them to be executed as a warning to the troops. But if everyone of our three forces are fearful, refrain from execution, which will gravely damage the troops' morale. We must treat them with kindness, display our fearlessness, make them understand the situation, explain our strategy for survival; thus the mind of the multitudes can be reassured. The principle goes, "Use execution to prohibit fear. When fear is excessive, refrain from execution but treat the troops kindly and inform them of the way of survival."

Ibid., "Battle of Fear" ("Wei Zhan")

There will be victory if soldiers are more afraid of their commander than of the enemy, and defeat if soldiers are more afraid of the enemy than of their commander. The way to predict victory or defeat is to compare the soldiers' fear for the commander and for the enemy.

Book of Master Wei Liao (Wei Liao Zi),
Chapter Twenty-Three

Duke Huan of Qi Becomes the Overlord of the All-Under-Heaven

Guan Yiwu, whose polite name was Zhong, was a native of Yingshang (in northwestern Anhui Province). He used to do business with a friend named Baoshu Ya and always took two-thirds of the profit. This caused much complaint among the servants of Baoshu Ya. But Baoshu Ya defended his friend, saying, "Do not think that Zhong is greedy. I let him take the better part of our profit because his family is poor."

Once, Guan Yiwu took part in an expedition as a low-ranking officer. He stayed in the rear when the army advanced to give battle and joined the vanguard when his army returned from war. Some thought him a coward and laughed at him, but Baoshu Ya again spoke out for his friend. "Zhong has his old mother at home, so he has to stay alive to look after her. Actually, he is not in the least afraid to fight."

Though the two friends had frequent quarrels and disagreed on many things, their friendship remained unimpaired. Baoshu Ya once announced, "A wise person can achieve nothing if he is born in the wrong time. I am sure that Zhong will make a great figure if only he is given the chance." Guan Yiwu was greatly moved to hear these words and said, "It is my parents who gave me life, but it is Baoshu who really understands me!"

Later, Guan Yiwu and Baoshu Ya were appointed by the Duke of Qi to tutor his eldest son, Jiu, and second son,

Xiaobai, respectively. The two friends agreed that the one whose pupil succeeded to the dukedom should recommend his friend to the new duke so that they could enjoy high positions together.

Formerly, Qi had defeated the joint forces led by a minister of the Zhou court. The Duke of Qi feared that the King of Zhou might seek revenge, so he sent two generals to guard the southeast border against a possible invasion. He promised to have the two generals replaced after a year, but then he went back on his word. The two generals got so angry that they assassinated the duke and set up his cousin as the ruler of Qi. This cousin failed to win support from the courtiers and was soon murdered in his turn. Then followed a fierce contest for succession to the dukedom between Jiu and Xiaobai, the eldest and second sons of the late duke. Xiaobai, the second son, was the luckier of the two. With the help of Baoshu Ya, he finally put his brother Jiu to death and ascended the dukedom in 685 B.C. Known as Duke Huan of Qi, he ruled for forty-three years and turned Qi into the most powerful among the various feudal states.

Duke Huan thanked those who aided his ascension with generous gifts of land and court positions. Baoshu Ya, the most meritorious of them, was offered the position of chief minister. But he declined, saying, "I know nothing more than to follow the rituals and obey the law as an ordinary minister should do; I do not have the abilities for running a state."

Surprised, the duke asked if there was any person who had such abilities. Thereupon Baoshu Ya recommended his friend Guan Yiwu. "No!" the duke exclaimed. "Do you not remember how he tried every means to kill me?"

"That does not mean anything." replied Baoshu Ya.

"At that time he was serving his own master. But if he serves you, the all-under-heaven will be brought under your command!"

"All right. I will send for him and find out for myself if he is really worthy of your praise," said the duke.

"The chief minister is second only to the duke in the state," Baoshu Ya said. "You will injure your own reputation by treating your chief minister with such insolence. Why not choose an auspicious day to hold a grand ceremony for the reception of Guan Yiwu into the court? In this way you will obtain a matchless minister. Moreover, by treating with great respect someone who has offended you in the past, you will conquer the world with your generosity, and people with outstanding merits will come to Qi like rivers flowing into the ocean!"

Following Baoshu Ya's advice, Duke Huan appointed Guan Yiwu as chief minister and asked for his opinion on the management of the state. He found the words of Guan Yiwu so enlightening that they talked for three days and nights on end. Guan Yiwu gave his systematic view on how to achieve internal stability, increase the wealth of the state, strengthen military power and contend for supremacy among the vassal states. The uniqueness of his ideas was shown by his reply to the duke's blunt question: "I love hunting and women. Will this impede my plan to rule the all-under-heaven?"

"Not at all," replied Guan Yiwu. "If you cannot recognize an able person, or if you recognize him but fail to use him, or if you use him but fail to trust him—only then will your cause be endangered."

In spring of 681 B.C., Duke Huan summoned his ministers and announced his intention to organize an alliance, of which he was to be the leader, with the other states. Guan Yiwu offered his plan, saying, "At least three states surpass Qi in strength: Chu in the south and Qin and Jin in the west. Each of them holds sway over a large area, but in their ignorance they fail to pay proper respect to the King of Zhou. Therefore, none of them has been successful in dominating the all-under-heaven. Now the state of Song has just recovered from an internecine fight. Though the treacherous minister was executed, no ceremony has been conducted for the ascension of the new duke. Therefore you may send an envoy to the court of Zhou and ask the king to issue an edict calling for a meeting of the vassal lords to instate the new duke of Song. After the meeting, you will have firmly established your connection with the king and be able to command the other lords in his name. Then you can lead the other lords to pay homage to the court of Zhou regularly, fight away the four barbarians, and punish any lord who dare disobey the king. All the rulers within the four seas will hear of the lofty prestige of Qi and come together to pay their tribute. In this way, you will become the overlord without resorting to war chariots."

Duke Huan was pleased with this advice and immediately had it carried out. With no difficulty he obtained the edict from the King of Zhou, who was only too glad that the intransigent Qi showed its allegiance by such an act. Then Duke Huan had the edict proclaimed to the states of Song, Lu, Chen, Cai, Wei, Zheng, Cao, and Zhu. He had a huge platform constructed for the occasion, with spacious inns around to accommodate the lords. To show his sincerity and friendliness, he did not bring a single war chariot to the meeting place.

However, of the eight lords expected, only four showed up. Disappointed, Duke Huan intended to put off the meeting. At this Guan Yiwu said, "As an ancient saying goes, 'Three people make a crowd.' Now we have four lords come for the meeting, and that should be enough. By putting it off, we would only ruin Qi's credence."

Thus the ceremony was held in the third month among the five states of Qi, Song, Chen, Cai, and Zhu. Naturally, Duke Huan of Qi was elected leader of the alliance.

At the conclusion of the ceremony, Guan Yiwu suggested that since Lu, Wei, Zheng, and Cao deliberately disobeyed the king by failing to attend the meeting, a punitive campaign should be launched against them. Duke Huan turned to the other four lords and said, "As my poor city has few war chariots, I beg you to join this expedition." The lords of Chen, Cai, and Zhu all nodded their agreement, but the new Duke of Song remained silent.

Back at the inn, the Duke of Song complained to his minister Dai Shupi, "The Marquis of Qi has too high an opinion of himself! He has merely conducted a meeting in the king's name, and now he wants to command the troops of other states! If we obey him this time, I fear that we will be kept constantly on the run afterwards!"

Dai Shupi agreed with the duke, observing, "Half of the states invited failed to attend the meeting, therefore Qi's attempt to gain supremacy over the world has not worked out. Among the states present, Song is the biggest. If Song drops out, the other three states will follow suit. Thus Qi's expedition plan will go under. Besides, you have come here only to receive the formal appointment of the King of Zhou. Now that your purpose is achieved, why should we stay on?"

Late that night, the Duke of Song mounted his chariot

and left in secret.

On hearing of the Duke of Song's abscondence, Duke Huan became furious and intended to send a general to pursue him. But Guan Yiwu advised against it, reminding the duke that an order from the king was needed to take action against a state as big as Song. "Besides, something more urgent needs to be done," he added.

"What is that?" asked the duke.

"The punishment of Lu. The Duke of Lu belongs to a lateral branch of the royal house of Zhou, and the land of Lu is also easier to reach. How shall we bring Song to submission if we can do nothing about Lu?"

"By which route shall we send our army?" the duke asked eagerly.

"We need not sent the army to Lu," replied Guan Yiwu. "The state of Sui to the northeast of River Ji is a vassal of Lu. It is so small and weak that our army can capture it in a single day. This display of strength and determination will not fail to affect Lu and Song. Lu will in all probability ask to join our alliance. After that, Song will become isolated and easy to manage."

Duke Huan of Qi adopted this plan. He led an army in person and marched on the city of Sui, seizing it after the first round of battle drums. In consternation the Duke of Lu called an audience to discuss the matter with his ministers. Most of them agreed that it was unwise to offend the powerful Qi. So the Duke of Lu, in reply to a letter from Duke Huan, explained that an untimely illness had prevented him from attending the meeting. He offered to go and meet Duke Huan if the latter would first withdraw his troops back to Qi.

Thus a meeting between the dukes of Lu and Qi was duly held. It went on smoothly until an incident occurred.

When Duke Huan was carrying out the rituals on the platform, a follower of the Duke of Lu grabbed him by the sleeve and pointed a sword at him, demanding the return of a piece of land that Qi had formerly taken from Lu by force. Taken by surprise, Duke Huan had no choice but to concede.

After the meeting, Duke Huan was urged by some indignant courtiers to revenge the insult by detaining the Duke of Lu, but he would not listen to them. "I have made a promise and I will keep it," he declared. "Even an ordinary man knows enough to keep his word, and as the Duke of Qi how can I go back on mine?"

Duke Huan's reputation for honor as well as resolution spread far and wide among the various states. Soon afterwards, Wei and Cao sent envoys to Qi to apologize for their absence from the meeting and ask to join the alliance under Qi. Therefore only Song remained to be chastised. Duke Huan, after obtaining approval from the King of Zhou, led a band of joint forces and advanced on Song.

Passing by a mountain village, Guan Yiwu met a cowboy named Ning Qi and found him very knowledgeable. He recommended Ning Qi to Duke Huan, who appointed him a minister. When the troops arrived at the border of Song, the duke held a conference to discuss the plan for attack. At this, Ning Qi offered to go to see the Duke of Song and persuade him to yield without fighting. "It would be better to establish your authority by virtue than by force," he said. This idea appealed greatly to Duke Huan. So Ning Qi set out for the capital of Song in a small chariot with a few attendants.

Upon his arrival, Ning Qi requested an audience with the Duke of Song. The duke asked Dai Shupi, "Who is this Ning Qi? I do not think I have ever heard of him."

Dai Shupi replied, "He used to be a herdsman and has only recently received a position in the Qi court. He must have come to canvass for Qi with his glib tongue."

The Duke of Song had Ning Qi brought to his presence and tried to humiliate him by not returning his salute. At this, Ning Qi shook his head and heaved a deep sigh. "What a great danger Song is facing!"

"I enjoy the most prestigious title among the various lords," observed the duke. "How can any danger come to me?"

"How do you compare yourself with the Duke of Zhou?"* asked Ning Qi.

"The Duke of Zhou is a saint. I do not suppose I can compare with him."

"Duke of Zhou lived in a glorious age, when the all-under-heaven enjoyed peace and even the four barbarians paid tribute to the king. Yet he was so fearful of missing a capable man or a useful suggestion that, when someone called on him while he was eating, he would spit out the food and hurried out to receive the visitor. You live at a troublesome age when the various states are vying for power and Song has had two dukes murdered in succession. Yet you treat your guests with such arrogance and disrespect. Was I not right in saying that Song is in great danger?"

The Duke of Song left his seat and apologized. "Only recently did I assume my humble position, and I have hardly received any instruction from gentlemen like you. Now, what is it that you are going to teach me?"

"The King of Zhou has lost his supreme authority and

---

*Duke of Zhou, a statesman in early Zhou Dynasty, was held in great respect by Confucius.

the vassal lords have grown disrespectful," Ning Qi said. "To prevent the world from falling into chaos, Duke Huan of Qi has been entrusted by the king to establish an alliance of the states. However, you took leave without notice before the meeting was concluded. Enraged, the king has sent a joint army to attack you. If Song puts up resistance by force, the outcome of the battle is only too obvious."

"Well," the duke said, "I might have made a mistake in leaving the meeting a little early. Now what should I do?"

"In the opinion of your humble servant, you might send an envoy with a few simple gifts to Qi and ask to join the alliance. Duke Huan of Qi is not a man who remembers old grudges and will surely grant your request. In this way, Song will be rid of its danger without fighting."

The Duke of Song was satisfied and acted upon Ning Qi's advice. Consequently, Duke Huan of Qi succeeded in establishing an alliance of eight states with barely any fighting. Afterwards he was to sponsor eight more such alliances. He is thus known as one of the "Five Overlords" in the Spring and Autumn period.

Adapted from *Record of Events Based on "Zuo's Spring and Autumn Annals"* (Zuo Zhuan Ji Shi Ben Mo), Tome Eighteen

Strategy Twenty-Seven
Feign Folly Instead of Madness

第二十七计 **假痴不癫**　宁伪作不知不为，不伪作
假知妄为。静不露机，云雷屯也。

Translation

Feign ignorance and make no move rather than feign
knowledge and make rash moves. Stay motionless and
hide one's intention. Clouds and thunder symbolize
Tun.*

Purport

In warfare, suddenness can be achieved either by
secrecy, concealing one's maneuvers from the enemy, or
deception, making the enemy misinterpret the purpose of
one's open maneuvers. Secrecy is the normal method and
is widely applicable. One who is not ready to take action

---

* *Tun* (Difficult Beginning), the third hexagram in *I Ching*, consists
of *Kan* (water) above *Zhen* (thunder). It signifies tension and difficulty
when clouds and thunder gather in the sky. But after the rain, the
thunder will stop, the clouds will disperse, and the sky will become clear
again. Therefore a difficult and chaotic beginning will lead to order and
improvement in the end. The symbol of the hexagram reads, "Clouds
and thunder symbolize Difficult Beginning. The superior man brings
order out of chaos." When *Tun* appears on the astrological chart, it
means that the time is inopportune for one to take action.

may make wild gestures to distract the enemy. Yet such a strategy of "feigning madness" often provides a clue for the enemy to detect one's real intention. In general, a military leader tends to act by the Chinese saying, "When still, be quiet like a maiden; when moving, be agile like a rabbit just released." When not ready to fight, he plays the fool. Also, the strategy instructs the commander not to explain his orders to the troops.

Quotations for Reference

To undertake military operations, the army must prefer stillness to movement. It reveals no shape when still but exposes its shape in movement. When a rash movement leads to exposure of the shape of the army, it will fall victim to the enemy. But for movement, the tiger and leopard will not fall into trap, the deer will not run into snare, the birds will not be stuck by net, and the fish and turtles will not be caught by hooks. All these animals become prey to man because of their movement. Therefore the wise man treasures stillness. By keeping still, he can dispel temerity and cope with the temerarious enemy. When the enemy exposes a vulnerable shape, seize the chance to subdue it. *The Book of Master Weiliao* observes, "The army achieves victory by stillness." Indeed, the army should not move without careful thought, much less take reckless action.

Essentials of War (Bing Lei), Chapter Nine

Superb military maneuvers leave no trace. When leaving no trace, they cannot even be detected by deep-probing spies nor be counteracted by persons of wisdom. It is in conformity with circumstances that I place victory in front of the multitudes, who cannot comprehend this. They all know the shape in which I achieve victory but know not why I achieve victory in this shape. Therefore, to achieve victory I never repeat my methods but adapt them according to the infinite variety of situations.

Art of War (Sun Zi Bing Fa), Chapter Six.

The duty of the commander is to achieve secrecy by quietness and discipline by justice. Delude the soldiers' eyes and ears to make them ignorant.

Zhang Yu's Note: "Make plans quietly and secretly so that the enemy cannot find them out; command the troops justly and regularly so that the soldiers dare not neglect orders."

Li Quan's Note: "When the plot has not yet worked out, the soldiers should not be allowed to know it. You can enjoy success with them but should not lay plans with them. Therefore you have to delude their eyes and ears to make them ignorant."

Mei Yaochen's Note: "The troops should be made to carry out orders but not given to understand the plans of battle."

Ibid., Chapter Eleven

Emperor Taizong asked: "As for the trick of yin-yang and mystical numbers, can it be done away with?"

Li Jing replied: "No, it cannot. War is an art of deceits. We can issue orders in the name of yin-yang and mystical numbers to employ the greedy and the stupid. Therefore they should not be abolished."

Li Jing's Reply to Emperor Taizong of Tang (Tang Tai Zong Li Jing Wen Dui), Tome Three

The Establishment of a Unified Xiongnu Regime

The nomads known as the Xiongnu lived under primitive conditions in the north of modern Inner Mongolia. The turmoil in central China during the Warring States period gave them the opportunity to expand their influence. Their sporadic plundering expeditions were a constant threat to the states that bordered on their territory.

After his conquest of the six rival states and the establishment of a unified empire, the First Emperor of Qin launched a series of grand construction projects. One of them was to connect and strengthen the defense works in the north. First he sent his general-in-chief, Meng Tian, with a hundred thousand troops to drive the Xiongnu to the north of the Yellow River. Garrisons were restored and some of the best troops of the empire stationed along the extensive line of fortifications, known as the Great Wall, to protect central China from the incursions of the Xiongnu. Sandwiched between the Donghu (Eastern Barbarians) to the east and the Ruzhi to the west and no longer capable of infiltrating into the defense line of the Qin, the Xiongnu people were compelled to retreat further north.

About a dozen years later, Meng Tian died of illness. As rebellions against Qin broke out and spread all over the empire, the defense of the northern frontier was considerably weakened. The Xiongnu seized the chance to penetrate again to the south of the Yellow River.

The Xiongnu chieftain was named Touman and his heir apparent, Modu. Infatuated with a concubine who had given birth to a younger son, Touman planned to get rid of Modu and set up the son of his favorite as his heir.

On one occasion Touman sent Modu to the Ruzhi

nation as a hostage. Then he led his men to attack the Ruzhi, intending to enrage them into killing Modu in retaliation. A man of exceptional strength and agility, Modu managed to steal a fine horse and ride back to his own tribe. Impressed, Touman put Modu in command of ten thousand horsemen.

After this incident, Modu realized his precarious position and, with the aim of replacing his father, undertook to create out of the unruly, assorted men under his command an army with absolute loyalty to himself only. He made some arrows that whistled in flight and used them to train his followers in mounted archery. He ordered, "Shoot wherever my whistling arrow is directed! Anyone who fails to do so will have his head cut off!"

At the beginning Modu drilled his mounted archers during routine hunting trips. Whenever he shot a whistling arrow at a bird or an animal, his men were to immediately shoot at the same object. When any of them failed to respond promptly, Modu had him beheaded on the spot.

During a hunting excursion sometime later, Modu tested the discipline of his trained horsemen by shooting a whistling arrow at one of his favorite horses. Some faltered and dared not shoot at the horse; those were beheaded on the spot. Thus Modu gave his men to understand that he required absolute obedience to his orders regardless of their content.

On another occasion, Modu directed his whistling arrow at his favorite concubine. Again some of his men grew fearful and dared not shoot their arrows, and again Modu punished them with death. In a last test, Modu went out hunting and shot his whistling arrow at one of his father's best steeds. Without the least hesitation, all his followers shot their arrows in the same direction. Thereupon Modu knew that his men could be counted on to do anything at his order.

Modu's opportunity came when he accompanied his father on a hunting trip. All of a sudden, he shot a whistling arrow at Touman. His men discharged a shower of arrows in the same direction, and the chieftain was instantly killed. Modu then executed his stepmother, younger brother, and all the officials who refused to obey his orders. He set up himself as the new chieftain of the Xiongnu tribes.

At that time the Donghu nation was very powerful. On hearing of Modu's arrogation, the King of Donghu decided to size up this new Xiongnu chieftain. Thus he sent an envoy to Modu, asking for a famous horse. The horse, which had belonged to Touman, could reputedly cover a thousand *li* in a single day. When Modu summoned his ministers to discuss the matter, all of them advised him not to grant such an exorbitant request. They argued, "The thousand-*li* horse is a treasure of our people. You should not give it away."

However, Modu did not agree with them. He announced in a calm tone, "How can a mere horse compare with our relationship with our neighbor?" With this he gave the horse to the envoy to be brought to the Donghu.

This reaction of Modu caused the King of Donghu to take him as a weakling. A short time afterwards, the king sent another envoy to Modu to ask for one of his concubines. Again Modu consulted his ministers. They all burst into rage and exclaimed, "What degenerate beasts these Eastern Barbarians are to make such a shameless demand! Let's launch an attack at once to teach them a lesson!"

To their perplexity, Modu remained as unperturbed as

ever. He declared in a calm tone, "How can a mere woman compare with our good relationship with a neighboring country?" So he parted with his favorite concubine, who was taken away by the Donghu envoy.

Further convinced of Modu's cowardice, the King of Donghu grew more and more arrogant and launched invasions to the west. Between the areas inhabited by the Xiongnu and the Donghu there stretched over a thousand *li* of unpopulated land, which was the Gobi Desert. The King of Donghu sent an envoy to Modu, saying, "The stretch of wasteland that lies between our borders is beyond the reach of the Xiongnu. Our king desires to take possession of it."

As usual, Modu brought up the matter at an audience with his ministers. Some of them who had become accustomed to their chieftain's concessional responses replied noncommittally, "That is no more than a piece of desert land. It does not matter much whether we allow the Donghu to take it or not."

On hearing this, Modu flew into a fit of uncontrolled rage. "Land is the very basis of our nation," he roared angrily. "How can we surrender it to the Eastern Barbarians?" And he ordered the ministers who gave that reply decapitated.

Then he mounted his steed, summoned all his soldiers, and without a moment of delay set out on a major campaign against the Donghu. The people of Donghu, who had long held the Xiongnu in contempt, were totally unprepared to resist such a swift, overwhelming attack. Thus Modu and his powerful and well-disciplined troops inflicted a crushing defeat on his enemy. They killed the King of Donghu and destroyed his nation.

Returning home, Modu brought back the people, farm

animals, and other booty captured from the Donghu. Thus strengthened, he proceeded on to the west and defeated the Ruzhi people, driving them away from their land. Having disposed of the two foes on his flanks, Modu marched south across the Yellow River to recover the land formerly seized from the Xiongnu by the Qin general Meng Tian. By this time the resources of central China had been depleted in the contest for supremacy between Liu Bang and Xiang Yu. As a result, Modu's military ventures went virtually unopposed. He had under his command over three hundred thousand skilled bowmen.

Modu's masterstroke in his military career was yet to come. At the founding of the Han Dynasty, Liu Bang transferred Xin, the former King of Hann, to rule the area of Dai with his capital at Mayi. A powerful Xiongnu army laid siege to Mayi, and Xin surrendered to them. With a Han general at his service, Modu led his troops on a march southward to attack Taiyuan, finally reaching the city of Jinyang.

Liu Bang set out in person to lead an expedition against the Xiongnu invaders. It was winter time and they encountered heavy snow. Two or three out of every ten soldiers lost their fingers from the frost. Modu, feigning defeat to lure the Han army, retreated northward. He concealed his best troops and left his weak and decrepit men to be seen or captured by the Han soldiers. At this the entire Han army, numbering three hundred and twenty thousand, mostly infantry, pushed north in hot pursuit. Leading the vanguard, Liu Bang arrived at Pingcheng.

Before the arrival of his main force, Liu Bang found himself surrounded by four hundred thousand Xiongnu cavalrymen. Unable to break out the encirclement or to get aid from the outside, Liu Bang and his men remained there for seven days, suffering from cold and hunger. Finally, Liu Bang sent a spy in secret to bribe Modu's consort, who went to the chieftain and persuaded him to lift the siege. "Even if you gain possession of the Han lands," she said, "you will not be able to rule them. So why should you and the ruler of Han fight each other in such a way?"

Modu was already growing doubtful because two of Xin's generals failed to meet him as scheduled. And now, reluctant to displease his consort, he opened a corner of his encirclement. Thus Liu Bang's men were able to withdraw and join the main force of the Han army. For dozens of years after this ignominious defeat, the Han court was compelled to court peaceful relations with the Xiongnu at the price of gold, silk, and occasionally an imperial princess.

Adapted from *Records of the Historian* (Shi Ji), Tome One Hundred and Ten

Strategy Twenty-Eight

Climb up the Roof and Remove the Ladder

第二十八计 上屋抽梯　假之以便，唆之使前，断其援应，陷之死地。遇毒，位不当也。

Translation

Provide the army with an apparent chance, entice it to advance, cut it off from coordination or reinforcement, and place it in an impasse. One gets poisoned at an improper position.*

* This is the symbol of the yin line in the third place of *Shi He* (Chewing), the twenty-first hexagram in *I Ching*. *Yi* (Nourishment), the twenty-seventh hexagram, has two yang lines at its top and bottom and four yin lines in between them. Thus it represents two jaws that move together to chew food and thereby obtain nourishment. Compared with *Yi*, *Shi He* has its fourth line turned into yang, which means that the teeth have met an obstruction in the food. In order to digest the food and obtain nourishment, one must chew forcefully to break up the obstruction. The hexagram therefore indicates that one has to work hard through difficulties before one can hope to achieve one's goal. A yin line in a yang place, the third line represents a person lacking in strength who has embarked upon a strenuous task. This can lead to some misfortune. However, by perseverance one will finally achieve success. Therefore the judgement of the line observes, "One chews upon dried salty meat and gets poisoned. Small misfortune, no blame."

Purport

This strategy underscores the employment of a "ladder" in an ambush planned to annihilate the enemy. Ladder refers to the means by which the enemy is lured into the ambush ring. It may be a gesture of weakness if the enemy commander is arrogant, an enticement of gain if the enemy commander is greedy, or repeated defeats if the enemy commander is hesitant.

The strategy can also be used to discipline one's own troops in the manner of another familiar expression, "Break the caldrons and sink the boats." Faced with superior enemy forces, one may put his own soldiers in a position with no way of retreat so that they will fight with all their might. "Beasts at bay will put up a desperate fight." A commander who understands this strategy is able to contend with inferior forces against a powerful enemy. Conversely, when he lays siege to a weak enemy, he will leave a breach in the encirclement to prevent the enemy from fighting to death.

Quotations for Reference

When engaged in battle with the enemy, if our troops are stuck in a perilous place, encourage the officers and men to fight to the death instead of clinging to life. Only in this way can we achieve victory. The principle goes, "Soldiers lose fear when placed in a position of great peril."

A Hundred Marvelous Battle Plans, "Battle of Danger" (Bai Zhan Qi Fa, "Wei Zhan")

If the enemy is strong and our soldiers are hesitant to commit themselves, throw them into a fatal position and give them to understand the exigency of the situation. Slaughter the oxen and use carts as firewood to feast the soldiers. Burn up our provisions and destroy our wells and cooking stoves, and burn up the boats and break the cooking pots in order to eliminate all hope of survival by chance. In this way we will certainly achieve victory. The principle goes, "The troops prepared to die will survive."

A Hundred Marvelous Battle Plans, "Battle of Death" (Bai Zhan Qi Fa, "Si Zhan")

Place the troops in a position with no way of escape and they will not flee even if faced with death. When they are prepared to die, what can they not accomplish? They will exercise to the utmost of their power. Thus, soldiers lose fear when placed in a position of great peril, stand firm when left with no way out, unite together when venturing deep into the enemy's territory, and engage in close combat with the enemy when there is no other option.

Art of War (Sun Zi Bing Fa), Chapter Eleven

The Rise of Xiang Yu as Generalissimo

Xiang Ji, whose polite name was Yu, was born in Xiaxiang in the area of Chu. He had an uncle named Xiang Liang, the son of the renowned Chu general Xiang Yan who had died in a battle against the invaders from Qin. For generations the Xiang family had served as generals of Chu.

When young, Xiang Yu first studied the art of writing but could not finish it. Then he turned to swordsmanship but again quit without much accomplishment. This made his uncle disappointed and angry. At this Xiang Yu argued, "The study of writing only enables one to keep records of people's names, and swordsmanship only enables one to deal with a single enemy. So both are unworthy of my effort. What I want to learn is the art of fighting ten thousand men."

Accordingly, his uncle began to teach him military strategy. Xiang Yu was elated. However, once he grasped the general idea of the art, he did not bother to pursue it to the end.

Later, Xiang Liang killed a man and had to flee to the area of Wu with his nephew. As he was more capable than any of the local gentlemen, he took general charge of labor conscriptions and major funerals in the area. He seized the chance to enlist capable people into his service and trained them in the art of war.

In the meantime Xiang Yu grew into a youth of imposing stature and matchless strength. The young men of Wu all held him in awe.

On one occasion, the First Emperor of Qin crossed the Zhe River on his trip to Kuaiji. Xiang Yu and his uncle were among the crowds of people that gathered to watch the magnificent procession of the Son of Heaven. Then Xiang Yu blurted out, "He can be replaced!"

Aghast, Xiang Liang covered his nephew's mouth and cautioned in a whisper, "Do not talk that way! It would cause our entire family to be executed!" But the incident made the uncle realize that Xiang Yu cherished unusual aspirations.

In the seventh month of the first year under the Second Emperor (209 B.C.), Chen Sheng and Wu Guang raised an uprising at Daze Township. In the ninth month the defender of Kuaiji summoned Xiang Liang and said, "All regions west of the Yangtze have risen up in rebellion. It must be time when Heaven will destroy the rule of Qin. I have heard that, by striking first, one leads the others, whereas by striking too late one has to be led by others. So I've decided to raise troops, and I need you and Huan Chu as my generals."

At that time Huan Chu had gone into hiding in the marshes. So Xiang Liang replied, "Huan Chu has hid himself in the marshes, and no one but Xiang Yu knows how to find him." He went out and fetched Xiang Yu, telling him to wait outside with his sword. Then Xiang Liang returned to sit with the defender and said, "You may send for my nephew and order him to seek Huan Chu."

The defender gave his consent, and Xiang Liang had Xiang Yu ushered into the house. After a while he glanced at his nephew and said, "The time has come!" At this, Xiang Yu suddenly drew his sword and cut off the defender's head. Xiang Liang picked up the head and hung the seals of office on his own belt. The defender's men were frightened, and the entire house fell into commotion. After Xiang Yu cut down nearly a hundred of them, no one dared move anymore.

Thereupon Xiang Liang summoned all the local celebrities with whom he had made acquaintance and declared his intention to raise a revolt against Qin. He took command of the army of Wu and sent men to conscript soldiers from the various districts. Thus he was able to assemble a picked force of eight thousand men and appoint the distinguished locals of Wu to be his officers. He set up himself as the defender of Kuaiji and Xiang Yu as his assistant general.

Xiang Liang led troops on a westward march against the Qin army. He was soon joined by many people and had several tens of thousands of men under his command. At this time Fan Zeng, a wise man of seventy, went to see Xiang Liang to offer his suggestion, saying, "Of the six states destroyed by Qin, Chu was the most innocent. The people of Chu have always mourned for King Huai, who went to Qin and never returned. Thus a saying goes, 'Even if only three households are left in Chu, it is Chu that will eventually destroy Qin.' When Chen She started the revolt, he did not set up the descendant of Chu but took the royal title for himself. It is all too natural that he did not last long. Since you rose up east of the Yangtze, the people of Chu have been swarming to put themselves under your command. This is because you come from a family of Chu generals, and people expect you to restore the royal house of Chu to power. Only thus will you be able to obtain the absolute loyalty of your followers and attract more talented people under your banners."

Xiang Liang adopted this plan and sent men to seek out the grandson of the late King Huai of Chu. The noble heir turned out to be herding sheep as a commoner. Xiang Liang set him up as King Huai to gratify the people's hope and took the title Lord Wuxin for himself.

After defeating the Qin forces several times, Xiang Liang grew arrogant and began to underestimate his enemy. A subordinate named Song Yi cautioned him, "A victorious army may tend to defeat as its generals are arrogant and its soldiers tired. Now your men have slacked off while the Qin forces keep growing in number. I am afraid that you are in a perilous situation." But Xiang Liang paid no attention to him. Then the Qin mustered all its forces to reinforce general Zhang Han at Dingtao. There Zhang Han attacked the Chu army and routed it, killing Xiang Liang.

Zhang Han believed that the death of Xiang Liang put an end to the threat of Chu. Thereupon he crossed the Yellow River to attack Zhao, inflicting a grave defeat. The King of Zhao, with Chen Yu as his general and Zhang Er as his chief minister, retired to the city of Julu. The two armies confronted each other across the river. Zhang Han ordered his generals Wang Li and She Jian to surround Julu, while he camped with his army to the south. He had a fortified path built to provide the troops with grain. The Zhao general Chen Yu, leading a few tens of thousands of soldiers, pitched to the north of Julu.

King Huai of Chu made Song Yi his chief general to rescue the Zhao army at Julu, with Xiang Yu as the second general and Fan Zeng as the third general. They reached Anyang and stayed there for forty-six days without advancing. Xiang Yu got impatient and advised Song Yi, "If we cross the river immediately and attack the Chu army from the outside while the men of Zhao take concerted action from the inside, Qin is bound to be defeated."

To this Song Yi replied, "It is not so. Qin is now attacking Zhao in force. If it gains victory, its troops will be exhausted. Then I can take advantage of its weakness. If it fails to gain victory, I can march west with sounding drums and defeat the men of Qin for certain. Therefore it is better to wait and let Qin and Zhao fight it out first. I am no match to you in the use of weapons, but you are no match to me in devising strategy." With this he issued an order to the troops: "Anyone who is fierce as a tiger, headstrong as a sheep, greedy as a wolf, and therefore disobedient to orders will be beheaded." Then he appointed his son the chief minister of Qi and saw him to Wuyan, where he gave a sumptuous feast.

A chilly rain was falling. For lack of food and clothing, the Chu soldiers shuddered with cold and hunger. At this, Xiang Yu spoke up. "We joined together to attack Qin but have been stuck here for so many days without advancing. The year is barren, the people are poor, and the soldiers have only taro roots to eat. The army has no food, yet the chief general is treating himself to a feast! He will not lead troops across the river so that we may get food from Zhao and join forces with the men of Zhao to attack Qin. Instead, he tells us to 'wait for the enemy to be exhausted and take advantage of its weakness.' Actually, the powerful Qin army is bound to rout the newly founded Zhao and will grow ever stronger after that. And what kind of weakness will we be able to take advantage of? Besides, our last defeat has worried the king so much that he can hardly sit squarely on his seat. Now the king has summoned all the men within the borders and put them under Song Yi's command, thereby entrusting him with the destiny of our nation. But Song Yi only seeks personal gain and shows no consideration toward the soldiers. Such behavior is unworthy of a minister of the state!"

The next morning Xiang Yu paid a routine visit to Song Yi and cut off his head in the tent. Then he went out and announced to the troops: "Song Yi made a plot with Qi against Chu, and the King of Chu secretly ordered me to behead him." The officers all cowered in submission; none dared challenge Xiang Yu's words. They said in unison, "Your family restored the state of Chu. Now you have executed a traitor." They all agreed to elect Xiang Yu as their acting chief general and then sent someone to pursue Song Yi's son and kill him when he arrived in Qi. An envoy was dispatched to inform King

Huai of Chu of what had taken place. The king had no choice but to issue an edict confirming Xiang Yu's appointment as the chief general in command of the Chu army.

Xiang Yu sent two generals with twenty thousand troops to cross the river and rescue Julu. They gained some minor victories, and the Zhao general Chen Yu begged Xiang Yu to intensify his attack. Thereupon Xiang Yu led the entire Chu army across the river. Then he sank all his boats, broke the cooking caldrons, burned up the tents and packed along food rations that could last only three days. In this way he made it clear to his men that they must fight to the death and think nothing about retreat. Then he advanced to attack the Qin forces.

By that time more than ten armies from various states had arrived to rescue Julu. But they all entrenched themselves outside the city and dared not venture out to challenge the army of Qin. They remained behind their ramparts, merely looking on as Xiang Yu launched his attack. The Chu soldiers threw themselves on the enemy with overwhelming intrepidity, and each of them was a match for ten men of Qin. They fought ferociously amid resounding battle cries, striking terror into anyone who heard them. Thus Xiang Yu engaged the Qin army in nine battles, destroying its fortified path of supply and defeating it completely. The Qin general Wang Li was captured alive, and She Jian took his own life.

After he had routed the Qin forces, Xiang Yu summoned the generals of the various states to come to his tent for a meeting. Arriving at the gate, they all knelt down and entered on their knees. They lowered their heads in submission and dared not look up. Henceforth Xiang Yu became the generalissimo of all the forces of various states, whose rulers took orders from him without exception.

Adapted from *Records of the Historian* (Shi Ji), Tome Seven

Strategy Twenty-Nine
Flowers Bloom in the Tree

第二十九计 树上开花　借局布势，力小势大。鸿渐于陆，其羽可用为仪也。

Translation

Exploit external forces to create favorable conditions, so that a small army acquires great energy. The wild goose gradually approaches the cloudy paths. Its feathers can be used in ritual decoration.*

Purport

Attach lifelike silk flowers to a flowerless tree, and any but the most discerning people will think the tree capable of bearing flowers. In warfare, one who lacks strength may resort to external forces (natural conditions,

---

*Jian (Gradual Development), the fifty-third hexagram in I Ching, consists of Xun (wood) above Gen (mountain). Trees grow slowly on the mountain, taking roots deep into the earth. Likewise, gradual development is the correct way to achieve a lasting cause. The judgement for each line of the hexagram describes a wild goose that, leaving the water, sets out to explore its surroundings. In the sixth line, the wild goose soars high into the sky. As the feathers of wild geese can be used in ritual decoration, so a hermit who keeps aloof from the society nevertheless exerts a favorable influence on the people by his exalted morals. In military contexts, mere outward appearance can sometimes produce concrete effects.

allies, or even unwitting enemies) to achieve his strategic goal. At the least, one will be able to intimidate or distract the enemy and delay its attack at one's weak point. At the most, one can turn the external forces into powerful weapons to destroy the enemy, as shown in the story below.

Quotations for Reference

Displaying power to intimidate the enemy is a timeless strategy. Feign advantages that you have not secured, achievements that you have not made, strength that you lack, and maneuvers to mislead the enemy. Flaunt your strength, subdue the spirit of the enemy, and use extraordinary plans to gain victory. This is the practical use of false gestures and a good policy for one in a weak position.

A Hundred War Maxims, "Display"
(Bing Fa Bai Yan, "Zhang")

People are accustomed to what they often see and are startled by what they rarely see. When a fisherman picks the earthworm and a woman shifts the silkworm, neither feels the slightest fear since they have been accustomed to such sights. An unexpected encounter with monsters and demons, however, will strike terror in almost everyone and send one to one's heels.

Essentials of War (Bing Lei),
Chapter Nineteen

Victory in war can be achieved by ingenuity. One who is conversant with a minor skill can launch great causes, and one who is versed in a minor art can attain great achievements. No skill is too lowly and no art too humble; this rings especially true in war.

Carve wood into birds, bind artemisia into human figures, set up fences into a city, and fasten grass into a battle formation: We can thereby perplex the enemy by false shapes.

Direct river courses, tunnel through great mountains, move away small mounds, and transfer bridges: We can thereby ward off harm and tend toward benefit.

Start the gear to move vehicles, lash at the wheels to propel vessels, slit the cloth into suspending drapes, and set the slings on fire before hurling them: We can thereby enhance our capabilities.

Tie up chickens to start fire, lock up pigeons to reconnoiter, train monkeys to surprise the enemy's camp, drive beasts to break out of an encirclement: We can thereby exploit the use of various things.

Splash water to freeze the ground, spread dust to conceal the marshland, build a deceptive bridge to trap the enemy cavalry, and dig gullies to enmesh the enemy troops: We can thereby hurt the enemy by various traps.

Set the enemy's ships on fire, conduct water to flood its city, sling stones to destroy the city wall, toss hooks to seize objects: We can thereby compensate for the inadequacy of our weapons.

Link up oxen to ford across the river, lie prostrate in front of a well to plead for water, accumulate ice into a rampart, and establish stakes to assuage the waves: We can thereby supplement the incapacity of our weapons.

Fire can set off the gear, water can rotate the axle, things can be transformed and moved, and people can appear and vanish: We can thereby fool the enemy and deprive it of judgement.

It follows that the troops can take the form of demons, monsters, gods, and ghosts.

The fox and birds can be made to signal good fortune, ghosts and accidents to forebode catastrophe, divine troops to appear in the day and fiendish hosts to appear at night: We can thereby confound the enemy's eyes and ears, confuse its heart and resolution, and make it flee in panic and lose the esprit to fight with us.

Furthermore, wind can be acquired by sacrifice, rain can be obtained by prayer, and cloud, fog, thunder and lightening can be summoned by conjuration. We can employ a myriad of ruses to ensure our victory.

A Scholar's Dilettante Remarks on War
(Tou Bi Fu Tan), Chapter Ten

Tian Dan Uses "Fire-Bull" Troops to Defeat the Yan Army

The Warring States period (475-221 B.C.), as its designation suggests, was a time of incessant battles among the various rival states. At the beginning, just as in the previous Spring and Autumn era, the interstate warfare was conducted on a limited scale to achieve limited purposes, causing a few walled cities to change allegiance and providing a pretext for one or the other party to launch "punitive campaigns" afterwards. However, as the prestige and power of the ruling house of Zhou continued to dwindle, all-out invasions gradually became the order of the day. The ambitious vassal lords sought not merely the position of "overlord" to command the neighboring states in the name of the King of Zhou, but the actual control of the entire empire. This meant cruel wars of conquest and annexation. Such was the case when Qi took advantage of the internecine strife in Yan to launch a major invasion, which nearly succeeded in a complete conquest.

The King of Yan had only himself to blame for the catastrophe, and he paid for it with his life. He was too gullible a ruler for that treacherous age. He inherited the throne from his father, who, as the legitimate heir of the dukedom of Yan, had usurped the title of king in 332 B.C. He placed complete faith in his chief minister, Zi Zhi, a man of ruthless ambition. Wheedled by Zi Zhi's cohorts, the king was made to believe that he could achieve universal fame by passing his throne to his chief minister after the example of the ancient sage kings.

Soon after the king handed over state affairs to the management of Zi Zhi, Yan was plunged into chaos. It seemed that Zi Zhi's ability to govern was far inferior to his lust for power. His unpopular policies caused widespread complaints among the common people as well as members of the nobility. Finally, a general raised a revolt in an attempt to depose Zi Zhi. The revolt was put down in the end, but tens of thousands of people died in the process, and state resources were vastly depleted.

The King of Qi seized the opportunity to launch a major campaign against Yan. Disgusted with the rule of Zi Zhi, the soldiers of Yan put up no resistance, and city after city surrendered to the Qi army with wide-open gates. The King of Yan was killed, and Zi Zhi was captured. He was then escorted to the state of Qi, where he was cruelly put to death with his body dismembered. Had this happened a few hundred years earlier, the Qi general would have undoubtedly sought out the legitimate heir of Yan and set him up to be the new sovereign. This would then result in a relatively long period of friendly relations between Qi and Yan. But times had changed; propriety was rarely observed, and then only when it contributed to practical interests. So the Qi general simply stationed his troops at the capital of Yan and proceeded to bring the entire state of Yan under his command.

The people of Yan grew indignant. Two years later the son of the former King of Yan established himself as King Zhao of Yan. The people of Yan did not hesitate to turn against Qi and pledge their allegiance to the new king. The Qi general grew fearful and pulled away from Yan. In 311 B.C. King Zhao of Yan returned to his capital.

Like many rulers who had suffered humiliation, King Zhao was determined to take revenge and willing to work hard for it. He curtailed the royal luxuries and professed to share both comforts and hardships with his subjects. Then he ordered an advisor named Guo Huai to seek out persons of wisdom to assist in state management. Guo Huai suggested, "Why not start with me?"

The king was pleased with this suggestion and immediately carried it out. He had a stately mansion built for Guo Huai and afforded him the honor and respect due to a master. By his handsome treatment of Guo Huai, whose talent was no more than average, the king displayed to the world his sincerity in enlisting capable people into his service.

When the news spread out, several men of exceptional abilities arrived from various states to offer their service to the King of Yan. Among them was Yue Yi, one of the best generals in Chinese history. As he was a native of Zhao, the King of Yan intended to treat him as an honored guest. But Yue Yi was willing to serve in the court of Yan, and the king appointed him a minister.

In the meantime the state of Qi grew even more powerful and belligerent and became a constant threat to its neighbors both far and near. This enabled Yan to organize a temporary military alliance with Zhao, Chu, Wei, and Hann. In 284 B.C. Yue Yi led the joint army of the five states and defeated the Qi forces to the west of Ji River. After this victory, the troops of Zhao, Chu, Wei, and Hann withdrew to plunder the areas along the borders they shared with Qi. Bent on revenge, however, the Yan army fought all the way to Linzi, the capital of Qi. The King of Qi sneaked across the border and went to several states to seek refuge, but was refused admission. Finally he returned to Qi and gathered some troops to defend the walled city of Lü.

After capturing Linzi, Yue Yi gathered the treasures and ceremonial vessels of Qi and had them transported back to Yan. Exceedingly pleased, King Zhao of Yan went in person to the Ji River to reward the victorious Yan troops. He conferred on Yue Yi the title Lord Chang-guo and ordered him to stay at Qi and subdue those cities that refused to yield.

In the next five years Yue Yi seized over seventy cities of Qi, which he turned into districts under the rule of Yan. Only two cities still held out: Lü, where the King of Yan was staying, and Jimo under the command of Tian Dan.

Tian Dan had been a minor official in Linzi. At the invasion of Yan, he fled from the capital to the city of Anping. There he told his clansmen to reinforce their chariots by cutting off the protruding ends of the wheel axles and attaching iron baskets to the stumps. Then the Yan army arrived and laid siege to Anping. The city succumbed, and the more affluent residents rode in carriages to flee. On the crowded road, the carriages bumped against one another and many of their axles were broken. The occupants were thereby captured by the men of Yan. But Tian Dan and his kinsmen managed to escape thanks to the iron boxes that protected their chariots. They went east to defend the city of Jimo.

Upon the arrival of the Yan army, the defender of Jimo went out to give battle. But he was defeated and killed. Thereupon the people of Jimo unanimously elected Tian Dan as their commander, saying, "In the battle of Anping, Tian Dan and his kinsmen preserved themselves by fitting iron boxes to the wheel axles of their chariots. He certainly understands warfare."

Aiming to bring Qi to complete, everlasting subjugation, Yue Yi surrounded the two cities of Lü and Jimo but did not assail them vigorously. In the meantime he carried out a conciliatory policy to bring the conquered land of Qi under control.

Then King Zhao of Yan died and King Hui succeeded to the throne. As the crown prince, King Hui used to be at odds with Yue Yi. On hearing of King Hui's ascension, Tian Dan sent men to spread rumors in Yan, declaring, "Yue Yi wants to set himself up as the King of Qi. Therefore he leaves two cities unconquered as a pretext to stay in Qi and carry out his plan. The people of Jimo are afraid that the King of Yan may come to his senses and replace Yue Yi with another general."

On hearing this, King Hui of Yan immediately appointed a general named Qi Jie to take Yue Yi's place. Fearing persecution, Yue Yi did not return to Yan but took refuge in Zhao, his native state. This caused much agitation and discontent among the Yan troops. Qi Jie took command of the Yan army and immediately resumed the assault against Jimo.

One morning, Tian Dan got up and declared to his men, "Last night I dreamed of the Jade Emperor of Heaven. He promised to send a god to teach me strategy." A quick-witted soldier approached Tian Dan and said in a whisper, "May I be that teacher?"

He was running off when Tian Dan grabbed him and exclaimed in great excitement, "You are the god that I saw in my dream!" He then led the soldier to his house and treated him as a divine master. When they were alone, the soldier confessed, "I have cheated you. I know practically nothing about strategy." To this Tian Dan replied, "Keep your mouth shut!"

Henceforth, whatever order Tian Dan issued, he proclaimed it to be the will of the "divine master." He then announced to the people, "The divine master has commanded you to present sacrificial offerings to your ancestors at mealtime in your courtyards. Thus you can obtain the blessing of your forefathers and beat the enemy." The people acted accordingly, and the men of Yan outside the city were dismayed to see swarms of birds gathering over the city twice a day at mealtime. This unordinary phenomenon seemed to confirm the rumor that a god had descended in the city of Jimo to help the people of Qi against Yan.

Though Yue Yi's policy of conciliation failed to achieve the aim of complete subjugation of Qi, it did produce some effect in that the people of Qi did not bear intense hatred against the invaders of Yan. To countervail this unfavorable influence and further boost the morale of his troops, Tian Dan again employed his secret agents to spread rumors among the Yan army, saying, "Yue Yi failed to capture the cities of Jimo and Lü because he was too kindly toward the people of Qi. If the Yan army cut off the nose of each Qi prisoner and then put the prisoners at the front when attacking the city, the Qi soldiers would become afraid and Jimo would succumb of its own accord."

The unwitting Yan general Qi Jie swallowed the bait and acted upon it. But when the people of Qi saw how the prisoners were being treated, they felt more anger than fear and put up a desperate resistance. They preferred fighting to death to being captured.

Then Tian Dan spread another rumor, saying, "The people of Jimo feel secure behind the city wall. The graves of their ancestors, however, are outside the city. They will grow despondent and lose their courage to fight if the men of Yan dig up the graves and destroy the bodies in them."

Again, Qi Jie acted as he was informed. He had his men dig up the graves and set fire to the corpses. Watching the sight from the city wall, the people of Jimo were filled with rage and from that moment bore against the men of Yan an intense hatred that cut into their very bones. They all begged Tian Dan to lead them out of the city to fight.

Thus assured that his men were ready to fight, Tian Dan began to carry out his plan for a major counterblow. First he enrolled his wife and concubines in the ranks of the army and shared all his food and wine with the soldiers. He ordered the fully equipped soldiers to keep out of sight and the old, the weak, and women to take up the defense on the city wall. He collected a thousand *yi* of gold from the city residents and sent several wealthy men to see the Yan general. They presented him with the gold and said, "Jimo is about to yield. Please command your soldiers not to seize our wives and concubines and let us live in peace." Highly pleased, the Yan general accepted the gold and granted their request. The men of Yan were glad to learn that the siege was coming to an end at last.

In the meantime Tian Dan distributed to the troops what food was left in the city so that they could eat a few proper meals before the major action. He then collected all the bulls in the city, which amounted to over a thousand. He covered them with purple silk, painted them in fantastic stripes of various colors, and bound daggers to their horns and oil-soaked straw to their tails. He also had his men make dozens of breaches in the city wall through which the bulls could pass.

At night, the Yan soldiers were roused from their sleep to find a host of strange beasts rushing out of the city toward them. The fiery tails of the beasts cast a ghastly light and revealed them to be dragon-like monsters with colorfully striped hides, sharp, pointed horns and uncontrollable temper. They were followed by five thousand dark, noiseless, stalwart figures with five-color faces, who brandished big swords and axes to cut down the bewildered men of Yan. Meanwhile, there rose from the city a deafening racket that shook heaven and earth. The men of Yan retreated in terror, and after General Qi Jie was killed amid the confusion, the entire Yan army collapsed.

Tian Dan went on to restore other cities occupied by the Yan army. They all revolted against Yan officials to join Tian Dan. Before long the more than seventy cities captured by Yue Yi returned to the rule of Qi. The entire state of Qi was restored and King Xiang of Qi was received to the capital city of Linzi. He rewarded Tian Dan by enfeoffing him as Lord of Anping.

Adapted from *Records of the Historian*
(Shi Ji), Tome Eighty-Two

Strategy Thirty
Reverse the Positions of Host and Guest

第三十计 反客为主　　乘隙插足，扼其主机。渐之进也。

Translation

Take the opportunity to put in your foot and seize the heart of the enemy. Proceed step by step.*

Purport

When a host is so awkward that he does not know how to accommodate a guest, the guest may dictate the necessary proceedings on the host's behalf. Thus the roles of the host and guest are reversed. The expression can also describe a presumptuous person who takes someone else's job into his own hands.

In this strategy, the guest is advised to usurp the host's role. For instance, a warlord attacked by superior enemy forces may be compelled to seek help from his allies. He thereby assumes the role of the host, and the ally who comes to the rescue acts as the guest. Finding the host weak, the guest may secretly subvert the host's authority and seize control of his troops. Having completed this, the

---

*This phrase is taken from the comment of *Jian* (Gradual Development), the fifty-third hexagram in *I Ching* (cf. Strategy Twenty-Nine).

guest becomes the host.

In Chinese military terminology, guest may refer to the party that launches an attack into the territory of its enemy, who consequently assumes the role of the host by taking up the defensive in its own territory. Though the guest holds the initiative of the attacker, he suffers from many disadvantages. He has to transport provisions over great distances, fight on unfamiliar terrain, deal with a hostile populace, and lay siege to well-fortified cities. A skilled attacker can find various ways to overcome these difficulties. For instance, he can raid the enemy's base of provisions to provide for his own troops and befriend the local populace to acquire reliable guides and agents. Blocked by an impregnable stronghold, he can feign weakness and lure the defending army to venture out to attack him at his choicest position. In this way, the attacker who fights in his enemy's territory can nevertheless turn the enemy into the guest and obtain the advantageous position of the host for himself.

Quotation for Reference

Emperor Taizong asked, "In war, we prefer the position of the host to that of the guest and swiftness to duration. Why is it so?"

Li Jing replied, "War is used only under great exigence. That is why we dislike the position of the guest and duration. Sun Zi said, 'Transport over long distances impoverishes the populace.' This is the setback of being the guest. And also, 'Conscription cannot be carried out twice and food cannot be transported more than twice.' This is why we should not fight a protracted war. Sizing up the situation of the host and guest, your servant discovers the method to turn the guest into the host and vice versa."

Taizong asked, "What do you mean?"

Li Jing said, "'Procure food from the enemy' is the method to turn the guest into the host. 'Starve a well-fed enemy and exhaust a well-rested enemy' is the method to turn the host into the guest. Therefore the key point in war lies neither in the position of host or guest nor in swiftness or duration, but in striking at the right place at the right moment."

Li Jing's Reply to Emperor Taizong of Tang (Tang Tai Zong Li Jing Wen Dui), Second Part

Duke of Zheng Captures a Small State Without Fighting

After it was compelled to move east to Luoyang in 770 B.C., the ruling house of the Zhou Dynasty gradually lost its control over the feudal lords. The next three hundred years, called the Spring and Autumn period, unveiled a turbulent drama of usurpation, annexation, treason, murder, as well as of wisdom, courage, and loyalty.

In the first year of King Huan of Zhou (719 B.C.), the Duke of Wei was murdered by his brother Zhou Xu, who thereby usurped the dukedom. Zhou Xu learned that his act was much talked about among the people and sought for a way to stop this. "I want to launch an expedition against a neighbor state to intimidate my subjects," he told Shi Hou, a minister who had conspired in the usurpation. "Which one should we pick for this purpose?"

"The state of Zheng, which invaded us some years ago."

"Qi and Zheng are close allies and will surely join forces against us. How can we cope with them?"

"We can seek alliance with the big states of Song and Lu and the small states of Chen and Cai. With the strength of five states, victory will certainly be ours."

"It will not be difficult to manipulate Chen and Cai in the name of the King of Zhou, but Song and Lu are no easy game. How can we obtain their assistance?"

"Duke Shang of Song has a cousin named Feng, who is the son of the late duke. Now he has taken refuge in Zheng and is trying to secure help from the Duke of Zheng to depose the Duke of Song. Therefore the Duke of Song will be glad to have a chance to attack Zheng and seize his cousin. As for Lu, its duke is a weakling and has no actual control over the army. To get a band of troops from Lu, we need only bribe Lord Hui, the commander of its army."

The plan of Shi Hou worked out smoothly. About thirteen hundred war chariots from the five states assembled at the eastern gate of Zheng. But the Duke of Zheng remained very calm. "Zhou Xu started all this on the pretext of settling a grudge with us. His real aim is not to invade Zheng but to intimidate his own subjects into silence. The lords of Chen and Cai hold no grudge against us and will not fight us wholeheartedly. Lord Hui of Lu has come only because he had accepted handsome bribes. As for the Duke of Song, he just wants to seize Feng, his cousin. I know how to cope with this motley band."

Thereupon the Duke of Zheng had Feng transferred to the city of Changge and sent an envoy to inform the Duke of Song, who accordingly led his troops to attack Changge. After the Song army had left, the men from Cai, Chen, and Lu became dubious of the venture and decided not to actively support Wei. So when a band of Zheng soldiers came out of the city gate, they were only confronted by the Wei army. After a short engagement, the men of Zheng feigned defeat and pulled back into the city. Shi Hou had his soldiers harvest the rice and wheat fields outside the city. Then he issued the order to withdraw.

"Our men are in high spirits after the victory. Why not advance to attack the city?" asked Zhou Xu.

"The Duke of Zheng serves as minister in the court of Zhou, and his army is very strong. We have already made our reputation by defeating the men of Zheng. If we stay away from Wei for too long, internal trouble may arise."

"Right!" Zhou Xu said. So the Wei army returned home, singing songs of victory. How could they predict that Shi Hou's father, a retired minister who remained loyal to the former duke, had a trick in store for them? Both Shi Hou and Zhou Xu were caught and executed, and the younger brother of the former duke was set up as the ruler of Wei.

After Zheng was relieved of the siege from the five states, the duke started to make plans for revenge. He summoned his ministers and said, "The invasion was started by Zhou Xu, who has been executed by the new Duke of Wei. But the main force of the invading army came from Song. I will teach Song a lesson first."

"Formerly, five states joined forces to attack us," observed Ji Zu, the chief minister. "Now if we attack Song, the other four states will become afraid and send troops to rescue Song. So we had better secure the help of Chen and Lu before taking action."

The Duke of Zheng accepted this advice and sent an envoy to seek an alliance with Chen. However, as Zheng was strong and Chen weak, the Marquis of Chen felt suspicious and refused to see the envoy. At this the Duke of Zheng secretly ordered a group of soldiers, disguised as hunters, to march across the border into the territory of Chen on a raid. The Marquis of Chen, startled at the news, was then told that another envoy from Zheng was waiting to see him. The envoy brought a letter from Duke of Zheng, saying that Chen's refusal to receive the last envoy from Zheng had caused some misunderstanding among the frontier officers of Zheng, who then committed the looting without the duke's knowledge. Therefore the duke sent his envoy to apologize and offer to establish a brotherly alliance with Chen. The Marquis of Chen decided to accept the offer.

"Now that Chen is on our side, shall we attack Song?" asked the Duke of Zheng.

Ji Zu replied, "Song is a very big state, and even the King of Zhou treats the Duke of Song with respect. Therefore we have to find a proper excuse for our expedition. I suggest that we go and pay a visit to the King of Zhou. On our way back, we will send envoys to Qi, Lu, and other states, announcing that we have received the order from the king to attack Song."

"Excellent idea!" the duke exclaimed. He set out to pay tribute to the King of Zhou in the eleventh lunar month that year. However, the king never liked the imperious Duke of Zheng very much. He could not help remembering that, just a few years before, a band of Zheng troops had looted the crops from the royal domain of Zhou.

"How is this year's harvest?" the King of Zhou asked the Duke of Zheng.

"By Your Majesty's blessing, there has been neither drought nor flood," replied the duke.

"How fortunate! Then I can keep my rice and wheat for my own use," the king said sarcastically. He did not endow the duke with the usual gift of silk but instead gave him ten carts of grain, saying, "Please accept this just in case of your future need."

Angry and ashamed, the Duke of Zheng regretted that he had come. At this juncture, a minister of the Zhou court called on the duke and presented him with two carts of silk. After the unexpected visitor had gone, the duke asked Ji Zu, "What does this mean?"

"This minister plans to help the king's second son succeed to the throne," Ji Zu replied. "He wants to secure our support when the time comes. But he cannot realize what a great help his gift will be for us. We can distribute the silk cloth among the ten carts of grain and then cover them with brocade. These we will claim to be gifts from the king and evidence of our mandate to punish Song for evading payment of tribute. Thus any state who does not join the expedition will be guilty of disobeying the king's order. Though Song is big and strong, how will it be able to withstand the attack of the king's army?"

Acting upon this plan, the Duke of Zheng made a display of the ten carts of "silk" and sent men to spread the word that the king was angry with Song and had ordered the Duke of Zheng to lead the other lords on a punitive expedition against it. Thus he succeeded in getting three hundred war chariots from Qi and two hundred from Lu. The joint army of the three states marched towards Song, upholding a giant flag embroidered with the words, "Punish the sinner by the order of Heaven." They defeated the Song army on the first engagement and marched into the Song territory.

Startled at the news, the Duke of Song hastily sent for

his minister Kong Jia and asked his advice. "I have sent men to the royal city," replied Kong Jia, "and learned that the king did not issue any order to attack Song; Qi and Lu are being fooled by Zheng. Even so, we cannot withhold such a powerful joint army by force. Now I have a plan that will make Zheng retreat without fighting."

"How can that be achieved?"

"Formerly, Wei, Cai, Chen, and Lu joined us in attacking Zheng. Though Chen and Lu have now become the allies of Zheng, Cai and Wei are still friendly with us. Why not present the Duke of Wei with valuable gifts and ask him to join force with Cai to attack Zheng? The Duke of Zheng will have no choice but to withdraw when his homeland is besieged. If the men of Zheng retreat, how can Qi and Lu stay on?"

The Duke of Song adopted this plan. Thereupon Kong Jia proceeded at night to Wei and presented the Duke of Wei with gifts of gold, jade, and colored silk. In return he obtained a band of Wei soldiers to assist in attacking Zheng.

Kong Jia marched on Zheng along a bypath and suddenly emerged in front of the city of Yingyang, taking the men of Zheng by complete surprise. The Wei troops looted and plundered in the area around the city. The Wei general wanted to attack the city, but Kong Jia stopped him, saying, "A surprise attack can be carried out only once. Now that the Zheng army is ready to fight, it will be very difficult for us to capture the city. When the Duke of Zheng returns, we will be attacked on both sides. So we had better retreat by way of Dai. By the time we have left Zheng, the Duke of Zheng will have lifted his siege of Song."

It was a wise and sensible plan, but to Kong Jia's

surprise and anger, the men of Dai were suspicious and refused to let the Wei army pass through their territory. Kong Jia lost his temper and proceeded to attack Dai, but was not able to overcome the city.

By this time the Duke of Zheng had already seized two cities of Song. On hearing of the invasion of the Wei army, he at once ordered his men to stop the attack and retreat. When questioned by the commanders of the Qi and Lu troops, the duke replied that the loss of two cities was enough punishment for Song. With this he led his troops homeward. On his way, he learned that the Song and Wei troops had left Zheng and turned against Dai instead. "Kong Jia knows nothing about warfare!" he laughed. "Why does he vent his anger against irrelevant people when his own safety is at stake? I know how to handle him now." He divided his troops into four columns and advanced on Dai quietly.

The troops of Song and Wei, joined by reinforcements from Cai, were about to capture the city of Dai. Then they got news that Lord Lü, the supreme commander of Zheng, was coming to relieve Dai. Some time later, it was reported that the Duke of Dai had opened the gate and conducted the Zheng army into the city. At this Kong Jia climbed up the rampart to have a look. He was astonished to see the banners of Zheng unfurling all over the city, accompanied by several cannon shots. Then he saw Lord Lü standing on the city tower and laughing aloud. "I must thank you for helping us take the city of Dai," Lord Lü shouted. "Thanks to you all!"

The whole trick had been contrived by the Duke of Zheng. Disguised, he had hid himself in a war chariot and let Lord Lü lead the army, claiming to come to rescue Dai. Overjoyed, the men of Dai opened the gate and received them into the city. Then the Duke of Zheng ordered the troops to seize control of Dai and drive away its ruler. Inferior in number and tired out in their fight against Wei, the men of Dai panicked and scattered at the attack of the Zheng army. The ruler of Dai fled west to take refuge in Qin. Thus the Duke of Zheng captured Dai at practically no cost.

Enraged, Kong Jia swore aloud, "I shall not live under the same sky with Zheng!" At this juncture he got a letter of challenge from the Duke of Zheng. Kong Jia replied that he was willing to fight it out with Zheng the next day. Then he withdrew the troops for twenty *li* to make camp and rest.

The following day the two armies, arrayed in battle formations, confronted each other. Impatient to take revenge, Kong Jia was the first to order a charge at the enemy. The men of Zheng did not rush forth to meet them but stood their ground and took the defensive. After six such charges were repulsed, the Wei and Song troops had grown tired and much discouraged. Then the Duke of Zheng issued orders for an attack. In the meantime he sent a band of troops to reach the rear of the enemy by a roundabout route. The tired men of Wei and Song, attacked at both the front and rear, were defeated and fled in all directions. The Wei general was killed, while Kong Jia managed to escape on his chariot with a few followers.

The Duke of Zheng returned home and gave a sumptuous feast to his meritorious officers. He had much to celebrate: At small expenses, he had taken two cities from Song, seized the city of Dai, and defeated the joint army of Wei, Song, and Cai. Then he was reminded by one of his generals that two small states had failed to obey his order to attack Song even though the campaign had been proclaimed in the king's name. Therefore the duke began to lay out plans for more "punitive" campaigns.

Adapted from *Record of Events Based on "Zuo's Spring and Autumn Annals"* (Zuo Zhuan Ji Shi Ben Mo), Tome Forty-One

Strategy Thirty-One
Beauty Trap

第三十一计 美人计　兵强者，攻其将；将弱者，伐其情。将弱兵颓，其势自萎。利用御寇，顺相保也。

Translation

If the enemy forces are strong, try to subdue their general; if the general is wise, try to crush his willpower. When the general becomes infirm and the soldiers listless, their combat power will dwindle. It is of benefit to resist an invasion; security can be attained by internal unity.*

Purport

War is a continuation of politics; its result can therefore be affected by political maneuvers outside the battlefield. There are two practices often adopted by military leaders in ancient China: the use of double agents to sow

---

*This phrase is taken from the symbol of the third line of *Jian* (Gradual Development), the fifty-third hexagram in *I Ching* (cf. Strategy Twenty-Nine). The line's judgement observes, "The wild goose gradually approaches the land. The man sets out but does not return. The woman becomes pregnant but does not give birth. Calamity. It is of benefit to resist an invasion." When one does not observe the law of gradual development but plunges headlong into a struggle, calamity will result. Therefore one is advised to maintain one's own position and secure good relations with one's allies and subordinates to fend off invasive attacks.

discord among the enemy troops, and the use of beautiful women to infatuate the sovereign of the enemy state.

The official history of China contains many stories of women whose beauty was so ravishing that they could topple kingdoms. Sent to a hostile state, such a matchless beauty had the task not of collecting military information but of corrupting the sovereign, making him indulge in lascivious pleasures to the neglect of his duties.

Man, yang (firm and strong) in nature, fights with his fists. Woman, yin (weak and yielding) in nature, fights with her smiles and tears. As dripping water wears through rock, so the weak and yielding can subdue the firm and strong. The strategy therefore points to the general principle of employing the weak to subdue the strong, and the beauty trap is just one of its many applications.

Quotations for Reference

Men are staunch and women are soft. Chief commanders in ancient times sometimes made use of the softness of women. Employed in civil affairs, women can mislead and fool the enemy. Employed in military affairs, they can ride chariots to combat and relieve danger and difficulty. They are able to adapt to changing circumstances. Women move in where men are incompetent.

A Hundred War Maxims, "Women"
(Bing Fa Bai Yan, "Nü")

The twelfth method is to cultivate the enemy's faithless courtiers to mislead him, offer beautiful women and lascivious music to infatuate him, present fine dogs and horses to fatigue him, submit flattering reports to blunt him, and seize a favorable opportunity and summon the people under Heaven to overcome him.

Six Strategies (Liu Tao), Tome Two

Yue Exterminates Wu

Yue and Wu, two neighboring states in southeast China, were once vassals of the powerful Chu. They were on friendly terms. In the middle of the Spring and Autumn period, Chu was contending for supremacy with Jin, the great power of the central plain. To undermine Chu's strength, Jin sent men to Wu to train the people there in combat. After that, Wu launched a series of campaigns against Chu. In retaliation, Chu dispatched two of its ablest men, Fan Li and Wen Zhong, to help train Yue troops and make them attack Wu. Thus Wu and Yue were transformed into enemies.

In 506 B.C. He Lü, the King of Wu, launched an all-out expedition against Chu and marched victoriously into its capital. The King of Chu fled to a neighboring state. He Lü intended to subdue the state of Chu completely, but then he received news that the Yue army had invaded Wu. He had to leave the defeated Chu unconquered and rush back to Wu. Upon his return, the Yue army had already withdrawn of their own accord.

In 496 B.C., the old King of Yue died and his son Gou Jian succeeded to the throne. He Lü was by then a churlish old man who kept his mind busy with old grudges. He decided to seize the chance to launch an expedition against Yue. A minister named Wu Zixu objected, saying, "Though Yue has sinned against Wu, it is inexpedient for us to attack a state in mourning. We can bide our time."

But the old king was too intent upon his purpose to listen to even his most trusted courtier. He led thirty thousand troops in person and marched on Yue. Gou Jian put some convicts in front of his army. They approached the men of Wu and said in unison, "We are willing to die to amend for the mistake of our king." With this, each of them drew his sword and cut his own throat. The men of Wu were bewildered at this unusual sight. Just then, Gou Jian led his army to attack and inflicted a grave defeat. He Lü returned to Wu but soon died of a sword injury.

He Lü's son was named Fu Chai. To spur on his determination for revenge, he had ten special guards stand duty at the court. Whenever he passed in front of them, they would shout in one voice, "Fu Chai, have you forgotten how the King of Yue murdered your father?" At this Fu Chai would burst into tears and answer aloud, "No! I dare not forget."

After three years' mourning was over, Fu Chai mustered all the troops in Wu to attack Yue by way of the Tai Lake. At word of the Wu invasion, Gou Jian consulted his ministers on how to meet the enemy.

"For three years Wu has been preparing for this action," Fan Li said. "It is unwise to deal with such a strong and determined enemy directly. We have to hold on to our fortified cities and refuse to engage in battle until the Wu army withdraws for lack of provisions."

The other chief minister, Wen Zhong, was more pessimistic. "In my opinion, we had better sue for peace in humble terms. It will not be late for us to plan revenge after the Wu army has retreated."

Gou Jian dismissed their arguments impatiently. "Wu is our old enemy. If we yield to it without giving a single battle, the lords of other states will hold us in contempt."

287

So he assembled all the able-bodied men in Yue and led them to meet the Wu army. He suffered a severe defeat and retreated into a walled city with five thousand men. The men of Wu soon arrived to encircle and besiege the city. Gou Jian again summoned his ministers to ask their advice. This time, he was more ready to listen.

"Fate is against us," Wen Zhong observed. "But it is not too late to sue for peace even now."

"What if the King of Wu refuses?"

"There is a Wu minister named Bo Pi, who has a weakness for wealth and women. He is also very jealous of the other ministers, especially Wu Zixu. The King of Wu is a little afraid of Wu Zixu but is very fond of Bo Pi. If we win over Bo Pi with gifts of gold, jewelry, and beautiful women, he will certainly help us by talking his king into accepting our terms for peace."

Sure enough, Bo Pi was easily bought over with twenty pairs of jade, a thousand catties of gold, and eight beautiful maidens. He went to see Fu Chai at once, talking in favor of Yue. At first, Fu Chai was uncompromising. "Wu and Yue are old enemies that cannot live under the same sky," he said. "How can we conclude peace with the men of Yue?"

"Do you still remember the favorite remark of Sun Wu? 'War is a lethal instrument that should only be used temporarily.' Yue has committed grave offenses against Wu, but now its king is asking to be a mere subject. He asks only that we allow him to continue to worship his ancestors. If we refuse, he will organize the remnants of the Yue army for a last-ditch resistance, and this will result in heavy losses on the side of Wu. Then he will burn up his treasures and flee to a neighboring state. That would be in no wise beneficial to Wu. But if we accept the

King of Yue's surrender, we will get a vassal state paying substantial tributes and earn a reputation for generosity among the various rulers."

The last argument moved Fu Chai, for he had the ambition to expand his influence into central China and for this purpose wanted to create for himself an image of benevolence as well as strength. He therefore agreed to give Wen Zhong an audience. The latter, on behalf of the King of Yue, pledged complete allegiance to Wu. Fu Chai agreed to withdraw the troops on the condition that Gou Jian and his wife arrive in Wu within three months. Wu Zixu tried to persuade Fu Chai to change his mind about compromising with Yue, but in vain. As he stumbled out, Wu Zixu remarked angrily to another minister, "In twenty years, the palace of Wu will become a stretch of wasteland!"

Gou Jian, his wife, and Fan Li spent the next three years in a stone house by the tomb of He Lü, the late King of Wu, tending horses for Fu Chai. Though they lived a life of misery and humiliation, they looked submissive and content, free of homesickness. Fu Chai was gradually mollified. In spite of Wu Zixu's protests, Fu Chai finally allowed Gou Jian and his wife to return to Yue.

Back in his home country, Gou Jian immediately started planning for revenge. To strengthen his resolve to wipe out the national humiliation, he tasted a bitter gall that he hung in his sitting room several times a day and slept on brushwood at night. He enacted various decrees to enhance the population of Yue. It was forbidden for an able-bodied man to have an old wife or an old man to have a young wife. If a girl was still unmarried at the age of 17 or a boy at 20, their parents would be held responsible and severely punished. When a woman was to give birth, a physician would be sent to look after her at the expense of the local authorities. In a family with three sons, two would be brought up at the expense of the state. The whole populace was exempt from tax for seven years.

Wen Zhong told the King of Yue that, since Wu was much stronger than Yue, they should attempt to undermine its strength by every possible means as well as build up their own. To this purpose he suggested seven methods: First, give Wu money to please its king and ministers; second, import grain from Wu at a high price to deplete its food reserves; third, present the King of Wu with beautiful women to demoralize his daily activities; fourth, send skillful artisans to build palaces in Wu to drain its wealth; fifth, employ the sycophants who served the King of Wu to mess up his policies; sixth, sow dissension between the King of Wu and his capable ministers to debilitate his reign; seventh, accumulate wealth and train soldiers to enable Yue to strike when the opportunity came.

It is hard to say which of the seven methods turned out the most effective, but later historians tend to stress the fulfillment of the third as a warning against the grave danger of beautiful women who can topple kingdoms and dynasties. In folklore and legend, the hapless woman of Yue is regarded as a victim rather than a victimizer. She came from the Shi family in West Village of Mount Zhuluo (to the south of modern Zhuji County in Zhejiang Province); therefore she was called Xi Shi (West Shi). She was discovered by a beauty-hunting team, which comprised a hundred court servants disguised as street performers. At the order of Gou Jian, they had traveled all over the state of Yue on a secret beauty hunt. It took three years to tutor Xi Shi on courtly manners, singing and dancing, the playing of Chinese zither, and various other womanly arts that would enhance her charm and qualify her for her court debut. When she was finally sent to Wu as a gift from the King of Yue, Fu Chai became so enamored of her that he spent days on end with her alone in a temporary palace on a hill near the capital, where Bo Pi the flatterer attended him from time to time but Wu Zixu the carper was seldom granted an audience.

One year, Yue had a poor harvest and its people were on the verge of starvation. Gou Jian sent Wen Zhong to borrow grain from Wu. In spite of Wu Zixu's forceful objection, Fu Chai agreed to loan ten thousand bushels of grain on condition that Yue returned the same amount of grain the next year. Little did he suspect that Wen Zhong had a vicious trick in store.

The next year, Yue enjoyed a bumper harvest. Wen Zhong had ten thousand bushels of the best grain cooked and dried. Then he had them transported to Wu. The King of Wu was pleased that Yue had kept its word and, finding the grain to be of the best quality, ordered it to be used as seed. As a result, Wu suffered a severe famine the following year, and its grain reserves were depleted. Even then, Fu Chai did not realize he had been duped. He could only imagine that the failure was a result of the differences between the climate and soil of Wu and Yue.

While using every opportunity to weaken Wu, Gou Jian also busied himself to build Yue's military strength and make ready for an all-out invasion against Wu. The military training reached such a grand scale as to draw the attention of Fu Chai, who then began to doubt Yue's loyalty. When urged by Zi Gong, a disciple of Confucius, to attack Qi, Fu Chai decided to launch a preemptive strike against Yue. However, he was conciliated when Gou Jian hastily sent three thousand Yue soldiers and some fine weapons to assist Wu in its expedition against Qi, which turned out a success.

Back from his victory, Fu Chai indulged in a three days' orgy with Xi Shi in his temporary palace and then held a regal banquet to feast the generals and ministers who had achieved merits. Wu Zixu, who had advised against the expedition, was the only high official to receive no reward. When Fu Chai teasingly asked if he was ashamed of his worthlessness, Wu Zixu did not hesitate to give an acrid reply. "When the downfall of a kingdom is determined in Heaven," he said, "it will have some small luck before receiving the deadly blow. The victory over Qi is just such a piece of small luck, and I fear that the deadly blow will soon come."

The outraged Fu Chai drove Wu Zixu out of the court. A few more words from the jealous Bo Pi incited the king to send Wu Zixu a sword, a polite but unmistakable gesture by which a sovereign announced the death penalty of a high-ranking official. Before cutting his throat with the sword, Wu Zixu ran out of his house and exclaimed, "Heaven! O Heaven! It is I who helped you succeed your father as the King of Wu, and it is I who helped you defeat Qi and enjoy high prestige among the neighboring states. Now, after lending a deaf ear to my words for so long, you endow me with death! Well, today I die, and tomorrow the Yue army will arrive and destroy your kingdom!"

Like every ruler of a strong state at the time, Fu Chai aspired to become the overlord of all China. He arranged a meeting of various lords at Huangchi (near modern Fengqiu County, Henan Province) and for this purpose had a grand canal constructed leading northward to the central plain. In 482 B.C. he led the crack troops of Wu to Huangchi to vie with the Duke of Jin for predominance.

At the meeting, both Wu and Jin cited their relation to the royal house of Zhou as well as military exploits to prove their legitimacy as the leader of all lords. Many days passed, but no agreement was achieved. At last a messenger arrived from Wu with the news of Yue's invasion. As Fu Chai had taken the best Wu soldiers with him, only the old and weak remained to defend the Wu capital. They were overwhelmed by the Yue army and the crown prince was captured alive.

On hearing this, Bo Pi drew his sword and killed the messenger on the spot. "We have to prevent the word from spreading among our soldiers," he told the astonished Fu Chai. "If the lords of Jin and Qi heard about this, they will seize the chance to intimidate us."

"What shall we do?" Fu Chai asked. "Quit the meeting at once or let Jin preside over the ceremony for the moment?"

"We can beat drums and challenge Jin to settle the dispute by battle," another minister suggested.

At the meeting place, the Wu army outmatched the Jin army in both number and strength. Therefore Fu Chai acted upon the advice and was able to obtain the Duke of Jin's oath to recognize Wu as his superior. As soon as the ceremony was concluded, Fu Chai headed home in great haste. However, news of Yue's successful invasion had already spread among the Wu soldiers, and they grew sad and frightful. Such a despondent and tired army proved no match for the Yue soldiers riding the tide of victory. After losing a battle, Fu Chai dispatched Bo Pi to sue for peace. "You told me that Yue would never revolt, so I allowed Gou Jian to return home. Now if you fail to talk him into retreat, I will have a fine sword waiting for you!"

Gou Jian did withdraw his troops, for he knew that a complete subjugation of Wu was still beyond his power. From then on, however, Yue continued to grow in strength, whereas Wu declined steadily. Four years later, Gou Jian attacked Wu in full force and seized its capital.

Fu Chai begged Gou Jian to accept Wu as a vassal state rather than annex it. But Gou Jian responded by offering to exile him to an island with a hundred households to support his family. Finding the humiliation impossible to swallow, Fu Chai wept bitterly and, shouting out his remorse for his unfair treatment of Wu Zixu, cut his throat.

Thus the state of Yue emerged as a formidable power in the southeast, having gained equal footing with Jin and Qi. Fan Li did not stay in the court but absconded. He left a letter to Wen Zhong, saying, "After all the birds are shot down, the good bow will be tucked away; after the rabbit is caught, the hunting dog will be cooked by his master. The King of Yue is the kind of man with whom one can share misfortunes but not success. Why not leave him?"

Wen Zhong failed to adopt this advice. He only declined to attend the king's audience, pleading illness. A jealous courtier informed Gou Jian that Wen Zhong was plotting revolt. Thereupon the King of Yue endowed Wen Zhong with a sword, saying, "You taught me seven methods, and by using three of them I have destroyed Wu. You may recommend the other four to our late king." Thus Wen Zhong came to the same end as Wu Zixu.

Adapted from *Record of Events Based on "Zuo's Spring and Autumn Annals"* (Zuo Zhuan Ji Shi Ben Mo), Tome Fifty-One

Strategy Thirty-Two
Empty-City Scheme

第三十二计 空城计　　虚者虚之，疑中生疑。刚柔之际，奇而复奇。

Translation

Bear a weak appearance when in a weak position to create doubts in the already doubtful enemy. Used by the weak against the strong, it works wonders of the most wondrous kind.

Purport

Deception in warfare is aimed to present the enemy with a false impression of one's strength and intention. The normal practice is to feign weakness when strong and feign strength when weak. But such deception has become so commonplace that even a commander with average talents will not take the appearance of his opponent at face value. This results in the unordinary plan of deception by displaying one's true strength and weakness. Deception is achieved if the enemy takes what it observes for false appearance.

The empty-city scheme is a risky plan, adopted only in a desperate situation to intimidate the enemy by revealing one's weakness. The strategy is usually employed when a poorly defended city is suddenly enveloped by superior enemy forces. The city defender realizes that by putting up resistance he cannot hold out until reinforcements arrive. An attempt to escape would only result in total annihilation by the pursuing enemy. Of course he can have many banners erected over the city wall and battle drums beaten aloud, but to a crafty enemy such pretense of power is exactly a sign of weakness. So he finally decides to adopt the empty-city scheme. He withdraws the soldiers from the city wall, opens the city gate, and orders the people to make no noise. Suspecting a trap, the enemy dare not advance to attack at once. Ideally, it may even be scared into escape. Because of the danger involved, the scheme is used only in emergencies when one can find no other way to defend oneself and, preferably, when the enemy general is known to be overcautious.

Quotation for Reference

In a battle against the enemy, if our position is weak, display a powerful appearance so that the enemy cannot decide where our strength lies and dare not engage us lightly. Thus we are able to preserve our troops. The principle goes, "The enemy fails to engage you because you have misled it toward somewhere else."

A Hundred Marvelous Battle Plans, "Battle of Weakness" (Bai Zhan Qi Fa, "Xu Zhan")

Li Guang, the "Flying General" of Han

Li Guang, born in Chengji of Longxi, was descended from Li Xin, the famous general who served the First

Emperor of Qin. Superb archery skills were passed down for generations in the Li family, with Li Guang emerging as the best archer in China's history.

On one occasion, Li Guang went out hunting and saw a tiger crouched in the tall grass. He took his powerful bow and discharged his arrow, which hit the target squarely and cut right into it so that the entire arrowhead was buried. On a closer look, the "tiger" turned out to be a huge boulder in the shape of a tiger. Li Guang then tried several more shots but could not make his arrow pierce the rock again.

At that time the young empire of Han was suffering from incessant harassment of the nomadic Xiongnu people along the northern frontier. The teenaged Li Guang joined the army and took part in many battles against the Xiongnu invaders. He won merits as a superb archer and was promoted to be a mounted attendant of Emperor Wendi. He often accompanied the emperor on his trips across the country. His outstanding ability in fighting battles as well as in grappling with wild beasts prompted the emperor to sigh deeply, observing, "What a pity you live in an inopportune time! If you had lived in Emperor Gaozu's reign, you would have easily gained the title of Marquis with a fief of ten thousand households!"

In 154 B.C. the rebellion of seven princes broke out. Li Guang joined the pacifying expedition and won distinction by charging into the enemy's formation and seizing its commander's banner. But he received no reward on his return, because he had accepted an appointment as a general from Prince Liang without the emperor's approval. So he was made governor of Shanggu Commandery, which bordered on the Xiongnu territory. He took every chance to lead the troops in person to fight the Xiongnu, and his reputation for valor and surpassing combat skills spread far and wide along the border.

An official named Gongsun Kunxie was worried over Li Guang's safety and went to plead with the emperor, saying, "Li Guang has matchless abilities and courage, but he tends to overexert himself and loses no chance of engaging the Xiongnu in close combat. I am afraid we may lose him someday!" Thereupon Emperor Jingdi transferred Li Guang to Shang Commandery, which lay closer to the capital city of Chang'an but still bordered on the land of the Xiongnu. Subsequently Li Guang held posts in various frontier regions, and wherever he went he won distinction for his vigorous fighting.

Li Guang was kind and generous to his men. He had enjoyed an emolument of two thousand bushels of grain for forty years but had accumulated no personal property. He shared whatever rewards he received with his troops. If the army was short of water or food, Li Guang would not drink until all of his men had drunk or eat until they had eaten. Therefore they served him wholeheartedly and would risk their lives to carry out his orders.

However, Li Guang never had a chance to gain a major victory and be honored with a noble title. There were men less talented than he who enjoyed much higher positions, and even some of his subordinates became enfeoffed as marquises. He once consulted an astrologer, asking why he was so unfortunate. "Is my visage unsuitable for a marquis?"

The astrologer asked, "Have you ever done anything you regret?"

"When I was governor of Longxi, the Qiang people raised a revolt. I tricked eight hundred of them into surrender, but I broke my promise and had them executed the same day. This is the one thing I regret the most."

"Nothing can be worse than killing the surrendered. This is why you have never become a marquis," announced the astrologer.

Once, the Xiongnu horsemen pushed into Shang Commandery in a major offensive. Emperor Jingdi ordered Li Guang to organize a counterattack and sent a favored eunuch to accompany him. After the troops had made camp, the eunuch went for a ride with several dozen attendants. On seeing three Xiongnu soldiers, they charged forth to capture them. The Xiongnu soldiers turned, drew their bows and finished off most of the eunuch's attendants in a matter of minutes. The eunuch himself was wounded but, thanks to his fine horse, managed to flee back to the camp.

On hearing the report, Li Guang remarked, "They must be eagle shooters." He summoned a hundred cavalrymen and rode out with them in pursuit.

The three Xiongnu soldiers had lost their horses and had gone on foot for a few dozen *li* when Li Guang and his men caught up with them. Li Guang ordered his men to close in from the left and right while he used his powerful bow to shoot the enemy. He killed two and captured the third alive. On interrogation, the Xiongnu soldier confessed that he and his companions were indeed eagle shooters, the best Xiongnu archers.

They bound the Xiongnu archer on a horse and were about to head back to the camp, when several thousand Xiongnu horsemen suddenly came into sight. The Xiongnu were startled to see a small band of Han army and suspected it to be a trap. In great haste they mounted a nearby hill and arrayed themselves in a defensive formation.

Li Guang's men were struck with terror and wanted to flee at top speed. But Li Guang observed calmly, "We are now a few dozen *li* from our main force. If the hundred of us attempt to flee, the Xiongnu will make a hot pursuit and shoot down all of us quickly. But if we stay here, they will take us for a scouting band sent by our main force that is close behind. Thus they will not dare advance to attack us."

Li Guang and his men rode casually toward the enemy and halted when they were only two *li* from its formation. Then he ordered his men to dismount and remove the saddles. Again they exclaimed in dismay, "The enemy forces are so numerous and near. What shall we do if they attack us?"

Li Guang replied, "The Xiongnu expect us to move away. Now that we have unsaddled our horses to make clear we will stop here, they will be convinced that we are playing a trick."

The Xiongnu dared not advance, but an officer on a white steed rode forth to reconnoiter. Li Guang jumped onto his horse and led a dozen of his men to meet the officer, shooting him dead on the spot. Then he returned, dismounted and ordered his men to lie down and rest. By this time it was growing dark. The Xiongnu remained apprehensive and dared take no move. They grew more and more fearful, suspecting that the Han army must be plotting a surprise night attack. So they pulled away at midnight.

At dawn the next day Li Guang got up and led his hundred cavalrymen back to the camp of the Han army, which had not come to his rescue because no one knew where he had gone.

Altogether, Li Guang fought more than seventy battles against the Xiongnu. He did not die on the battlefield but at his own sword. In the fourth year of the Yuanshou reign (119 B.C.), General-in-Chief Wei Qing led a northward expedition. By this time Li Guang was over sixty. After repeated entreaties to the emperor, he at last got appointed as the vanguard commander.

However, as Li Guang was old and his luck always bad, the emperor secretly ordered Wei Qing not to allow him to fight the Xiongnu chieftain. As soon as they crossed the frontier, Wei Qing learned the whereabouts of the Xiongnu chieftain. He decided to lead the crack army in person to attack but sent Li Guang to take a circuitous road. After pleading in vain, Li Guang took leave in great indignation. Having no guide, he and his men lost their way and did not arrive at the destination on time.

Wei Qing sent men to summon Li Guang to the headquarters to stand trial. At this Li Guang announced to his officers, "I am too old to face the questions of those clerks." He then drew his sword and cut his throat.

Adapted from *Records of the Historian*
(Shi Ji), Tome One Hundred and Nine

Strategy Thirty-Three
Turn the Enemy's Agents Against Him

第三十三计 反间计　　疑中之疑。比之自内，不自失也。

Translation

Lead the enemy into his own trap. Union from within; one will not lose oneself.*

Purport

On detecting a secret enemy agent, one can arrest him and try to win him over with handsome bribes, thereby obtaining information of the enemy forces. Or, as this strategy advocates, one may feign ignorance, expose the agent to false information, and allow him to return and

*This is the symbol of the yin line at the second place of *Bi* (Union), the eighth hexagram in *I Ching*. The upper trigram is *Kan* (water), and the lower is *Kun* (earth). The earth supports water on its surface and water flows on the earth into rivers and oceans. Thus the symbol of the hexagram observes, "Water over the earth symbolizes *Bi*. The ancient kings established numerous states and cultivated relationship with feudal lords." The yin line at the second place, which receives complemental support as well as instructions from the yang line in the fifth place, represents one who abides consistently by the orders of the strong, generous ruler. Quoted in the text of the strategy, the symbol of this line signifies that one has secured the honest service of a person within the enemy camp.

report to the enemy commmander. Taking the false information for facts, the enemy will make wrong judgement and therefore commit strategic errors in its battle plans. The strategy points to the general principle of feigning ignorance when informed. Knowledge is a vital component of military strength, and one should generally hide one's strength until the moment to take decisive action. On learning of the enemy's secret maneuvers, one had better feign ignorance and at the same time carry out countermeasures in secret.

Quotation for Reference

Uncover the enemy agents who have come to spy on you. Tempt them with bribes, give them instructions, and accommodate them well so that they can be won over and employed as double agents.

Wang Xi's Note: "Retain enemy agents and ask them for information. They should be accommodated properly, persuaded with involved arguments, afforded ample appreciation, and then tempted with handsome bribes or intimidated with severe punishment. You will then be able to employ all except those most faithful to their sovereign.

Du Mu's Note: "Find out promptly the enemy agents sent to spy on you. Either tempt them with handsome bribes and enlist them in your service, or feign ignorance and expose them to false information before releasing them. Thus the enemy agents can be employed to your advantage.

Art of War (Sun Zi Bing Fa),
Chapter Thirteen

The Story of General Han Shizhong

Han Shizhong (1089-1151), a native of Yan'an in Shaanxi, was born of a poor family in the late Northern Song Dynasty. He joined the army at the age of seventeen and soon distinguished himself in a battle against Xia by charging alone into the enemy forces and cutting down several officers.

In 1122 the Emperor of Liao, who had just ascended the throne, suddenly died of illness. Contests over succession broke out, plunging the Liao court into disorder. The Song considered it a good chance to recover Yanjing (modern Beijing) and sent a force of two hundred thousand on a northern expedition. The Jin, the empire of the semi-nomadic Nuzhen people, also launched an attack against Liao, gaining many victories. But the commander of the Song expedition was still afraid of the enfeebled Liao, and poor coordination caused his vanguard to collapse at the first engagement.

At this juncture Han Shizhong, who had joined the expedition as a low-ranking officer, volunteered to lead a shock force of fifty cavalrymen to march on Yanjing. After crossing the Hutuo River, they suddenly ran into two thousand Jin troops. Han Shizhong quickly surveyed the surrounding field and ordered his men to climb up a nearby hill. When the men of Jin approached to attack, he broke into their ranks all by himself and killed two standard-bears. Thereupon his fifty cavalrymen galloped down the hill, cut down many enemy soldiers and sent the rest of them flying. Soon after, Han Shizhong was promoted to be a general with the power to lead his own army to carry out independent tasks.

The Northern Song was on the decline. As the imperial court was losing effective control over the beleaguered empire, it grew increasingly arbitrary, eager to use what power it retained at every opportunity. In 1125 a Song general was executed for having lost a battle against Jin. Indignant and fearful of persecution, his officers and men raised a revolt under Li Fu, who was able to muster a force of several tens of thousands in a few days. The bewildered Song court assigned the task of subjugating the rebels to Han Shizhong, who at that time commanded fewer than a thousand men. As usual, Han Shizhong undertook the task with courage and intrepidity. He announced to the troops, "Advance, and we will win. Retreat, and we will die. Anyone who falls back against orders will be cut down on the spot!" Thus they engaged the superior rebel forces in battle and routed them, killing Li Fu.

Trailing the rebels, they approached Suqian at dusk. There scouts reported that the retreating rebels had joined forces with about ten thousand rebel soldiers and had made camp outside the city. Han Shizhong ordered his men to come along the next morning and then rode into the rebels' camp all alone. "The great Song army is come!" he shouted. "Resist and you shall meet certain death with no burial ground! But if you take off your armor and bundle up the weapons, I promise to spare you all!" The rebels, who did not expect the Song army to arrive so quickly, were enjoying themselves with wine and women. They were so scared at the abrupt appearance of Han Shizhong that they got down on their knees in submission. An officer poured a cup of wine and with shaking hands offered it to Han Shizhong. "Please accept our respects," he said. "We will follow your orders."

Han Shizhong dismounted, unsaddled his horse, and

sat down at the table to enjoy heartily the wine and beef. All the rebels surrendered to him and, at his order, took off their armor and tied their weapons in bundles. Their astonishment was beyond measure when they discovered the next morning that Han Shizhong had only a few hundred men. But it was too late for them to regret, for they had already been disarmed.

By that time the military power of the Jin had reached its peak. It destroyed the Liao in 1125. The next year it took Bianliang and captured the ruling Song Emperor, putting an end to the Northern Song Dynasty. In 1127 the Southern Song was set up under Emperor Gaozong, who set out to restore centralized control over south China. He proved capable at this task, and the Southern Song prospered under his rule. However, to the indignation and disillusionment of many people both in and out of the imperial court, he showed no interest in recovering the central plains and always maintained a defensive posture toward the sporadic incursions of the Jin. The frequent reverses of the Song army on the battlefield convinced him that war against the Jin was a losing game. He rejoiced at occasional victories of the Song army, but he did not want the military leaders to consolidate their fame and power by exploiting these victories. When appointing officials, he placed ability above moral character, so that quite a few people who had cooperated with the Nuzhen held high positions in the court. Some of them maintained clandestine connections with the Jin.

In the tenth month of 1134, the Jin prince Wuzhu launched a major southward incursion. As a Song governor fled south without fighting, the men of Jin marched across the Huai River valley encountering little resistance and quickly pushed to the Yangtze River. Han Shizhong, then a pacification commissioner of the Huai River area, was compelled to abandon his position and fell back to defend the city of Yangzhou by the Yangtze River.

Just as Han Shizhong was busily organizing the troops into a defensive position, the Song court solicitously sent two envoys, Wei Liangchen and Wang Hui, to sue for peace with the Jin army. They set out with a few followers and reached Yangzhou at the end of the month.

Now a seasoned general, Han Shizhong had no illusions about such peace negotiations. He knew all too well that a peace offer would lead nowhere unless it was accompanied by effective resistance on the battleground. He did not trust Wei Liangchen, Vice Minister of Personnel, who had a reputation of getting along well with the men of Jin. Therefore, when he was informed that the imperial envoys were coming, he secretly arranged for a few trusted guards to put the envoys under surveillance. In the meantime he laid out a plan to make use of Wei Liangchen's disloyalty.

On reaching the eastern gate of Yangzhou, Wei Liangchen saw the vanguard of the Song army leaving the city. He inquired where they were heading and learned that they were dispatched by Han Shizhong to defend the passage at the river mouth. Upon entering Yangzhou, Wei was received by Han Shizhong at the observation tower of the city. A short while later, board after board of imperial edicts turned up. Han Shizhong deliberately let Wei look at the boards, which ordered Han to withdraw the army to defend the river mouth.

Wei Liangchen, Wang Hui, and their attendants left Yangzhou and spent the night at the town of Dayi. The next morning, after riding for a few *li*, they ran into over a hundred mounted archers of Jin. Wei Liangchen ordered his men to dismount and then shouted, "Don't shoot! We have come to make peace!" The Jin soldiers then escorted Wei and his followers to the city of Tianchang.

"Where is the emperor?" asked the Jin soldiers.

"At Hangzhou," replied Wei.

"Where is General Han? How many men and horses does he have?"

"He was at Yangzhou. When we took leave he was heading for Zhenjiang," replied Wang Hui.

"Maybe he is playing a trick and will return to attack?"

"Who knows?" Wang Hui said defensively. "We are not supposed to know anything about warfare."

They met a Jin general on the way and entered Tianchang together. After exchanging a few words about peacemaking, the Jin general asked, "Where is General Han's army?"

"Before I left, I saw them go out through the eastern gate and head for Guazhou."

After Wei and his followers had taken leave of Dayi, Han Shizhong mounted his horse and summoned the troops. "Advance in the direction of my whip!" he ordered. They proceeded to Dayi, which lay between Yangzhou and Tianchang, and dispersed into five battle formations comprising more than twenty ambush rings. Han admonished the officers and men, "Rise and beat the enemy when you hear the drums!"

The Jin general took Wei Liangchen at his word and sent him off to meet Prince Wuzhu, commander of the Jin expedition. Then he led his men toward Yangzhou, which he believed to be poorly guarded. His officer Tuobujia led a band of cavalrymen and marched by way of

Dayi, where he was challenged by a small band of Song army led by Han Shizhong himself. Tuobujia repulsed the unexpected attack and pushed forth with his superior force right into the ambush rings of the Song army. At the sounding of battle drums, the Song soldiers suddenly rose out of hiding in every direction and cut the Jin troops into small sections.

In the tangled fight that ensued, the Jin horsemen found little use for their bows, arrows, and long swords. They became easy prey to the Song infantrymen, who wielded big axes to break first the horse legs and then the ribs of the fallen Jin horsemen. The band of Jin cavalry was completely wiped out, and Tuobujia was captured alive.

The Jin general returned to Tianchang, swearing fiercely against Wei Liangchen. He sent a report of his defeat to Wuzhu, who immediately locked up Wei Liangchen and his attendants.

Adapted from *Sequel to History as a Mirror*
(Xu Zi Zhi Tong Jian), Tome One
Hundred and Fourteen

Strategy Thirty-Four
Self-Torture Scheme

第三十四计 苦肉计　　人不自害，受害必真；假真真假，间以得行。童蒙之吉，顺以巽也。

Translation

Man does not inflict injury on himself, and a person's injury proves him a victim. Espionage can be conducted when the enemy takes a false injury to be genuine. The callow youth submits. Good fortune.*

Purport

To enable an agent to gain the trust of the enemy, one can punish him severely in public, throw him into prison and then secretly allow him to escape to the enemy camp. Thus the agent can gain the confidence of the enemy and bring about its downfall by various means, ranging from the supply of false information to the assassination of the enemy commander. In a broader sense, the strategy points

---

*This is the symbol of the yin line in the fifth place of *Meng* (Immaturity), the fourth hexagram in *I Ching* (cf. Strategy Fourteen). This line, holding the position of leadership, which is the middle place in the upper trigram, gains support from the yang line above as well as coordination from the yang line in the second place. Thus a young and inexperienced ruler who deals with the others in an ingenous, modest way will receive ample support in return and therefore achieve good fortune. In this strategy, however, the line is compared to an enemy general who is gullible because of his naive, simplistic judgement.

to the method of deception by self-inflicted loss. For instance, in the primeval Zhou Dynasty there was a ruler who planned to invade a neighboring state. First he executed a courtier who was a warm advocator of the invasion. As a result, the neighboring state lost its vigilance. Thereupon the ruler launched a surprise attack and destroyed the neighboring state at a single stroke. There are also instances in which a commander first sent a high-ranking official to negotiate with the enemy, making it feel secure. Then he launched a surprise attack to gain a major victory.

King of Wu Employs an Assassin to Get Rid of His Rival

The state of Wu covered the lower reaches of the Yangtze River. It bordered on Chu to the west, Yue to the south, and the sea to the east. The King of Wu had four sons. The throne was passed to his eldest son, Zhu Fan, then the second son, Yu Ji, then the third son, Yu Mei. When Yu Mei died of illness, it was the turn of the fourth son, Ji Zha, to ascend the throne. But Ji Zha declined. Thereupon Liao, the son of Yu Mei, took the throne for himself. He Lü, the son of Zhu Fan, was indignant but dared say nothing because Liao had powerful connections in the court and a very strong and brave son, Qing Ji.

He Lü worked in secret to enlist capable people into his service. Wu Zixu, a man of Chu, came to join him and became his chief advisor. It was Wu Zixu who planned for Zhuan Zhu, a very brave warrior, to assassinate Liao. Hiding his dagger in a fish, Zhuan Zhu killed Liao at a feast and was immediately killed himself by Liao's bodyguards. Then He Lü led his men into the palace and set himself up as the King of Wu.

After his ascension to the throne, He Lü never ceased to worry about Qing Ji. He said to Wu Zixu, "I am greatly indebted to you on the matter of Zhuan Zhu. Now I feel anxious that Qing Ji is plotting with the other lords against me. When eating, I can hardly tell the taste of my food; when resting, I can hardly keep still on the mattress. I entrust this matter to you."

"I know what my lord has in mind," Wu Zixu replied. "I have been looking for a man to run the errand, and I have found one at last."

"But Qing Ji is strong enough to wrestle with ten thousand men. How can the man you found be his rival?" He Lü asked.

"This brave man is named Yao Li," replied Wu Zixu. "I happened to see him humiliate another brave man named Shu Qiuxin."

"Tell me about it," said He Lü. So Wu Zixu recounted the tale of Yao Li.

Shu Qiuxin came from the eastern sea. Once, he was sent by the King of Qi as a messenger to Wu. On passing the Huai River, he intended to let his horse drink water at the ford, but was stopped by a local official. "Do not let your horse approach the water," the local warned. "There is a river god here who will come to eat the horse."

"I am a brave man," Shu Qiuxin announced. "What god dare provoke me?" With this he let his horse drink water from the river. All of a sudden, a monster emerged from the river, snatched the horse, and instantly vanished. Thereupon Shu Qiuxin flew into a rage. He undressed, took his sword, and jumped into the river to pursue the monster. He fought in water for three days on end but failed to recover his horse. When he finally got out, he had been blinded in his left eye.

Upon his arrival in Wu, he learned that a friend of his had just died. So he went to attend his friend's funeral. At the banquet after the funeral, he assumed an insolent air, bragging of his exploits in fighting with the river god for three days. People who shared the table with him were annoyed. Yao Li, who was sitting opposite Shu Qiuxin, spoke up to snub him, saying, "Now, this is what I have heard about a brave man: When fighting the sun, he stops the sundial from moving. When fighting gods and ghosts, he never turns his heels. When fighting men, he does not utter a single cry. He would rather die in the fighting than suffer humilation from his opponent. In fighting the river god, you failed to recover your horse and lost your left eye. But instead of fighting to death, you returned alive. What makes you, with your handicapped body, believe you have made a great fame and thereby come to boast at us?"

At these words Shu Qiuxin was struck speechless with shame and anger. On returning home, Yao Li said to his wife, "Today at the banquet I humilated a brave man named Shu Qiuxin. He is very angry with me and will surely come tonight. Do not lock the door."

When he arrived at Yao Li's house that night, Shu Qiuxin found the door wide open. He slipped quietly into the house, walked up the hall, and, entering Yao Li's room, found him lying motionless in bed. He grabbed Yao Li and pointed his sword at him. "You deserve to die for committing three wrongs," Shu Qiuxin said. "Do you understand?"

"No," Yao Li replied calmly.

"You humilated me in public and should die for it. On returning home you did not lock the door and should die for it. You lay motionless in bed when I approached and should die for it."

To this Yao Li replied, "I have done nothing to deserve death. But you have done three things that are shameful. Do you understand?"

"No," Shu Qiuxin said.

"First, I humiliated you in front of many people and you dared not retaliate on the spot. Second, you entered the door without coughing and ascended the hallway without noise. Who but thieves act in this way? Third, you have come to abuse me, but you dared not speak up until you had drawn your sword and grabbed my neck. You have done such shameful things, and yet you mean to overwhelm me with your bravery!"

On hearing this, Shu Qiuxin dropped his sword and sighed, "I always took pride in my bravery, and no one challenged me. But now I know Yao Li must be a matchless brave man under heaven."

Impressed, He Lü ordered a banquet to be prepared and told Wu Zixu to bring Yao Li. When Yao Li was brought to his presence, He Lü was surprised to see a gaunt man. He asked doubtfully, "What can you do?"

"I come from the remote east," replied Yao Li. "I am so lean and weak that, when a gust blows toward me, I will fall down on my back. If the wind comes from behind, I will then fall down on my stomach. But just give the order, my lord, and I will carry it out with all my ability."

He Lü thought he had been duped by Wu Zixu. He sulked and did not speak for several minutes. Then Yao Li approached him and said, "Are you worrying about Qing Ji? I can dispatch him."

"But Qing Ji is famous for his bravery," said He Lü.

"He runs so fast that he can catch beasts on foot, and he jumps so high that he can catch birds in the sky. Once, I pursued him with a four-horse chariot and could not catch up with him. When I ordered my men to shoot arrows, he snatched them from the air with his bare hands. You are no match for him."

"I can dispatch him, if that is what you want." insisted Yao Li.

"I cannot see how that is possible," He Lü said. "As an exile, Jingji is very alert and cautious. A person from Wu is the last one he will trust. So you have little chance to get close to him."

To this Yao Li replied, "He will trust me if you have my wife and children executed and my right arm cut off."

The next day, a rumor swiftly spread in the Wu capital, enumerating He Lü's crimes as a despot. He Lü sent men to seek out the rumormonger. Two days later, Yao Li was captured and brought to He Lü, who immediately called an audience to interrogate him. Yao Li not only admitted to having started the rumor but vigorously berated He Lü at the court. The courtiers all thought that Yao Li must be a madman. Wu Zixu suggested to He Lü, "Such a maniac should be beheaded!"

"No," He Lü said. "This man has barely enough strength to bind a chicken, yet he dare challenge us at court. He must have other, more powerful conspirators and may even have connection with Qing Ji. I want to get more information out of him." He ordered the guards to cut off Yao Li's right arm. He also sent men to arrest Yao Li's wife and children and throw them into prison.

A few days later, Yao Li escaped from prison. Thereupon He Lü had Yao Li's wife and children beheaded and their bodies burned up in public. This created a furor in the Wu capital. Many people thought the King of Wu was too cruel to Yao Li.

After breaking prison, Yao Li proceeded to Wei. On his way, he told everyone he met how he had been treated by He Lü. He reached Wei and called on Qing Ji, who did not believe him at first. Later, people from Wu confirmed Yao Li's story, and Qing Ji came to trust him and consulted him on matters about Wu.

Yao Li advised Qing Ji to attack Wu, saying, "He Lü usurped the throne by murdering your father. The courtiers of Wu feel indignant though they dare not show it. Even the common people are dissatisfied. I only spoke a few words against He Lü, and he killed my wife and children and cut off my arm. If you summon your followers and march on Wu, I will be your guide. By seizing the Wu capital and deposing that despot, you will avenge your father and I will avenge my wife and children."

"But I have heard that Wu Zixu is a very capable man. With him as the chief minister, He Lü has built a strong army and accumulated plentiful resources. I fear that we are not strong enough to challenge him now."

To this Yao Li replied, "Wu Zixu went to Wu after the King of Chu killed his father and brother. He is now much dissatisfied with He Lü, who refrains from taking action against Chu. Therefore he will not help defend Wu wholeheartedly."

Qing Ji was at last convinced and started to prepare for an expedition. Three months later they set out to attack Wu. When crossing the Yangtze River, Qing Ji and Yao Li shared the same boat. As Yao Li was weak in strength, he sat windward and stabbed Qing Ji with a spear, penetrating his chest. Qing Ji turned, grabbed Yao Li and dunked him in water three times until Yao Li became unconscious. Then he put Yao Li across his knees and said, "Humph! A real brave man, indeed, who dare apply his weapon against me!"

Coming to their senses, his guards drew their swords to kill Yao Li. But Qing Ji stopped them, saying, "This is a brave man. Why should two brave men die on the same day? Let him return to Wu and be extolled for his loyalty to his king." Then he pulled out the spear in his chest and died.

Having completed his mission, Yao Li drew his sword and cut his own throat.

Adapted from *Record of Events Based on "Zuo's Spring and Autumn Annals"* (Zuo Zhuan Ji Shi Ben Mo), Tome Fifty

Strategy Thirty-Five
Interlaced Stratagems

第三十五计 连环计　　将多兵众，不可以敌，使其自累，以杀其势。在师中吉，承天宠也。

Translation

Do not engage an enemy that has many generals and numerous soldiers. Weaken its position by making its troops interlaced. The general secures his rule in the army: Good fortune, with the blessing of Heaven.*

Purport

A victory often results from a circumspect battle plan consisting of several interrelated ruses. Promptly carried out, they bring about a succession of chain reactions to demoralize, weaken and finally defeat the enemy troops. Typically, two adjoined operations are taken. The first aims to reduce the enemy's maneuverability, and the second to annihilate its effective strength.

---

*This phrase is quoted from the symbol of the yang line in the second place of *Shi* (The Army), the seventh hexagram in *I Ching* (cf. Strategy Twenty-Six). The second line represents the general of the army who has gained the necessary authority to fulfill his task, as all the other five lines are broken, or submissive. Working within the army, he receives the assistance and support of his officers and men. He can thereby trust the troops to strictly carry out his battle plans.

Interlaced stratagems has found its most successful application in fighting against cavalry, the power of which relies mainly on its mobility. Confronted with the enemy in the morning, one challenges it to battle and soon feigns defeat. After retreating for some distances, one stops and turns to challenge the enemy again, then feigns defeat and retreats. Eagerly seeking for a decision, the enemy follows in hot pursuit, with no time to take a rest. On the other hand, one has planned the repeated retreats beforehand and is therefore able to use the intervals to rest and feed the troops. At nightfall, the enemy has become tired and hungry. Feigning defeat for the last time, one scatters cooked beans on the ground. When the enemy cavalry arrives, the horses are attracted by the fragrant beans and stop to feed. A great victory can be achieved if one fights back at this moment.

The Battle of Shunchang

The fall of its capital Bianliang (modern Kaifeng in Henan Province) to the invading Jin forces in 1127 marked the end of the Northern Song Dynasty. That same year the Southern Song was established under Emperor Gaozong, who was to rule for thirty-five years. Several Song generals, notably Yue Fei, Han Shizhong, and Liu Qi, distinguished themselves in fighting against the Jin, gaining quite a few victories with inferior forces. But Emperor Gaozong's policy of reconciliation with the Jin and his inveterate mistrust of military commanders forestalled any prospect of recovering the lost north. In a treaty signed in 1139, Song lowered itself to the status of a tributary state of Jin in exchange for temporary peace. Emperor Gaozong was elated, but the men of Jin did not take the treaty seriously.

In the third month of 1140 Liu Qi was appointed assistant regent of Bianliang. He departed from the capital Lin'an (modern Hangzhou in Zhejiang Province) with forty thousand troops. Many officers and men, expecting a period of peace in Bianliang, took their families with them. They boarded nine hundred boats in Lin'an and rode upstream along the tributaries of the Yangtze River toward the north.

After traveling slowly for more than a month, they approached Shunchang, where they got news that the men of Jin had torn up the peace treaty and launched another southward invasion. Thereupon Liu Qi ordered the troops to abandon the boats and march swiftly on land to take hold of the city. Upon arrival at Shunchang on the eighteenth of the fifth month, he learned that the Jin army had already captured Bianliang and Luoyang. Wuzhu, the commander-in-chief of the Jin expedition, was strengthening his control of Bianliang and in the meantime had dispatched some troops to march east toward Shunchang.

Liu Qi met the governor of Shunchang, who asked if the city could be defended. Liu Qi asked in return, "How much food do you have in the city?"

"Several tens of thousands of *hu* of rice," replied the governor.

"We can defend the city then," Liu Qi declared. He consulted his officers on plans to meet the men of Jin. However, many officers, worrying over their families, offered to desert the city, get back on the boats and ride downstream back to the south. Liu Qi retorted, "I was made assistant regent of Bianliang and have led you to guard the city. Though Bianliang is now lost to the enemy, we are fortunate enough to arrive here at Shunchang. How can we surrender it to the enemy gratuitously? Whoever talks more of retreat will be beheaded!"

With this he destroyed all the boats to make clear to his men that there was no turning back. He put up his family in a temple and had firewood stacked at the gate. "When the city is about to yield," he told the guards, "set fire to the temple so that my family members will not suffer humiliation in the hands of the enemy." Inspired by the courage of their commander, the troops shook off their initial shock and fear and prepared to defend the city against invaders.

The defense works of Shunchang were incomplete and dilapidated, unable to withstand the attack of superior enemy forces. Liu Qi ordered his men to reinforce the city and went in person to supervise the work. Cart wheels and door planks were used to strengthen the city wall and some makeshift earthen ramparts were constructed in front of the main gate. Just outside the city there were a few thousand households. Liu Qi had the houses burnt to the ground and moved the inhabitants into the city. Thus, when the Jin troops came to besiege the city, they would have to stay in the open field, for the nearest village was more than a dozen *li* from the city. Liu Qi also sent many scouts to find out the whereabouts of the coming Jin troops so that he could plan for preemptive actions.

Six days later, the vanguard of the Jin army crossed the Ying river to attack Shunchang. Before that, Liu Qi had dispatched some men to lie in ambush behind the earthen ramparts outside the city gate. Upon the arrival of the Jin vanguard, they suddenly rushed out of their hiding place to charge the enemy lines. The men of Jin did not expect an ambush just outside the city and, unable to cope with the attack, took to their heels. Two of the officers were captured alive. Upon interrogating them, Liu Qi learned that a Jin general named Han Chang had stationed his troops at Baishawo, about thirty *li* from the city. That same night Liu Qi sent a thousand men to attack Baishawo, inflicting great casualties upon Han Chang's army.

Soon afterward, two Jin generals joined forces to lay siege to Shunchang with thirty thousand men. Liu Qi ordered the troops to lie in ambush in the city and had all the gates opened. But the men of Jin were suspicious of a trap and dared not advance into the city. They stopped in front of the main gate and started to shoot arrows. The Song soldiers retaliated with bolts from powerful crossbows from the city wall or behind the ramparts. Failing to gain any advantage, the Jin troops pulled back. While crossing the Ying River, they were waylaid by a band of Song army that had reached their rear by a roundabout route. The men of Jin panicked and many were drowned in the river.

By this time the city had been besieged for four days. More and more Jin troops arrived, making camp at Li Village about twenty *li* from the city. On learning this, Liu Qi sent a brave officer with a select force of five hundred to attack Li Village at night. It was a typical summer night, with no rain but intermittent heat lightening. They approached the enemy camp quietly and suddenly broke into it, killing many of the sleepy Jin soldiers. They hid themselves in the darkness and jumped up to fight when the lightening flashed across the sky. The men of Jin grew fearful and pulled fifteen *li* further away from the city.

The Jin Commander-in-Chief, Wuzhu, was angry at

the unexpected reverses at Shunchang and left Bianliang with reinforcements of a hundred thousand infantry and cavalry troops. On the seventh of the sixth month, he arrived at Shunchang, finding it to be a small city with makeshift defense works. "I can topple the city with the tip of my boot!" He sneered with contempt. Then he sent for the officers and scolded them severely for failing to capture such a poorly defended city. "But these southerners here are so bold and crooked!" the officers exclaimed in unison. "They are different from those we fought in the past! You will believe us after you have tried for yourself."

On hearing of Wuzhu's arrival, Liu Qi sent an envoy to present him with a letter of challenge. "How dare Liu Qi challenge me to a fight!" Wuzhu roared. "With my invincible army I can smash his city into pieces!" To this the envoy responded, "Our general challenges you to a real fight in front of the city. He cannot be sure that you have enough courage even to cross the Ying River again, so he has ordered five floating bridges to be built to facilitate your advance. He hopes to see you tomorrow if you dare come at all."

Fighting back a snicker, Wuzhu accepted the letter and sent away the envoy. Then he summoned the troops and announced they would capture the city the next day. Early the next morning he led troops to advance on Shunchang and, on reaching the Ying River, saw five floating bridges across it. Making sure that the bridges were not booby-trapped, the men of Jin crossed them and arrived in front of the city.

The day was sultry. Though it was still early morning and the troops had marched for merely twenty *li*, they already felt very hot and thirsty. So they drank water from the river and let their horses browse on the grass by the riverbank. By the time Wuzhu realized that the water and grass had been poisoned, many of his men and horses had become sick to the stomach. The rest of the troops were then forbidden to drink from the river and had to go without water under the scorching sun.

Suffering from lack of strength and poor morale, the men of Jin attacked the city but failed to gain any ground. Intent on fulfilling his pledge to capture the city that day, Wuzhu was not prepared to withdraw. He was waiting for the Song troops to come out of the city so that he could destroy them with his powerful cavalry.

While the entire Jin force was exposed to the baking sun, Liu Qi arranged for his men to fight in relays. Every band of soldiers would defend the city gate for a shift and then return to a shelter to cool themselves. In this way they were able to repel the enemy's attack for several hours. The best Jin troops were dressed in metal armor. Liu Qi had such a suit of armor laid out in the sun; when it became scalding to the touch by noon, he decided it was time to fight back.

At this, some officers suggested that they charge at Han Chang's column, but Liu Qi disagreed. He observed, "After we have beaten back Han Chang's force, we will become fatigued and unable to cope with Wuzhu, who had the best part of the Jin army under his command. Wuzhu is also the commander-in-chief of the entire Jin army. It would be better for us to assault Wuzhu's force. After we have defeated him, the rest of the Jin troops will not be able to fight back."

Thereupon he ordered a few hundred men to march out of the western gate. They waved flags, beat drums and shouted loud battle cries. Then he sent five thousand picked troops out of the southern gate. Many of them carried bamboo tubes containing cooked peas. They advanced straight on Wuzhu and engaged his central force in close combat. Exposed to the scorching sun for hours, the men of Jin were no match for the well-rested Song soldiers and soon faltered. Wuzhu then pulled back his central force and ordered the wing forces to close in.

Wuzhu's crack legion, which he styled the "ever-victorious army," consisted of a central force of foot soldiers, mostly Han people who had been captured and forced to join the army, and the left and right wing forces, all of them fully equipped Nuzhen cavalrymen. Wuzhu was wont to use the central force to check and wear out the enemy and then send forth the cavalry as shock troops to outflank it and conclude the battle. By this tactic he gained numerous victories over the Song army, which consisted mainly of footmen.

Clad in white armor, Wuzhu led three thousand mounted guards and rode back and forth in the field to direct the troops. When his central force began to falter, Wuzhu ordered the cavalry to gallop onto the battle ground. At this, the Song soldiers opened the covers of the bamboo tubes and scattered them all over the ground. Both the Jin cavalrymen and their horses were sagging from hunger and thirst. Attracted by the fragrance of the cooked peas, some horses stopped to eat. Others tripped and fell over the bamboo tubes. Thus encumbered in movement, the Jin cavalry was penetrated and broken up by the Song soldiers, who brandished sharp axes to chop at the horses' legs. Once a horse was cut down, its rider fell to the ground and had difficulty getting up because of his heavy armor. Many Jin cavalrymen were finished off in this way.

The defeat of Wuzhu's force made all the Jin troops take to their heels. Wuzhu collected the army and found to his dismay that he had lost more than seventy percent of his best cavalry. The next day, Wuzhu broke camp and proceeded back to Bianliang. According to a secret report by a Song envoy staying in Jin territory, the men of Jin were so scared after the defeat at Shunchang that they sent all their booties back to the north and made ready to retreat. The Song emperor came to their rescue, ordering Liu Qi to withdraw. Thereupon Wuzhu decided to stay in Bianliang and give his army a rest; then he began to plan for new assaults the next year.

Adapted from *Record of Events Based on "History of the Song Dynasty"* (Song Shi Ji Shi Ben Mo), Tome Seventy-One

Strategy Thirty-Six
Running Away as the Best Choice

第三十六计 走为上　　全师避敌。左次无咎，未失常也。

Translation

Evade the enemy to preserve the troops. The army retreats: No blame. It does not violate the normal practice of war.*

Purport

Attacked by an overpowering enemy, one has only four choices: fight to death; sue for peace with the enemy; surrender; retreat. Either fighting to death or surrender results in total defeat, and negotiation with the enemy means half defeat. Retreat therefore turns out to be the best choice. By avoiding a defeat today, one gains an opportunity for a victory tomorrow.

---

*This is the symbol of the fourth line of *Shi* (The Army), the seventh hexagram in *I Ching* (cf. Strategy Twenty-Six). A yin line at a yin position, it represents a weak element that wisely conducts itself with modesty and submission. Thus, when confronted with a superior enemy, an army should make an orderly retreat to save itself from defeat. By such an act, which conforms to the normal practice of war, one can avoid misfortune that may otherwise result from a reckless fight against heavy odds.

An army should fight only at the right time, the right place, and with the right opponent; otherwise it must avoid any engagement with the enemy. The common image of a victorious army marching forward and a defeated army falling back can be misleading because of its implication that retreat is disgraceful. As indicated in *I Ching*, retreat, as well as advance, is a normal practice in war. Thus the strategy advocates the adoption of retreat as a preferable plan when a battle must be avoided.

Quotations for Reference

When engaged in battle with the enemy, if we have inferior troops and disadvantageous terrain and cannot rival the enemy in strength, withdraw quickly to avoid it and preserve our troops. The principle goes, "Beat a retreat in the face of difficulties."

A Hundred Marvelous Battle Plans, "Battle of Retreat" (Bai Zhan Qi Fa, "Tui Zhan")

King Wei asked, "How shall we cope with an enemy superior in number and strength?"

Master Sun replied, "The method is to avoid an enemy at the height of its potency ... and wait until it has become weakened."

Sun Bin's Art of War (Sun Bin Bing Fa)

The Tumubao Incident

The Oyrat Mongols, after their defeat by an expedition led by Emperor Chengzu of Ming in 1414, paid regular tributes to the Ming court. Then a distinguished leader emerged who extended Oyrat authority by subjugating other Mongol tribes. His son Esen continued the cause and succeeded in setting up a powerful Oyrat kingdom, the greatest Mongol regime since Genghis Khan. The territory under Oyrat control ranged from Central Asia in the west to the Kingdom of Korea in the east, and from Siberia in the north to the Great Wall in the south.

In the meantime the Ming Dynasty was already suffering from economic decline and military drawbacks. Several strongholds along the northern border were abandoned; the Great Wall became the foremost defensive line against invaders from the north, and strategic cities such as Datong and Xuanfu were exposed to the direct attack by the Oyrats. If anything untoward happened to any of these cities, the capital of Beijing could be readily threatened.

After Emperor Yingzong ascended the throne in 1435 at the age of nine, the Ming court was dominated by a eunuch named Wang Zhen, who easily manipulated the young emperor. Even after the emperor came of age, he continued to place complete trust in the eunuch, who had nothing to recommend himself except for arrogance, greed, and caprice.

Late in the thirteenth year of Emperor Yingzong's reign (1448), the Ming court sent some envoys to the Oyrat Kingdom. Esen asked for an imperial princess to marry his son. The Ming envoys consented, though it was beyond their power to make such a decision. Upon their return, they did not report the matter to the emperor.

In spring the next year Esen dispatched more than two thousand envoys to the Ming court. They brought some fine horses, claiming these to be Esen's betrothal gifts. Emperor Yingzong not only turned down the proposal but also cut the routine rewards by four-fifths. This provided a good pretext for Esen to launch an invasion he had been planning for years.

Esen first sent out three forces to attack Hebei, Liaodong, and Gansu in order to tie down the frontier troops of Ming. Then he led about a hundred thousand men in person on a march toward the city of Datong.

Early in the seventh month Esen arrived at a stronghold just outside the Great Wall. A general from Datong hastily ventured out to attack Esen but was defeated and killed. Esen then broke through the Great Wall and proceeded south to besiege the city of Yanghe. The Ming troops at Yanghe were supervised by a eunuch named Guo Jing, a close follower of Wang Zhen, who knew nothing about warfare but had strict control over the officers. The Mongols inflicted a crushing defeat and seized the city. After this, most of the Ming troops north of Datong panicked and abandoned their strongholds without fighting.

Emperor Yingzong decided to lead an expedition in person, though most ministers advised against it with ample arguments. The emperor stuck to his decision because it was suggested by his most trusted eunuch, Wang Zhen, whose hometown, Weizhou, was only a few dozen *li* south of Datong. Wang Zhen feared that the Mongols might pillage his hometown. He hoped to scare them away by the sheer size of an imperial army led by the emperor himself.

The emperor summoned all the forces he could conveniently get, which reportedly amounted to five hundred thousand. He opened the imperial treasury and armory and had silver, uniforms, food rations, and various weapons distributed to the troops. It was an impressive but confused army. The soldiers received new weapons, which they did not know how to use, and were led by unknown officers. They set out for Datong on the sixteenth day of the seventh month. There were several renowned generals in the expedition, but the emperor did not trust them. Instead, he put Wang Zhen in overall command of the army.

On hearing of the Ming army's advance, Esen quickly decided to avoid a head-on confrontation. He abandoned all the strongholds he had seized and retreated north, crossing the Great Wall. He hoped thereby to lure the Ming army into the frontier regions where the Mongol horsemen could give full play to their skills.

On the first day of the eighth month, the Ming expedition arrived at Datong. Wang Zhen urged the emperor to cross the Great Wall and march north in pursuit of the enemy. Most generals and officials objected, but in vain. Just then, the eunuch Guo Jing arrived to tell Wang Zhen about the grave defeats the Ming troops had suffered at Yanghe and other places. All of a sudden, Wang Zhen began to feel afraid. He was no longer certain that he could use the Ming emperor to scare the ferocious Mongols into escape. He hesitated a little while and then decided to withdraw the troops.

No one objected to him this time, since the army had already begun to run short of food and the soldiers had grown tired and fearful. Even then, Wang Zhen did not forget a major purpose for which he started the expedition. He wanted to invite the emperor to his hometown and thus prove his worthiness to his fellow townspeople. Therefore he ordered the troops to retreat by way of Weizhou. Again no one objected, since this happened to be the safer path for the army.

After they had marched for forty *li*, it suddenly occurred to Wang Zhen that the hundreds of thousands of troops would certainly trample his precious gardens and cultivated fields. He found that too exorbitant a price even for an emperor's visit. So he ordered the troops to proceed north by way of Xuanfu. It did not require expert military knowledge to perceive that the move would expose the flank of the Ming army to the Mongol invaders. The emperor ignored the objections of his generals and conceded to Wang Zhen's decision.

As soon as he learned of the Ming army's retreat by the northern route, Esen led his men in a hot pursuit, arrivng at Xuanfu on the tenth day of the eighth month. There he defeated the Ming generals sent to block his advance. On the fourteenth day the Ming army reached Tumubao. It was only twenty *li* from the city of Huailai, but Wang Zhen would not allow the army to advance further because he was waiting for his supply wagons that had lagged behind. Therefore the Ming troops had to dig trenches and construct fortified camps in the open field. That night, Esen arrived at Tumubao and quickly seized control of the strategic positions to the south and northwest.

Esen did not wait for dawn to launch his attack. Fighting all night, the Ming troops managed to maintain their position but could not repulse the enemy. By then the soldiers had not drunk for two days. There was a river just a dozen *li* to the south, but it was controlled by the men of Esen. Wang Zhen ordered the troops to dig wells, but they could get no water even at seven meters underground.

The next morning Esen ordered his troops to withdraw for a few *li* and sent an envoy to make peace. The emperor was only too glad to concede. He appointed two officials as his representatives to hold negotiations with Esen's envoy.

This was enough to make Wang Zhen believe that the battle was over. He hastily ordered the troops to move south to drink water from the river. The tired Ming soldiers swarmed out of their fortified camps and scrambled over trenches in disorderly formation, when the Mongol cavalry suddenly arrived from several directions. The Ming army fell into complete chaos and suffered a crushing defeat. More than fifty Ming ministers were killed and the emperor himself was captured. Before that, an attending officer named Fan Zhong smashed Wang Zhen with a hammer, killing him on the spot. "I have killed this traitor on behalf of the all-under-heaven!" he shouted. Then he charged into the enemy forces and cut down dozens of Mongol soldiers until he died of exhaustion.

Esen was overjoyed to have the Ming emperor in his hands and hoped to subdue the Ming empire without fighting. By this time the Ming court had been plunged into a tumult; the Ming troops were poorly prepared to defend Beijing. But instead of attacking in full force, Esen shuttled with Emperor Yingzong between Datong and Xuanfu, trying in vain to cajole the city defenders to open the gates to their emperor. "I have received orders to defend the city and know nothing else," declared a general at Datong.

In the meantime the Ming court, under the initiation of Yu Qian, Minister of Defense, had already sorted things out. The households of the hated Wang Zhen and his followers were wiped out, and a new emperor was enthroned. When Esen resumed his attack in the tenth month, the Ming capital was well prepared to defend itself. Failing to gain the advantage, Esen had to retreat north of the Great Wall and then sent envoys to sue for peace. The next year he had Emperor Yingzong escorted back to Beijing.

Adapted from *Record of Events Based on "History of the Ming Dynasty"* (Ming Shi Ji Shi Ben Mo), Tome Thirty-Two

Bibliography

Bai Zhan Qi Fa 百战奇法
A Hundred Marvelous Battle Plans

Bing Fa Bai Yan 兵法百言
A Hundred War Maxims

Bing Lei 兵礧
Essentials of War

Cao Lu Jing Lue 草庐经略
Strategies from the Thatched Cottage

Guan Zi 管子
Book of Master Guan

Hu Qian Jing 虎钤经
Canon of the General

Jiang Yuan 将苑
The Art of Generalship

Jie Zi Bing Jing 揭子兵经
Master Jie's Canon of War

Jiu Tang Shu 旧唐书
Old History of the Tang Dynasty

Liu Tao 六韬
Six Strategies

Ming Shi Ji Shi Ben Mo 明史记事本末
Record of Events Based on "History of the Ming Dynasty"

Qing Dai Qi Bai Ming Ren Zhuan 清代七百名人传
Biography of Seven Hundred Eminent Figures in Qing Times

Qing Shi Gao 清史稿
Draft History of the Qing Dynasty

San Guo Zhi 三国志
History of the Three Kingdoms

San Lue 三略
Three Strategies

Shi Ji 史记
Records of the Historian

Si Ma Fa 司马法
Law of Master Sima

Song Shi 宋史
History of the Song Dynasty

Song Shi Ji Shi Ben Mo 宋史记事本末
Record of Events Based on "History of the Song Dynasty"

Sun Bin Bing Fa 孙膑兵法
Sun Bin's Art of War

Sun Zi Bing Fa 孙子兵法
Art of War

Tai Bai Yin Jing 太白阴经
The Yin Canon of Vesper

Tang Tai Zong Li Jing Wen Dui 唐太宗李靖问对
Li Jing's Reply to Emperor Taizong of Tang

Tou Bi Fu Tan 投笔肤谈
A Scholar's Dilettante Remarks on War

Wei Liao Zi 尉缭子

Book of Master Wei Liao

Wu Bei Ji Yao 武备集要
An Abstract of Military Works

Wu Jing Zong Yao 武经总要
Summary of Military Canons

Wu Zi 吴子
Book of Master Wu

Xin Tang Shu 新唐书
New History of the Tang Dynasty

Xu Zi Zhi Tong Jian 续资治通鉴
Sequel to History as a Mirror

Yuan Hao Zhuan 元昊传
Biography of Yuanhao

Zi Zhi Tong Jian 资治通鉴
History as a Mirror

Zuo Zhuan 左传
Zuo's Spring and Autumn Annals

Zuo Zhuan Ji Shi Ben Mo 左传记事本末
Record of Events Based on "Zuo's Spring and Autumn Annals"

Index

The figures indicate strategy numbers.

三十六计例释

孙海晨编

*

外文出版社出版

（中国北京百万庄路 24 号）

邮政编码 100037

北京外文印刷厂印刷

中国国际图书贸易总公司发行

（中国北京车公庄西路 35 号）

北京邮政信箱第 399 号　邮政编码 100044

1991 年（34 开）第一版

（英）

ISBN 7—119—01399—8/E・1（外）

00810

5—E—2642P